reaching out

DATE DUE

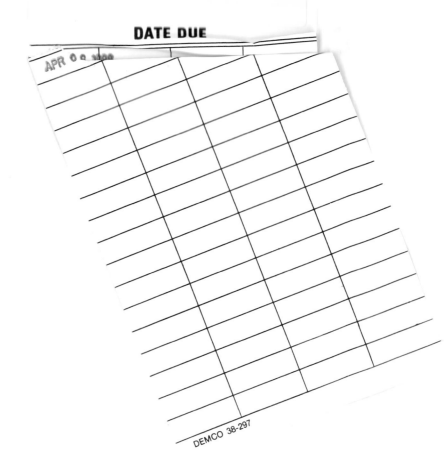

APR 0 9

DEMCO 38-297

reaching out

How academic leaders can communicate more effectively with their constituencies

by
Clay Schoenfeld
Linda Weimer
with Jean Lang

Magna Publications, Inc.
Madison, Wisconsin

Reaching out:
How academic leaders can communicate more effectively with their constituencies

by Clay Schoenfeld, and Linda L. Weimer, with Jean M. Lang

Magna Publications, Inc.
2718 Dryden Drive
Madison, WI 53704

Printed in the United States of America

02 01 00 99 98 97   8 7 6 5 4 3 2 1

Cover design by Tamara L. Cook

Illustration by Mark Roeder

Library of Congress Cataloging-in-Publication

Schoenfeld, Clay, 1918-1996

Reaching out: How academic leaders can communicate more effectively with their
constituencies/by Linda Weimer, Clay Schoenfeld, with Jean Lang.

P. Cm.

Includes bibliographical references (p.) and index.

ISBN 0-912150-38-6

1. Public relations—Universities and colleges—United States. 2. Communication in education—United States. I. Weimer, Linda, 1947- . II. Lang, Jean, 1943- . III. Title.

LB2342.8.W45 1997
659.2'937873—dc21   97-1218
                                                                  CIP

Table of contents

Chapter Twelve: From Crises To Campaigns
Communications tips for challenging situations 313

Chapter Thirteen: Driving the Information Superhighway
Leadership communications in the electronic age 349

Chapter Fourteen: How to Know When You Get There
Measuring the results of effective communications 373

Chapter Fifteen: The Sum of the Parts
The interplay of multiple communications strategies 389

Preface

Leadership is communication and communication is leadership. This truism could apply to no leaders more aptly than leaders in academia — from the faculty who are leaders in their fields and the department chairs who represent the faculty, to the deans, directors, provosts, vice presidents, and presidents who serve in the ranks of college and university administration.

Functioning in an atmosphere of collegiality and shared governance, campus leaders often do not enjoy the clout or decision-making authority of those who own a business or command a battleship. Campus leaders must depend almost entirely on effective communications to help translate concepts and goals into actions and desired outcomes.

This is a guide. It is meant to help you understand communications strategies and tools, and how to use them more effectively. It draws upon the latest findings of communication research, upon the considerable experience of the authors, and upon many real-life experiences of academicians and college communicators with whom you may identify. When you finish this guide, you will have a better sense of how communications can help you win the understanding and support of your constituents and thereby help you achieve your goals. Perhaps as important, you will have some idea how to garner assistance and support in meeting your communications needs.

This is not a communications textbook. We have designed this so you can read it from cover to cover or choose the chapters that interest you.

This is not a treatise about the future of academia — although it touches on issues that are critical to the future. More and more, our colleges and universities must rely on public understanding and support, on alumni involvement, on good employee morale, and on pride in the institution among all stakeholders — students, their parents, faculty, staff, alumni, community leaders, government sponsors, and the public. Proactive communications programs are vital to fostering those attitudes and relationships.

This is not a tale about spin doctors. We believe your reputation or public image is only as good as your character. Your image reflects what you really are and what you really do. To succeed, a communications program must first reflect that reality. Through its policies and practices and its formal and informal relationships, your institution, division, administrative unit, or department shows what it stands for and truly values. Accordingly, it cultivates a climate of public opinion that is favorable, or unfavorable, to its objectives. The essence of good public relations — a good image — is honesty.

This is not a book that will necessarily change your habits. But we hope it will make you more aware of how you communicate and more empathetic to those with whom you communicate. Do unto others as you would have them do unto you. Communicate with others as you would have them communicate with you. To put it on a personal level, think about how you get information, how you form opinions, and how you would like to be treated by your boss and your colleagues. Let your own experience be part of this guide.

This is a guide to help you develop your basic communication skills. It is a synthesis of many people's views and experiences, and the authors gratefully acknowledge the assistance of those colleagues for their contributions and reviews.

Clay A. Schoenfeld
Linda L. Weimer
Jean M. Lang

chapter one

Getting Started
Putting this guide to work for you

We all know how to communicate. We do it every day. So why this guide?

Because, we live in a world that increasingly insists on information and accountability, in a world where people are making their support for higher education more conditional — conditional on information, service, relevance, and responsiveness — whether they are students, parents, donors, research sponsors, alumni, or taxpayers.

The readers of this guide live in this environment of accountability, though they come to it from many different experiences and situations.

They may be in charge of a department, unit, or division with an established communication program, in which case their task may be to ensure that the program is making the most of its resources and opportunities for getting the message out. Some readers may be communications professionals working in such a program.

Other readers may have recently taken over departments or programs with no history of public relations or communications or, more challenging still, with public relations problems or phobias about self-promotion. In that role, the task is to figure out the unit's communications needs, to persuade colleagues that such needs exist, and to design a plan and launch a realistic program to address those needs.

Still others of you may be part of programs whose members demand more public visibility. The task in that case is to determine what expectations are reasonable and realistic in terms of strategies, costs, and time frames within which to achieve that goal. As in the case above, internal communications with colleagues will be as important as messages to external audiences.

Whatever the extent of your communications knowledge, experience, or responsibilities, this guide is designed to broaden your understanding of communications methods and strategies and to give you insight into the media, the audiences, and the tools that are available to help you achieve your goals.

Why is this important? Because all of us in higher education depend on our constituencies for support. We depend on students, parents, our staff and faculty, state and federal lawmakers, public agencies, alumni, business leaders, and donors for financial and political support. To win that support we must deliver a variety of messages — and do it well.

It is especially important that those who are leaders in higher education understand communications tactics and practices. As leaders, they are the most visible symbols of the organizations that they lead — whether those are research projects, administrative offices, departments, programs, divisions, colleges, or universities. The leader's actions and words often define for others the nature of that enterprise. The public and the press form their impressions from the people in charge.

This is the new world in which our colleges and universities find themselves. Those that succeed will be those that learn how to communicate effectively what they are, what they mean, and why their work is important. In a sense, we must learn to "market" higher education and market our programs and departments. It is ironic that, for all that is taught about marketing in our institutions of higher learning, leaders in those institutions have been slow to grasp the need for marketing or embrace it as a means to achieve their own ends, except in terms of very specific audiences, such as high school seniors or high-profile donors.

Based on her 15 years of experience as a department chair and dean at Southern Illinois University at Carbondale, Mary Lou Higgerson (1992) observes, "Marketing ... may be the single most important task of an academic leader."

By "marketing" Higgerson means "strategically advocating the mission and achievements of the academic unit in order to enhance its overall reputation" and thus engender support. This task can run the gamut from official actions to written, oral, and visual messages to chance personal contacts.

To keep this guide at a manageable size, we're going to focus on the formal information dissemination activities that are the life-blood of any communications program. Not that official actions and interpersonal relations are not important. They are. Indeed, they may overwhelm even the most carefully calculated and orchestrated communications program.

Witness, for example, the ill will directed at both Stanford University and the University of California System in the early 1990s when they were perceived to have taken special financial license with public funds — one through the use of federal overhead funds to host parties and operate a yacht, the other through a secretly bargained, financially rich severance package negotiated for the president and vice president at a time when the university system was in severe financial trouble. Students, parents, alumni, donors, lawmakers, and the public in general were upset, even outraged, by these actions, which created long-term repercussions for the images and public relations programs of the two universities.

At the other extreme, in the realm of informal communication, a junior faculty member's cordial and serendipitous conversation with the sister of a prospective donor has been known to have more positive impact on a department's endowment than the most elaborate fund-raising drive.

Nevertheless, this guide focuses on how to use the media and other communication channels to cast and deliver a message, and how to measure the response. As Madison Avenue executives remind us, the word "communication" implies that information flows *both* ways. Successful marketing is more than delivering a message. It also is listening and responding to the audience. We will indicate how to re-form the message as needed, and we will encourage you to make your own observations and refine your own communications.

While the task of communicating effectively with constituencies "is seldom listed in the printed job description," Higgerson notes, "it is a task which is imperative to the overall success of the academic leader and his or her academic unit." An effective communications program, she adds, "is essential to assure that the perceptions held by others are both positive and accurate." If the communications program is effective, "all remaining tasks are made easier."

Elements of effective communications

What makes an effective communications program? Drawing on the research and insights of the "dean" of college public relations, Scott Cutlip (1993), we lay out several principles that campus leaders ought to consider before launching their communications planning efforts.

Effective communications are basic to, integrated with, and a reflection of sound institutional policies and performance. As mentioned earlier, the most nimble communicator can't maintain an effective communications program in the shadow of shoddy campus conduct. On the other hand, if stellar performance isn't understood and appreciated by key constituencies, its impact is markedly diminished.

Effective communications are planned, created, proactive, timed, aimed, coordinated, lively, and continuous. Astute campus leaders eschew communications that are largely off-the-cuff, reactive, isolated, bland, and sporadic. There is a strategy behind effective communications programs. They are not random activities or serendipitous events.

It is the quality of communications, not the quantity, that counts in the long run. Mere "publicity-getting" accomplishes little unless you are a movie star. Yet the fallacy persists that you can measure a program's success by the quantity of newspaper clippings, radio spots, TV sound bites, brochures, and reports. There is only one test of a communications program: Does it help the organization accomplish its mission and achieve its goals?

Effective communications are tuned to constituency wavelengths. To even begin to ensure that their messages are assimilated, effective communicators frame their information in ways that attract attention, stimulate interest, and help each particular audience get the point.

Good relations with the mass media depend on winning the confidence and respect of media "gatekeepers." Reporters, editors, editorial writers, news producers, and other such media people must respect you and believe your credibility. They do not expect you to have all the answers or to do "investigative reporting" on your own unit, but they do expect you to deal with them promptly and honestly. If you don't, you can expect harsh treatment. It also helps to know *their* criteria for what is news and what isn't and to appreciate the constraints and pressures under which they operate.

Release of information may generate negative as well as positive reactions. By the very act of disseminating information and calling attention to your unit as a newsworthy entity, you can draw attention to its failings as well. It is naive to expect that you will get only favorable coverage. The only sure way to keep bad news out of the media is to prevent bad things from happening. In very large organizations, especially, that is impossible. Owning up to mistakes can earn you points with the media and the public — and attempts to suppress such information can invite a media searchlight and destroy media trust.

With modest efforts, any campus leader can become a more effective communicator. You must acknowledge that communication involves clearly defined principles, strategies, and skills that can be learned; be willing to focus on the concerns (real or imagined) of each constituent group that is important to you; and recognize that each group must be addressed in its own way and at its own knowledge level.

No campus leader is an island. It would be an idiosyncratic institution, indeed, in which a chair, dean, director, or provost could not call on a wide range of communication professionals who already are operating according to the principles of this book. If you don't know who they are, this guide can help you find out.

Don't re-invent the wheel. Use their skills, listen to their advice, and give them the institutional guidance and support they need to do their jobs well. Also, remember that administrators all around you are also constantly involved in communications with *their* particular constituencies. Specific goals and audiences may differ, but the challenge and concerns are basically the same.

Communications take money, time, and effort. It doesn't necessarily take a lot of money, but anyone who thinks it's possible to carry out an effective communications program without an adequate budget better think again.

Effective communications pay off. A clear, focused, and aggressive communications program describing your institution's accomplishments can go a long way toward winning the financial support and public understanding it merits.

The communications wheel

With these principles in mind, we suggest 14 elements that, together, constitute an effective communications process. The sequence in which they are presented as chapters in this guide represents a logical progression from start to finish. But, the elements are better considered as spokes in a wheel rather than rungs on a ladder, because in actual operations you may initially confront "spoke 5," for example, and then work around the wheel from there.

Whatever your point of entry, your communications program should encompass all 14 of these elements — and they form the essence of this guide:

1. *Recognize the mission, goals, and context:* The purpose of any communications program is to support the mission and the attendant goals or objectives of the academic unit. Communications flounder in the absence of a precisely stated purpose. What exactly is the task before you? Is it overt and clear? Or are there covert nuances? If it's a short-range mission, is it consonant with long-range plans?

   Analyze with a dispassionate eye the institution, the unit you serve, and the program or project you propose to foster. What is your unit's past record, present policies and practices, hopes for the future? What are its strengths, its weaknesses? What are your own special talents and shortcomings? Successful communications programs are built around what is there, not what one wishes were there.

2. *Identify key audiences:* Unless you have a very large program, you can't afford to communicate with everybody all the time. Define the generalized and specialized constituencies of your unit or project. Who are the key opinion leaders? Get to know them and assess how best to reach them. This task is an essential and fascinating aspect of communications.

3. *Research your audiences' attitudes:* If you don't know where you are going, you won't know when you get there. No scientist would begin a scientific experiment without carefully thinking through the hypothesis that she or he is setting out to prove or disprove. And yet, as program leaders, those same scientists frequently throw a brochure or press statement at an audience without thinking to assess what attitudes or what knowledge they are trying to influence. What is the caliber of your relationships with your various constituencies? What are their attitudes toward your institution, department, unit, or project? Relative unawareness? Enthusiastic support? Festering unhappiness? The answers to such questions will suggest varying tenors and techniques of communications.

4. *Get familiar with available media:* Which media are best suited to carry your messages to your audiences? Which of those media are available to you? Which can your budget afford? Which can you control? Which can accommodate your time frame? Frequently, the success or failure of a communications program lies in the matching of these elements.

5. *Define your needs and formulate a communications plan:* What do you need to communicate? Focus on your program goals and think about how communications with key audiences can help you reach those goals. Define your goals and objectives. Knowing your mission, assets, message, communications tools, audiences, and their attitudes, you should be able to describe in writing how the pieces of your communications program will come together coherently. Be specific and realistic.

6. *Marshal communications assistance:* What institutional talents can you mobilize? Upon what resources can you draw? Are there off-campus allies you can enlist? A diligent reconnaissance may turn up more help than you might expect.

7. *Find and budget funds:* How will you fund your plan? How will you allocate the funds you find? You may have to start small and launch your program in phases, but each success should help you win more funds.

8. *Distill and shape your message:* Reduce your information down to a compelling nub that can be adapted to varied constituencies. How do you want to project your message? As unadorned facts? Or in motivational terms that seek a response? This is a step that requires discipline and creativity. Advertisers found long ago that short is sweet and simple is successful.

9. *Match your medium to the audience and your message to the medium:* Choose the medium most likely to reach the majority of your target audience in a timely way. Then, make

sure your message is tailored to the selected medium in tone, style, content, and format — bold, eye-catching headlines and designs for posters, for example, or detailed facts, rationale, and budget for a funding proposal.

10. *Use the news media:* The news media — from the campus student newspaper to the "ABC Evening News" — can be vital players in your communications campaign. It pays to know how to work effectively with these "gatekeepers," who decide what is newsworthy and how to cover it — and who control your access to the public.

11. *Prepare yourself for "business as unusual," that is, the crisis and the campaign:* As a leader, you undoubtedly will find yourself, at some point, involved in planning a major celebration, fund-raising drive, or other campaign that entails well-orchestrated and continuous communications for an extended period of time. You also undoubtedly will find yourself in less pleasant situations — having to react to bad news or respond to a reporter's deadlines — where you are not in control of the message or the medium.

12. *Get out and drive on the information superhighway:* We are in the midst of a communications revolution. Technology is quickly changing the way we communicate. What might these changes mean to your constituencies and your program?

13. *Measure results:* The astute communicator uses a battery of assessment devices and procedures to determine the effectiveness of a communications plan, ready to change tactics

if necessary. The test of effective campus leaders is not that they don't make mistakes, but that they don't make the same mistakes twice.

14. *Bring principles and practices of multi-perspective public relations into play:* Communications don't exist in a vacuum; they are strands in the fabric of a unit's comprehensive life, in which deeds always speak louder than words.

Midland University — A mythical setting

While institutions of higher education vary considerably in their traditions, organizations, and aspirations, they do share enough attributes that it's possible to fabricate a hypothetical campus and department chair with whom we all can identify. To give this guide focus and verisimilitude, we have invented Midland University and Amanda Perkins, with communications issues and challenges similar to yours.

The institution

If our hypothetical institution were actually to be listed in a Higher Education Publications HEP Directory, its profile would look like this:

Midland University
P.O. Box 412, Midland, ST 53102 Con Dist 06

County: Pontiac FICI #: 00398
Telephone 606/263-2331 Entity #: 1-38-700-6942-78
FAX 606/263-6299 Calendar System: Quarter
Established: 1881 (as a private normal school for teachers)
Annual Undergrad Tuition & Fees $2,907
Enrollment: 21,627 Coed
Affiliation or Control: Independent Non-Profit
Highest Offering: Doctorate
Program: Comprehensive
Accreditation: NH, ARCH, BUS, CYPSY, ENG, LIB, MBA, MT, MUS, NSC, NUR, OT, SP, SW, TED
01 President
05 Vice President for Academic Affairs

Principal Divisions:
Allied Health Professions
Architecture and Urban Planning
Business Administration
Education
Engineering and Applied Science
Fine Arts
Forestry and Environmental Studies
Graduate School/Research
Letters and Science
Library and Information Science
Outreach and Continuing Education
Social Welfare

The community

Socioeconomics

With a population of 300,000-plus, the city of Midland is the metropolis of its heartland state — a transportation hub. Diversified mix of heavy industry, high-tech light industry, agribusiness, banking, and insurance. A relatively stable economy, yet with its vicissitudes. A growing gulf between the "haves" and the "have-nots": the former clustered around Burr Oaks Country Club (private) in a suburb, the latter in sub-standard housing literally on the other side of the Northwestern tracks. A reasonable array of cultural and recreational amenities, news media, churches, and service organizations. A small U.S. Air Force base sits on a prairie 10 miles to the south.

Town-gown relations

The Midland faculty used to be concentrated in College Heights near the campus but is now widely dispersed, although an enclave seems to be developing in Starlight Hills, 12 miles westward. Community support for "its" university varies with the times, but in general would be rated comparatively solid. Midland alumni are well represented in the city power structure.

In no sense, however, is the university subservient to municipal interests, its increasing national stature giving it a prestige and independence much envied by the local community college and Baptist seminary.

Nonetheless, Midland University lives politically in the shadow of the sprawling state university 77 miles down the turnpike in

Carthage, the state capital. State faculty steer clear of any entangling alliances, except when grant monies dictate a measure of collaboration.

An assistant president for university relations, a director of development, and an outreach dean work hard at cultivating Midland's publics. The graduate school/research dean has a part-time representative in Washington soliciting federal monies; a career development center under the chief academic officer (CAO) offers support services to faculty who seek them.

All told, the two Midlands — town and gown — are a microcosm of U.S. academia and its environs.

The department

The department traces its lineage to one of the original Midland chairs, that of natural history. It was one of the first to offer a Ph.D. (originally joint with zoology).

Stemming from its heavy teaching role in offering service courses to satisfy university science requirements and prerequisites for majors in related professional disciplines, the department is large, having a faculty of 31, and has a healthy roster of graduate students supported by teaching assistantships. The number of undergraduate majors was limping until the addition of the "applied ecology" moniker in 1972, responding to student demands for programs "relevant" to the environmental era (and to the threat of the rise of environmental studies in what had been a conservative forestry school across campus).

The department's research stature jumped during WWII when its faculty participated in the national search for a penicillin mold that could be mass-produced. Combining his background in bacteriology with serendipity, Professor E. Ronald Pendarvis identified a mutant strain found on rotting melon rinds and cultivated it into a major source of the life-saving antibiotic. A grateful Department of Defense built the laboratory wing where Pendarvis still keeps office hours at the age of 87.

Based on that reputation, the department "took off" in the 1960s by staffing up to meet the almost bewildering requirements of modern botany in a university setting.

A Mason-Dixon line

Today the department is less a department than a loose confederacy of two rival factions — the field or applied botany (taxonomy, dendrology, pathology, economic, agronomy, horticulture, and a revitalized ecology) and the laboratory or basic botany (genetics, molecular, morphology, cytology, histology, and biotechnology to include gene-splitting).

The two cultures are archrivals for funds, freshmen, and favors. The department chair position alternates between the two. At the moment it is a plant pathologist in her first year of a five-year term, so her proclivities are unknown and untested. The college dean does his best to help preserve civility by sponsoring departmental curriculum committees and so on. (Actually, from his perspective the department is no more split than a number of others in his domain.)

Your alter ego

Your alter ego at Midland University is Amanda Rule Perkins. She is 50 and the newly appointed chair of the university's department of botany and applied ecology. She wants her department to instigate a new master's program in biological conservation and sustainable development and generally to enhance departmental quality in both teaching and research. All these changes will require thoughtful communications with both internal and external audiences.

A little background on Perkins: She was born in 1946 in Barrington, Illinois, where she grew up on a truck farm that her parents owned and operated. Her childhood was filled with talk about potato scab, cabbage worm, and sweet-corn smut, so she naturally developed an interest in plant diseases and their cures. She earned a M.S. in plant pathology at the University of Wisconsin-Madison in 1970 and, after some research work for a seed company, she returned there to do pioneering work in alternatives to chemical pesticides in the control of alfalfa blight and received her Ph.D. in 1974.

After working in the private sector for a few years, Perkins came to Midland University as an assistant professor of botany in 1976. She rapidly established a research program, introduced a popular plant pathology survey course, built an impressive publication record, and served on committees in campus governance, her discipline, and the community.

By 1995 she had become chair of her department. Well-seasoned in department and campus affairs and recognized in international plant pathology circles, Perkins was a popular choice to preside over Midland's contentious department of botany and ecology.

With her university, department, and private-sector experience, Perkins has a solid feeling for administration and a flair for interpersonal communications. But she is relatively unfamiliar with the broader dimensions of organizing a communications program aimed at the manifold constituencies she now finds to be her responsibility.

Though Midland, Perkins, and her colleagues are all imaginary, the communications challenges and problems they will face in the course of this guide are not. They are based on actual experiences, though names have been changed to protect the innocent — or guilty!

For further consideration ...

Why reach out

Why would a campus leader want to "get the news out" about his or her unit or division? Robert S. Topor, in his book *Media and Marketing* (1993), supplies a battery of reasons:

- Support the academic missions of the institution

- Keep alumni informed

- Help recruit students and staff
- Build awareness among key constituentcies
- Help people understand changing campus trends
- Help development efforts
- Beat the competition
- Build internal morale
- Assist individuals in their projects
- Inculcate pride
- Promote income-producing programs
- Give higher-ups a sense that their investment is well-placed
- Attract attention to public events

chapter two

What Do We Do First?

Mission and context in communication planning

For many years Clay Schoenfeld has kept over his desk a painting to remind him of the overweening importance of recognizing the mission of any endeavor. The painting portrays Gen. George Washington at the first assembly of his Continental Army staff officers. Underneath is this captious caption: *"Now that we're organized, what do we do?"*

It's a question that more of us should ask ourselves more often. Though we don't generally think of our day-to-day activities as "fulfilling a mission," most of our decisions are constrained and directed by the historical relationships, mission, goals, and outside trends affecting our institution and our particular unit. Whether the activity of the moment is to submit a research proposal on time, interview a potential new faculty member, or teach a course, that activity is a thread in the fabric of the institution's larger purpose. How well we *personally* comprehend the nature of that fabric affects the success of our communications about those activities, whether within our institution or beyond. To understand the environment in which we operate, we need to know the institution's mission and context.

Understanding your institutional context

Every college and university, every academic unit, every program or project has a past, a present, and a future, each influencing its direction and image — each influencing your goals and communications strategies. By exploring the history, current culture, and probable future of your institution, unit, and community, you begin to know your environment.

Understanding your place in history

The past is a good place to begin the analysis of your environments. Nearly all colleges and universities are old enough to have historic mission statements as well as a plethora of information about the achievements and events that have shaped their modern character and mission. Whether captured in word, sentence, paragraph, or page, these statements are the institutions' touchstones in defining direction.

For example, since 1894 the University of Wisconsin-Madison has had a sweeping research mission under an umbrella of academic freedom, enunciated by its Board of Regents:

> Whatever may be the limitations which trammel inquiry elsewhere, we believe that the great state University of Wisconsin should ever encourage that continual and fearless sifting and winnowing by which alone the truth can be found.

In defining its specific goals for research, the university uses that mission statement to plot its course. The institution's refusal, for example, to accept grant money for classified research stems, in part, from the mission statement written a century ago.

It is interesting to see how the land grant colleges and universities word their missions. Most were established in the late 1800s when Congress granted tracts of land to the designated universities of each state in the Union. The purpose was to establish applied agricultural and engineering research, training, and service programs at these locations to help the nation's farmers and artisans. That act was tremendously important in developing public higher education in this country and in instilling in participating institutions a lasting commitment to public service.

Apart from the historic mission statement, most institutions and many departments have written histories, often prepared in connection with an anniversary or milestone. Some are popularized presentations, rich with graphics and hyperbole; others are more scholarly works, written by historians, often members of the faculty. Both kinds of publications will present basic facts, but their interpretations may be colored by nuances of tone, when they were written, the amount of space devoted to a topic, and the point of view of the author. They may gloss over, for example, internal rivalries that dismantled departments or changed their nature or position within the institution. For a richer sense of history, you may want to refer to the memoirs of historic campus figures or talk with senior colleagues or alumni who are still around.

Other sources of historical information and insight may be independent or campus documentary films, old student newspapers and yearbooks, oral histories, old issues of alumni magazines and departmental newsletters, and biographies of past deans, presidents, and chancellors. (If written by doctoral candidates bent on demonstrating their scholarly objectivity, these biographies can be particularly revealing.)

Whatever its caliber, a published campus history is likely your best single, readily available source for a broad overview of past campus "culture or practice" that may inform the institution's mission today. A state history book with a chapter on education may be helpful. Likewise, the history of your city, region, and state may give you insight into how your institution has evolved and how its priorities developed in response to local, regional, or national needs.

The same kind of historical review should be applied to your unit. In addition to the resources described above, you will want to give attention to your unit's annual reports, which commonly hold a gold mine of history. Look as well at memoirs or biographies of past unit leaders or at any national histories of your discipline.

(If it is difficult to trace your unit's history, that adversity may energize you to begin compiling one, to the everlasting gratitude of your successors.)

Your search through the past will not be boring and should produce at least one "Aha!" as you uncover the historical roots for puzzling peculiarities in the culture or organization of various units within the institution.

Midland's context

For example, Amanda Perkins found that, because of its direct lineage to Midland University's origin as a private normal school for teachers, Midland's School of Education has never really lost its emphasis on "teaching the teachers." This includes the education of undergraduates and the region's elementary and secondary school educators. However, in recent years, the school has tilted more toward research. This trend could create friction with a longstanding constituency of the school if the research does not have direct application to the needs and concerns of state teachers.

Perkins also found that her own department of botany and applied ecology, which has a tradition of active faculty governance and participation, is different from the zoology department, housed in the same building, which is more hierarchical, due to the 28-year tenure of a dominating chair.

This type of knowledge is very useful, especially if you are initiating a change, merger, or cooperative activity that others might find threatening.

In considering a new ecology education program, Perkins could, for example, use the School of Education's strong history of teaching teachers to her advantage and help that school show that it is not focusing exclusively on research.

It is also important to learn about major institutional scandals or communication gaffes that have occurred within recent memory. Attempted cover-ups of wrongdoing, highly publicized cases of academic fraud, poorly attended major events, embezzlements, and serious cases of cheating are just a few of the clouds that can hang over a department or division and affect its communications strategy. By the same token, be aware of the good things that have come out of your unit — best-selling books, major faculty or student prizes, prestigious alumni, and the like — that have created positive impressions upon which to build your communications program.

Understanding the present

You may feel you already know the current culture and forces at work in your institution and unit simply by being there, but a little study may produce more useful information and insights.

Just as the historic mission statement is a good place to gauge where your institution has come from, the current mission statement is a good way to gauge where it is going. At most institutions, such statements of purpose, while refined periodically, still reflect elements of the historic posture.

For example, Oregon State University revised its mission statement not too long ago to read as follows:

1. To serve people through instruction, research and extension.

2. To maintain a high quality and nurturing educational environment that aids students in achieving their fullest potential.

3. To sustain and expand research excellence and artistic creativity.

4. To attract, develop and retain faculty and staff committed to excellence.

5. To expand educational and professional opportunities for members of minority, female, disadvantaged and disabled populations.

6. To increase enrollments of outstanding students.

7. To sustain, coordinate and sharpen the university's international focus.

8. To improve facilities and equipment.

9. To expand and improve library and computing services.

10. To improve the university's relations with its many constituencies.

The above statement really represents a combined statement of mission and goals for the institution. The first three on the list — and perhaps number seven — are really more statements expressing an expansive vision for the university; the rest are, to some extent, goals that will enable that vision of excellence, creativity, a nurturing educational environment, international scope, and service to be realized. Taken together, these 10 items not only lay a common groundwork for everyone associated with Oregon State, but also can be traced back to earlier statements of institutional purpose. Indeed, those at public research universities will almost certainly see many of their own institution's goals articulated in this list.

The vision maps the highway; the goals bring you to the specific destinations along the way. Those executing a communications program aimed at advancing a particular agenda must be clear about how their agenda fits into the overall scheme of things, how it relates to the larger mission and goals.

Institutional missions and goals, though providing an overarching guide, lack the precision and focus needed at the operating level of a campus. They must be translated — by campus leaders, deans, department chairs, and their staffs — into specific, actionable items, into self-stated goals of a more explicit nature. We may not be accustomed to calling them "goals"; rather, we may think of them as opportunities or even problems we must solve. "Topics of concern" was the term used by *Academic Leader*, a national newsletter, when it solicited a long list from representative department chairs. Here are a few examples:

- Maintaining a high-quality teaching program in an institution where the reward structure tilts toward the research function, and matching instructional resources with undergraduate enrollment demands. (These "topics" would relate to items 2, 5, and 6 on Oregon State's list.)

- Balancing faculty autonomy with professional accountability — in other words, at one and the same time, allowing faculty to operate as entrepreneurs, which inspires creative scholarship, while holding them accountable as paid employees. (This "topic" would relate to items 3 and 4.)

- Recruiting and retaining superior graduate students, particularly in currently less attractive areas or among underrepresented groups of students. (Items 5, 6, and 7. Addressing this topic or achieving it as a goal might require Oregon State, for example, to first address items 8, 9, and 10.)

Most goals that a department chair or a dean pursues will be derived from both an analysis of immediate needs and an awareness of institutional goals. Indeed, a mark of successful administrators may well be that they recognize those goals needing attention and adopt them quickly and voluntarily.

As an example, when Donna Shalala became chancellor of the University of Wisconsin-Madison in 1988, she discovered that many legislators were unhappy with the university. This unhappiness stemmed from the feedback legislators were getting from their constituents, whose children on the large Madison campus (enrollment 40,000) felt they were more a number than a name and, worse, said they couldn't get the courses they needed to graduate.

Shalala quickly made undergraduate education one of her highest priorities as chancellor, getting ahead of a wave that has since swept many public colleges and universities in the U.S. She instituted new student orientation and mentoring programs and she placed far greater emphasis on teaching undergraduates. One could say that she simply revisited, restated, and emphasized the historic educational mission of UW-Madison, but her action won many friends among the university's constituencies, including parents and legislators.

The UW example illustrates the importance of understanding the context or environment of your institution or program. It also illustrates the fact that, while you may be in a position to define some aspects of your mission and goals, others will "come down from on high" or from the world around you.

There are many guides to understanding your college or university, division, or department. Some you come across regularly, as a member of the faculty or staff; others you may need to seek out.

Official sources

Official sources of information may include:

- An updated mission statement or charter

- A regular report from president to trustees (These often chart the fiscal picture in detail, but are unlikely to delve into the real story of the institution.)

- Reports from divisional deans and vice presidents to the president (These could be insightful and frank.)

- Reports from the faculty senate to the faculty (Usually these require some careful reading between the lines.)

- Periodic reports from trustees to the donors, policy-makers, or the public (These will give you an idea how the governing board wants the public to view the institution.)

- Special reports bearing on affirmative action, accreditation, admissions policy, athletic recruitment, etc. (These can be of considerable utility.)

- Faculty handbook of rules and regulations (This provides a quick entrée to campus culture and bureaucracy.)

- Guidelines for tenure (This tells you where the faculty's emphasis lies.)

- Union manual (This constitutes an essential guide to personnel relations.)

- Reports from the development office or foundation to its constituencies (Look for the kinds of messages donors are receiving.)

- Campus periodicals (regular newspapers or newsletters) produced by the administration for employees (These have many internal constituencies to please and tend to report things as they are, not as they could be. Though usually not a source of controversial news, they can nonetheless be a fairly reliable measure of what's going on, especially if they carry guest columns or letters to the editor.)

- Promotional videotapes (These offer interesting overviews but are not especially candid.)

- Student recruitment materials and student guides or handbooks (These give a good sense of how the institution or department wants to be seen by an important constituency.)

Unofficial sources

Unofficial sources of information about the institution include:

- A variety of news media ranging from daily or weekly student newspapers to local, state, and national newspapers, and electronic media (Though most practice responsible journalism, student papers are usually a proving ground for "journalists in training," with fewer quality controls, but often more provocative — if sometimes inaccurate — stories.)

- The grapevine (This tips you off to things you wouldn't find out from other sources, but it is also highly unreliable, like a game of "telephone.")

Other sources

As you look to characterize your context, that is, to understand your institution, division, department, or program, there are elements that help define the culture and thereby will help you assess which of your proposed strategies are most likely to succeed. Peter Seldin (1991) has identified 10 characteristics that may help focus your thinking about your environment:

1. *Individual autonomy.* What degree of responsibility, independence, and opportunity does a faculty member at your institution enjoy?

2. *Structure.* To what degree do rules and regulations govern the actions of faculty, students, administrators, and staff?

3. *Support.* How much warmth and helpfulness do administrators show to subordinates? Faculty to students?

4. *Identity.* To what degree do faculty and students identify with the institution as a whole, as opposed to a single department or discipline?

5. *Quality of personnel.* How much confidence do administrators, faculty, and students

display in each other's integrity and compe-
tence?

6. *Cooperation.* How effectively do people
throughout the campus work together toward
shared goals?

7. *Decision-making process.* How much genuine
consultation and collaboration exist in formulating functions and policies?

8. *Risk tolerance.* How much is an individual
or unit encouraged to be professionally ad-
venturous and innovative?

9. *Communication patterns.* How well does
complete, accurate, and meaningful information flow upward, downward, and across
the institution?

10. *Sense of community.* To what degree do members of the institution feel a sense of oneness,
a tone of genuine caring for and sharing with
each other?

These attributes or cultural characteristics, which vary from
institution to institution, will help you predict which of your goals
and strategies are likely to find fertile ground and which are not.
They also can help guide you toward communications strategies
that are likely to be most effective in helping realize those goals.

If, for example, your institution is highly centralized and tightly
controlled, the goal of doing your own independent fund-raising
program may be unrealistic. If your institution is very large and
decentralized, it will be much more difficult to generate widespread interest and participation in a particular activity, such as
your unit's anniversary.

Many of the above sources will help you assess your unit's current
cultural context. You will get additional information by perusing
the minutes of recent faculty meetings. Also very useful are

records of special budget requests that required a summarization of unit needs and objectives.

Understanding the climate for communications

Because this is a book specifically about communications in an academic environment, it is worth considering your institution's climate for communications.

The CEO's view

An important part of your context is your president's attitude and behavior regarding the role of communications and constituent relations in your institution. A random sample of 300 presidents and chancellors in the United States and Canada, conducted several years ago by the Council for the Advancement and Support of Education (CASE), found that 98% of college and university chief executive officers consider their institution's communications functions important. A full 82% anticipate a growth in the importance of communications in the next decade.

There was widespread agreement that communications should systematically inform the way an institution thinks and acts, with 80% of the CEOs saying they must consider the communications impact of most decisions and 88% saying that communications considerations should be a component of institutional policy-making.

Says CASE President Peter Buchanan (1991),

> The news of this study is that rather than being viewed as peripheral to the institution, communications has become wound into the very fabric of academic leadership.

While this finding is very encouraging, the reader should be cautioned. Despite all the good intentions reflected here, there often exists a gap between what is said and what is done. Too many CEOs still consider the only relevant communications to be the ones that they issue. They sometimes fail to support the communication needs of other parts of the institution.

Some CEOs, with their background in the more humble world of academe, are not comfortable with the hubris of public relations and so rely on the most minimal form of public pronouncements, such as the annual report, press release, or written statements issued to the press. Others hire talented public relations professionals, but do not include them in discussions of how to handle a "bad news" situation or implement new plans or policies — and consequently make easily avoidable miscalculations in communicating with important audiences. It should be said, however, that campus CEOs have become increasingly sophisticated in their external relations strategies and are acting in deed, as well as in word, to put more professionalism into these areas.

A department chair or unit head will also have specific communications goals. One survey of department chairs around the country, conducted by the late Allan Tucker, author of *Chairing the Academic Department* (1984), found that departmental leaders felt their major communications responsibilities or goals were to communicate department needs to the dean, improve and maintain the department's image and reputation, coordinate activities with outside groups, process department correspondence and requests for information, complete forms and surveys, initiate and maintain liaison with external agencies *and* institutions, and write statements of departmental missions, purposes, goals, and objectives.

The departmental context

Regarding that last item as perhaps the most important, Tucker said,

> Those who control the purse strings, especially university administrators and granting agencies, look for and expect to find clear mission and goal statements. So do accrediting agencies.

Understanding the shape of the future

Communicating about the present inevitably includes considerable discussion of and speculation about the future. A university or college would not survive long if it weren't constantly looking forward, assessing trends, and preparing to meet the changes ahead — and to capitalize on emerging opportunities.

The late, longtime academic administrator Richard M. Millard predicted (1991) that in the 1990s and beyond, the key issues for higher education will be to confront challenging conditions, provide contexts that make life-long learning possible, meet social requirements of adequate advanced education for minorities and the economically disadvantaged, and help the country surmount increasing international competition.

To deal successfully with those realities, Millard said that academicians must modify their assumptions in several areas. They must re-assess the "myths" about the normative character of the past, the nature of college students, the peripheral role of older students, and the focus on "the university" as the primary vehicle for higher education. They also must take a long hard look at "turf wars" — the current and often unproductive emphasis on institutional and unit autonomy, and the opposition to coordination and planning. This goes hand-in-hand with a new look at curriculum and the current confining and even arbitrary traditions about the relationship between the arts and sciences, and professional and occupational education.

New views will come into play concerning quality — how to measure it, and what does and does not undermine it. Also, what is to be the role of remedial education in enhancing access?

To view the development of computer-based educational technology as a threat to the sanctity of the classroom, job security, and quality control of long-distance learning will be naïve and costly. It will also be counterproductive to continue shunning business/industry relations for fear that such liaisons may dilute institutional integrity.

Whether or not you agree with Millard on the significance of these issues, our communications programs must deal with the world as it will be tomorrow, not as many of us know or remember it. We must deal, for example, with the fact that most students now are coming from the "new" suburbs that are home to half of America's population. These are the vast sprawling communities that spread miles beyond the edges of the old urban centers. Many of these new 'burbs boast sophisticated amenities and have drawn businesses that now employ 80% of white collar workers. Many of the adjoining metropolitan areas now experience what has been called a "reverse commute," as their residents go off to the suburbs to work.

Manufacturing also has moved increasingly to the suburbs, even though blue collar jobs now constitute only 18% of employment. While the Industrial Age has waned, the Information Age has blossomed and requires new skills.

We've gone through the greatest wave of immigration in 100 years. Most of those immigrants are being assimilated into society in the suburbs. Finally, a third of America's blacks are now members of the suburban middle class.

The new suburbs are now the "norm." They are what America looks like and how it functions. They also are the origin and destination of most of today's college students. Their families are also "new" in the sense that women are no longer housewives. More than half of all mothers with preschool children work outside the home, up from one in five in 1960. Today one in four babies is born to an unwed mother, compared with one in 30 in 1960. Those couples who marry (36% of households) are waiting longer to do so. Meanwhile, divorce continues to create a large number of single-parent families (the majority headed by the mother) and produce stepfamilies (one in three Americans is a member of a stepfamily, a number expected to reach one in two by the end of the century).

Aside from the changing character of families, students, and communities, there are major demographic, political, social, and economic factors that will affect the college and university environment in the coming decade.

For example, declines in state and federal support for higher education and for research programs are expected to continue. So are the trends toward cultural and racial diversity in the U.S. population. At the same time, the American public will become increasingly conservative.

The numbers of college-eligible students will bulge at the end of the decade, but fewer of the Ph.D. students who graduate will pursue futures in academia.

The baby boomer generation will begin retiring in the late 1990s, and many of those retirees will add to the continued rise in numbers of non-traditional students. They, like all sectors of society, will feel the impacts as new information technologies evolve.

When you view some of these trends working in concert — that is, declining state support, increasing enrollment pressures, and a trend toward more faculty and staff retirements toward the end of the 1990s — you can glimpse some potential "collision courses" for higher education institutions.

Corbin Gwaltney, editor of *The Chronicle of Higher Education*, has given a fair summary of the issues that will lie before us for some time to come, and have a strong bearing on communications with all our constituents (1992):

- The challenge that institutions now face is how to ensure student access and academic quality at a time when state appropriations, tuition revenues, and federal student aids are not likely to grow significantly.

- Such fiscal realities are driving what may be the most profound review of institutional priorities that many colleges have seen in a long time.

- Some critics ... are calling for fundamental changes and are challenging such sacred cows as how faculty workloads are determined.

- Many in academe say the problem is not faculty productivity, but a rigid faculty reward system that values research over teaching and service.

- Accreditation is likely to receive heightened scrutiny.

- Concerns about the quality of undergraduate education are expected to receive renewed attention.

- In this era of economic uncertainty, community colleges are taking on an increasingly important role in higher education.

- The outlook for significant increases in the federal government's student aid programs is bleak.

- Competition for scarce federal dollars will continue to heat up among scientists.

- Two recent Supreme Court decisions will resonate deeply on college campuses ... desegregation in 19 Southern and border states, and "hate speech" issues.

- College sports programs face ... how to comply with a law requiring them to provide equitable treatment for female athletes.

- The dim fiscal outlook will continue to put pressure on campus fund-raising staffs.

- Multiculturalism will continue to influence scholars in the humanities and social studies.

- Sustaining faculty interest and vitality at a time of retrenchment will be a major challenge for administrators.

Take the above thoughts for what they may be worth. The point is that, in our deeds and our words, we cannot ignore changes that the future will bring to our institutions and units, just as we cannot ignore the past or the present. In fact, our goals and plans must reflect the expected trends.

Understanding the community context

The community is a powerful cultural and historical force in the life of all institutions, public and private. But because it is not *of* the institution, the community must be viewed as an important *external constituent* with an interest in and influence upon the institution, but with, at best, mixed loyalties to it. Thus, much of your interaction with the community will focus on communications that aim toward maintaining goodwill. This is particularly true when your institution's or unit's activities involve some element of public understanding or public action.

You can get to know the community better by following some of the same steps we suggested earlier for getting to know your institution. Check the library for a local history or a guide for visitors. Both should give you a feeling for the cultural and historical climate of your community. Sometimes reading old accounts of local life will give you good ideas for themes or events that will resonate with your neighbors today.

What is the role of your community in the state? Is it the state capital? Is it a major tourist attraction? Is it the seat of a major state industry? Is it a metropolitan area? What distinguishes it from other communities? The answers to these questions will help you understand the environment in which you are conducting your events and information "campaigns."

There is also value in knowing how your campus history has meshed with community history. Are you the biggest game in town? Are you a small fish in a big pond? Is the alliance between town and gown a strong and easy one? Is it close? Cantankerous? Collegial? Conflicted? Confounding? What are the other major local industries and how does your institution interact with them?

Some of this information can be gleaned by reading the local newspapers or talking to colleagues, especially those who serve in community posts, like members of the city council or school board. You also might search out your campus' chief community relations person — be it the government affairs officer, the vice chancellor for institutional relations, or the director of community relations — and ask him or her to talk with you about the current relationship.

Understanding the state and national context

Depending on the circumstances of your college or university, it may be important to do a little sleuthing on the subject of your state or region. This is especially important for those in state-supported institutions, whether small state teachers colleges or large research universities.

The University of Wisconsin-Madison even goes so far as to run a seminar each spring, the Wisconsin Idea Seminar. New faculty and administrators are loaded on a bus and spend an entire week touring the state. They visit a dozen communities or more. They spend time with community and business leaders. They tour farms, schools, and factories. They sit in on sessions in the state capitol. They meet authors, alumni, artists, and all variety of people. They get an immersion course on the economy and culture of the state, as well as a keen idea of the state's needs. They also learn a great deal about the university from the few senior faculty and staff sprinkled among them. This experience is a win-win-win situation. The experience informs the faculty's research and teaching, often influencing them to undertake projects that will benefit the state in very specific ways. Participants bond with each other, forming a support network across disciplines. Finally, the project offers great visibility for the university. It sends the message, in a powerful way, that the university cares about state communities.

It may also be important to pay attention to regional, national, and even international trends — particularly economic, political, and demographic ones. They may significantly influence your situation and your communication needs and methods.

If, for example, your state is losing population and commerce, you may want to expand the scope of your communications program for student recruiting or fund-raising to include neighboring states where business and babies are booming. Amanda Perkins keeps a close eye on California. Several of her department's alumni have started very successful environmental technology businesses there and have been generous in giving to the department and in hiring new master's and Ph.D. graduates. When California's economy suffered a few years ago, the trend directly influenced Perkins' department 2000 miles away, as gifts dwindled and jobs in California became harder for her students to get. When the California economy rebounded, so did her department's fortunes.

Understanding the media environment

To communicate internally or externally, you must understand your media environment. Read the local newspapers and tune into the television and radio stations. Do an informal survey of what others are reading and watching. What kind of local TV coverage is there in your town? Do your local radio stations run community calendars or have local news broadcasts? Are there talk shows that welcome faculty experts as guests?

Is there more than one newspaper in your community? If so, you will need to be sensitive to that dynamic and not give all your "hot" news to just one paper. Is there a weekly paper and, if so, what is its role vis-à-vis the daily paper? In many communities, the weekly paper has more room for in-depth stories and is frequently a better source of news on the arts, community events, and entertainment.

One former college relations officer used to joke that people read the dailies, but they memorize the weeklies! People read most carefully and pay closest attention to their "neighborhood" news.

They are most interested in the news about people and places they know personally.

What does the student newspaper look like? How much attention do students, faculty, and staff pay to it? If you want the academic community to know about things, it is sometimes more important to get information into the campus newspaper than into the community newspaper? Hence, campus newspapers may play the role of a small-town weekly and might garner more of your colleagues' attention than a newspaper published in a big city miles away. In fact, there have been faculty in our experience who are more concerned about the announcement of their research or an academic award in the campus' faculty/staff newspaper than in the *Chicago Tribune*.

Are there strong ethnic groups within your community with their own newspapers or radio stations? Are there large local groups, like the Rotary Club, where town leaders gather to share information? That may not seem like a mass media channel, but it is, in fact, a "broadcast" mechanism and perhaps vitally important.

How to organize contextual information

Clearly, you can find an enormous amount of information about the context of your unit and institution. But how should you approach it to extract the greatest insight? One way is to pretend you're the leader of a site-visit team charged by an accrediting agency or professional association with making a hard-nosed assessment of your unit.

John B. Bennett, a provost and vice president of academic affairs at Quinnipiac College (CT), has developed (1991) this thoughtful outline of what a site-visit team should look for in assessing an institution/division/department/unit (IDDU):

- *Mission*. How does the IDDU stand historically/currently and directly/indirectly in relation to what the institution as a whole has been widely known for being and doing?

- *Demand for Services.* What is the current level of demand for the services of the IDDU in teaching, research, and service, to include trend lines, patterns, projections?

- *Societal Needs.* What are the societal needs — geographic, demographic, political — to which the IDDU should be responding as the ultimate rationale for claiming societal resources? How well is the IDDU addressing those needs?

- *Program Cost.* Is the IDDU cost-effective in terms of such factors as student-faculty ratio, cost of instruction per student credit hour, indirect costs, contributions to other programs, revenue generated by externally funded research projects and/or by outreach activities, size of faculty in relation to its teaching/research/service track record, and proportion in each faculty rank — in comparison with peer programs elsewhere and comparable in-house units?

- *Program Quality.* What is the IDDU's "Nielsen Rating" with respect to conventional measures of faculty caliber, relations among faculty members, trends regarding faculty turnover, assessments of student potential and achievement, evidences of learning by both students and professors, coherence of the curriculum as the nexus wherein faculty strengths and expertise are hooked to student needs, adequacy of such material requirements as instructional and research technology and physical plant, library resources, and outreach logistics, and faculty involvement in program planning and execution?

Depending on the scope of your responsibilities and mission, you can tailor your "IDDU assessment," as needed, to a set of narrower, more specific criteria.

To save yourself from going over the same ground later, build a card file of the historical, cultural, and statistical data you collect on your institution, unit, and community. It can be quite valuable when you need the details to give your various messages credibility and life.

For example, try making a short, written inventory of what you have gleaned from this initial look at the "information environment." Begin by jotting down the mission of your institution as you understand it. Write the first two or three words that come to mind in characterizing your institution and/or your department. Do the same thing in characterizing your community. These concepts will give you a sense of where your message might "fit the profile" or what stereotypes you must overcome.

Next, in reviewing your communications context, make a list of all the ways that *you personally* get information on your campus and in your community — including the word-of-mouth methods. Then expand that list to other campus and community sources.

There are two points that we will come back to many times in this guide.

First, "word-of-mouth" or interpersonal communications is the most influential source of information. You may not believe what you read in the newspaper, but you will believe what your trusted friends tell you, especially if they are close to the situation they are describing.

Second, you are often the first and best judge of how to communicate with your colleagues. Pay attention to how *you* take in and assess information, and how *you* form impressions and opinions. What you do with information is probably *very similar* to what others are doing.

When you have completed this analysis of context — within your community, media environment, institution, and department — you will have three or four pages of notes. These will serve as a useful guide as you frame your goals and move into action. The next step in the communications process is to determine whose help, expertise, goodwill, respect, and confidence you need in order to achieve your goals — and to understand the best ways to reach them.

A case study in mission and context

Don Detomasi, professor of economics and planning at the University of Calgary, Canada, knows about campus mission statements. As dean of the Faculty of Environmental Design and associate vice president for planning, he was part of a team that drafted a new mission statement for that institution (*Planning for Higher Education* Fall 1995).

Detomasi states that meaningful modern mission statements must satisfy three requirements: first, to meet state or provincial government demands for "accountability, quality measures, and performance indicators"; second, to meet administrative need for "succinctly stated operational aims" that reflect an institution's primary goals; and third, to serve as "a valuable public information and marketing document."

A mission statement is "both product and process," he says, and the latter is as important as the former.

Here's how Calgary applied Detomasi's prescription:

The president and a senior faculty member with much institutional experience prepared the first draft, which then went to vice presidents, deans, and heads of non-teaching units for comments, concerns, and suggestions for change.

Detomasi then negotiated changes to compose a second draft, which was printed and circulated widely with a call for comments and criticisms from student newspaper readers, faculty members, the board of governors, the alumni association, various community organizations, and the senate.

Comments from all participating individuals and bodies were incorporated in a third draft, which was again widely circulated on and off campus, and additional comments contributed to a fourth draft, drawn up by the University Planning Committee. That document inevitably "read as if it had been written by a hundred hands to please a hundred different minds," and the president then asked the council to approve the penultimate draft statement *in principle* but to allow the document to be rewritten in its entirety by a single, anonymous hand.

Out of this seemingly tedious 18-month process, says Detomasi, came a product that meets two ends: first, it "bought ownership" in the statement on the part of wide-ranging institutional clientele; and second, "despite some fuzzy language and some obligatory sentences," it provided "a policy framework and enunciated objectives" for the institutional planning process as well as for UC's first major fund-raising campaign.

For those who think that there's an inherent conflict between broad participation in constructing a mission statement and clear delineation of an institutional mission, Detomasi has this advice: "Conflict can be managed by education leaders who strongly insist on specific purposes over pleasing everybody."

chapter three

Who's Out There?
Your key audiences and opinion leaders

Just as you can't write a letter addressed to nobody in particular, neither can you formulate an effective communications program in the absence of a sure sense of your audience.

From one perspective, every audience or constituency is in reality composed of a score, a hundred, or a thousand or more individuals. And yet, for any educational institution larger than a country school to personally address each individual in a constituency is impractical, if not impossible. So we do the next best thing. We classify our constituents into meaningful groups, and within each of those audiences, we try to identify opinion leaders who both help us understand that constituency's viewpoint and help us communicate with it.

Identifying and classifying key audiences

You can classify audiences in numerous useful ways: according to functional relationships to your institution or unit or according to inherent characteristics, knowledge of a particular subject, susceptibility to a new idea, socioeconomic status, geographical location, age, occupation, and the like.

It's important to recognize that these classifications are not mutually exclusive; they overlap in constantly shifting patterns. For example, an audience in direct contact with your unit may or may not have real knowledge of what you do and may have a variety of attitudes about what you do that change with the situation. Individuals in that group may represent a diversity of backgrounds — ethnic, socioeconomic, educational — that influence their opinions. If you stop to think about your immediate co-workers, you should easily see those differences. This diversity makes it sometimes difficult to categorize your audiences or constituencies and to draw broad conclusions about their attitudes. Nevertheless, there are advantages to thinking about groups of constituents and analyzing their particular attitudes and information needs when tackling your communication priorities.

Functional audiences

Initially, the most useful way to identify your audiences is in terms of their functional relationship to you. Taking a sample department, you might think of the following categories of audiences:

- Students

- Employees

- Employers and/or Superiors

- Co-workers

- Alumni

- Granting Agencies

- Trustees

- Community Members

- General Public

Each of these categories can have as many refinements as you wish. For example, you can break down "Students" into the following categories: undergraduate students, graduate students (if yours is a graduate institution), prospective students, part-time students, student employees, students with disabilities, foreign students, re-entering students, and so on. Sometimes your message will be the same for all; sometimes you will want to target a message to a specific subcategory. By the same token, "Co-workers" can mean your colleagues in other areas of your institution or your colleagues at other colleges and universities. Both the "Students" and "Co-workers" categories could also be subcategorized into *internal* and *external*, an important distinction for many of your messages.

It is up to you to refine such lists as you wish. One director of public relations at a large research university had a "checklist for relationships with university constituencies" in which he identified 83 discrete audiences, ranging from churches, community service organizations, and vendors of equipment and supplies to bankers funding student loans.

Which of these functional audiences are most important depends to a large extent on where an academic leader sits in the campus hierarchy. Writing from the perspective of a president, former college leader Robert Birnbaum says that while "there are many strategic constituencies, ... most (presidents) would agree that trustees, faculty and administrative staff are the most prominent ... participants in institutional governance." (Many presidents would add "students" to that list, in the growing recognition that students very often set the tone for the campus environment. If the administration's priorities are not in sync with the students', major problems of unrest can consume an administrator's agenda, creating problems with the other important constituencies named by Birnbaum.)

By contrast, a department chair would generally list students, faculty, and the dean as his or her "most prominent" constituencies, while a faculty member might list graduate students, other faculty members, colleagues at other institutions, and research sponsors.

It is unwise to rank functional audiences too rigidly according to how you perceive their importance, lest you fail to recognize changes in the significance of any of your constituencies. Better to always keep in your sights a wide range of audiences, although naturally paying more attention to some than to others.

It is also unwise to assume that audiences closest to you understand you, know you, or love you most. In fact, as a rule of thumb, those audiences should garner a fair share of your attention, since their goodwill and trust are not a given. In fact, recent public opinion polling by James Harvey suggests that, while the public may hold an institution in very high regard, business and political leaders who work more closely with it will tend to be more critical of it.

Common-characteristic audiences

On occasion, you will find it helpful to break down the general public into groups having certain things in common (other than their relationships to your unit). These things might be:

- Occupation or profession
- Political beliefs
- Experiences
- Loyalty
- Causes
- Age
- Socioeconomic status
- Ethnic background

This methodology is skillfully employed by fund-raising professionals, who frequently communicate with very specialized audiences identified by these criteria. It is important to note that, while identifying categories of your constituency this way, you should avoid unconsciously stereotyping them. For example, not all teachers are women, not all laborers are poor, and not all professors are political liberals.

Knowledge audiences

Any general public audience can be broken down according to degrees of their knowledge about any subject on which you wish to communicate:

- Little or no understanding of the subject

- "Speaking acquaintance" with the subject

- Expert knowledge

Each such audience will require a message cast in a particular content and style. Keeping these categories in mind, research faculty would communicate their scholarly results in sophisticated ways to their graduate students and peers, in less detailed ways to scholars in related fields, and in entirely different and simpler terms to the general public. Communication research also suggests, however, that level of knowledge can be inversely related to a favorable attitude on an issue when economic self-interest or some other stance intervenes. In other words, educating your audience will not always bring those people around to a desired point of view.

Bear in mind also that the knowledge that audiences have of your department or institution might be misinformed or outdated.

Although friends and family of the members of a group may consider them "experts" on you, their expertise is unfortunately often flawed. This is the reason why many colleges and universities have put much more energy into communicating with their own employees in recent years. If your colleagues have a better knowledge of what is really happening in the institution, at least they won't spread misinformation to their family, friends, and acquaintances — and, usually, they will be very positive ambassadors for their employers.

Things change, but often early impressions remain. For example, during the 1960s and '70s, many television viewers took away an indelible impression of campus protests against the war in Vietnam. The University of Wisconsin-Madison and the University of California, Berkeley, were in the forefront of student unrest and experienced occasional violence. Many people still think of these campuses as hotbeds of radicalism — even though both have changed dramatically. On the Berkeley campus, for example, the students are generally very conservative; there are as many Republican students as there are Democrats. Even issues that provoke student demonstrations on other campuses in California often fail to ignite as much protest at UC-Berkeley, because students tend to be most occupied with academics. Nevertheless, the 25-year-old images remain and can be obstacles when it comes to fund-raising, legislative relations, or drawing well-known conservative speakers to campus.

Attitude audiences

Just as important as an understanding of your audience's prior knowledge is a sense of its probable reaction to your message. Is the group you are addressing likely to:

- Have no opinion at all?

- Have doubts about the subject?

- Be favorable to your message?

- Be hostile?

The fact that people will approach a given subject with this range of opinions leads to four forms of targeted communications:

Eliciting General Support. The continuous release of information about a particular subject, program, project, or institution that helps develop a floor of interest and understanding — a climate of support — among those who have no preconceived knowledge or attitude.

Eliciting Specific Support. The concentrated dissemination of information about a specific project, program, or subject aimed at those with doubts.

Reinforcing Established Views. Coordinated restatements of a previously established point of view, aimed at those already favorably disposed.

Interdictory Communications. Calculated approaches to those who likely oppose your stance, through rebuttal of misinformation spread by others.

Typically, you will engage in all four forms of communication simultaneously, with each type contributing to the others. For example, interdictory communications ordinarily will be effective only against a backdrop of general support communications. Those, in turn, use specific support communications techniques to focus public attention and use reinforcing communications to transform that attention into goodwill.

Communication researchers generally agree that communication takes place within a mix of factors, most of which are not amenable to simple manipulation. Hence, changes of attitude are rarely if ever achieved through short-term communication campaigns, nor do attitudes necessarily determine actual behavior.

Although the mass media may tell people what to think about, their thoughts and any resulting actions are rooted in their individual natures and experiences. An oft-repeated conclusion of communication scholars interested in persuasion is that you make your communications program much more effective by complementing media messages with local audience groups organized for listening, discussing, and deciding. (This may be why the cooperative agricultural extension program that uses this strategy constantly is considered among the most potent adult education forces in the world.)

Communication scholars also believe that, when there is a measure of covert coercion associated with a communication, it is more likely to persuade. For example, professors usually use a grading system to reinforce classroom exhortations about the importance of studying diligently. Similarly, if a store is offering a cash rebate or prize to the first hundred customers, it will draw more attention to a semi-annual sale and motivate customers to come to the store.

Triage audiences

One last point on this categorization of audiences: no matter how sound or persuasive your communication, many people will never come around to your point of view. With limited time and resources to commit to an information campaign on a particular issue, it is wise to assess this situation at the outset and perform a kind of communication triage. That is, put most of your effort into educating those with no knowledge and motivating to action those who are inclined to support your point of view. This strategy leads us to a discussion of "susceptibility audiences."

Susceptibility audiences

A good deal of research indicates that individuals can vary significantly in their susceptibility to adopting new ideas or practices. To adopt a new idea entails making a decision, which individuals do at different speeds and in different ways.

In general, researchers recognize five stages in the decision-making process. In the *awareness* stage, an individual is first exposed to an innovative idea. In the *interest* stage, individuals may seek more information and consider if and how an innovation might apply to them. Those who progress to the *evaluation* stage make a mental note of the applicability of the innovation, weighing benefits and costs, difficulty of adoption, measures of outcome, and so forth. Those who remain intrigued move next to the *trial* stage, in which they actually experiment with the innovation. Finally, they make a decision — *adoption*, in full or part, or *rejection*.

It doesn't always work that neatly, of course. For example, a person may start recycling cans, bottles, and newspapers, not because information has led her to adopt a concern about the environment and resource depletion, but because of some neighborhood pressure to conform. Then, to rationalize the action, she may begin to pay attention to information that will justify and reinforce these recycling practices, and eventually may even form an attitude of genuine ecological concern.

In other words, she begins by adopting recycling, then becomes concerned because of her actions, and not the other way around. This form of cognitive dissonance can also explain why, as tuition rates rise, parents and students become more receptive to an institution's claims of academic superiority. It is such behavioral phenomena that make the communications game so fascinating — and so challenging!

In a normal diffusion progression, mass media can be very effective in stimulating awareness, while specialized media serve well at the interest phase. But at the stages of evaluation and trial, interpersonal communication is key. Note that in our example, it was interpersonal communication with neighbors that led our homeowner to recycle. Research has shown that the most credible and influential forces at informing, persuading, and moving to action are other people — colleagues, friends, family, acquaintances, peers, and neighbors. This is why internal communications are so very important to colleges and universities. If your own employees do not understand the motivations or actions of your institution or unit, or, worse, if they are hostile toward them, no flood of positive press releases or "opinion leader" testimonials can prevail against the negative influences of those employees on all who are around them. The power of personal opinion and attitude is also the reason why, for example, a college's good relations with high school counselors continues to be so critical to student recruitment efforts.

While on the subject of susceptibility to message and motivation to action, it is well to note that people also generally fall into five categories of receptivity to action:

- Innovators (the venturesome, risk-takers)

- Early adopters ("community leaders," receptive to new ideas)

- Early majority (also receptive, but more deliberate and cautious)

- Late majority (the skeptical, who eventually "go with the flow")

- Non-adopters (defenders of tradition or laggards, depending on your point of view)

Where a particular individual appears on this scale depends heavily on the nature of the innovation in question. For example, a teacher who is quick to adopt new computer technologies may be very reluctant to go along with changes in how the school is managed. Or a farmer who quickly adopts a new high-producing strain of hybrid corn may be completely closed to the idea of modifying his political orientation. Too, a person's social system helps define his or her view of what is tolerable behavior and subsequently determines the effectiveness of diffusion and adoption strategies. Traditional norms may mean a negative attitude toward change; modern norms favor change. The present is a particularly difficult time for "non-adopters," as our society is in the midst of almost constant and dramatic change.

Socioeconomic audiences

An understanding of America's socioeconomic pyramid also can help shed light on some of the complexities involved in communications. In fact, in some of the examples we have mentioned, such as adoption of recycling or rejecting changes in political affiliations, the personal economic impact of the change in question often plays a major role in shaping attitudes. For example, polls show that elderly voters are much less inclined to vote for school taxes, figuring that their children are already educated and that they will receive little in return for this investment. Thus, it is well to consider the economic aspects when educating, informing, and moving a constituency to action.

It is not just rhetoric to say that America is becoming a country of extremes in economic terms. According to the Census Bureau, nearly 20% of America's workers now are earning annual wages that put them below the poverty line for a family of four ($13,091) and the size of this cohort has grown 50% since 1979. At the same time, 46% of those who live in rental housing in the U.S. cannot afford to pay the national average of $485 a month for rent on a two-bedroom apartment, according to an article in the *Wall Street Journal* (1994). There also is a growing gulf between those "doing well" and those "scraping by."

There is, in fact, a silent Great Depression of sorts going on. Since 1973, young families have seen their median income fall by a third and their children's poverty rate double. And according to Susan Dentzer (1992), in the 1980s families in households headed by those younger than age 35 lost 20% of their buying power, while families in households headed by those 55-64 years of age gained 8.2%.

This gap is worth noting and, despite the attention given to spending on welfare, housing projects, and the like, the government spends far more on middle- and upper-income families than on the poor. This middle-class bonus includes the amount spent on medical care and social security to comparatively well-off senior citizens and on mortgage interest deductions and other tax breaks for home ownership. One could conceivably include government support to colleges and universities, which disproportionately subsidizes the education of children from middle-, upper-middle-, and upper-class families.

The relevance of these differences is important to communications programs. For example, one clearly would not target a lower-middle-class family when looking for a major gift with which to construct a new library.

Assessing audiences

After classifying and refining audiences in these and other ways, what pertinent assessments can we make of them? Midland University's Amanda Perkins might go about it this way:

First, she will recognize that all classifications overlap. For example, her "expert public" will include some, but not all, faculty and trustees, depending on the subject. Her "community audience" will represent a wide range of incomes and attitudes.

Second, Perkins will spot the same individual in several audiences. For example, Joanne Dough is a parent, an alumna, a local banker, a member of the Midland City Council, and the daughter of an ex-trustee.

Third, Perkins will realize that each audience is in constant flux. Dough can move in and out of several categories, or up and down within a category, as her situation, interests, and age change.

Fourth, Perkins will rightly sense that for each audience there is a particular set of media "fits." Direct mail, for instance, is an economical way for her to communicate with a specific audience, such as the employers of department graduates; it is an exorbitantly expensive way to communicate with a large, general audience. Conversely, a video press release may be a good way to access a mass audience, but it is a relatively expensive and inefficient way to communicate with an internal audience.

Fifth, on any given issue, Perkins will find that some of her audiences will be more important, more interested, and more likely to respond in some way than other audiences. As an example, the launch of her master's degree program in biological conservation and sustainable development is much more important to prospective graduate students — and, she hopes, donors and funding agencies — than to a venerable alumnus in Sun City, Arizona (unless he or she is a potential donor!).

On some issues, an otherwise minor public may suddenly assume paramount importance. If chemical leaks from a city fuel storage area were suddenly found to be polluting Lake Midland, Perkins would quickly hear from the local chapter of the Izaak Walton League, the State Wildlife Federation, and the regional office of the Environmental Protection Agency, asking that a professor give expert testimony on the extent of the damage to the lake's ecology.

Sixth, as communication research colleagues have told her, Perkins knows that behavioral science is based much more on probabilities than on deterministic laws — more like rough outlines in sand than like chisel cuts in stone. Communications research has lacked systematic, cohesive programs of investigation. Thus, there are few immutable rules. We need to play our hunches and test our theories.

While there is very little empirical evidence that communications, attitudes, and behaviors are related in any predictable way, common sense tells us there is a fundamental relationship between attitude and behavior. Clearly, the better Perkins is able to sense ramifications of her interlocking audiences, the better she will be equipped to communicate with any group or individual.

Finally, in assessing audiences, it pays to remember what may seem only too evident — never overlook the obvious audience. More than one college president beloved by donors and regents alike has been run out of town on a rail for overlooking his or her relationship with the faculty. And one surly secretary can make life sheer hell for the unappreciative department chair.

In assessing audiences, you might think about communications in terms of concentric circles. Those in the circles closest to you are critical to your success. If they are not aware of your goals and supportive of them, you will have more problems reaching and affecting the attitudes of the audiences further away from the circle's center. It is a common maxim that good external relations begin with strong internal communications.

Identifying public opinion leaders

Identifying the opinion leaders within each audience isn't easy. Communication research shows them to be ephemeral, depending on time and topic, so that who leads and who follows depends a lot on the timing, the subject matter at hand, and/or the setting.

Opinion-molders are not necessarily the individuals who control the obvious channels of communication within an audience. For example, Clay Schoenfeld recalls that for many years one of the key opinion leaders in his small home town was a local barber, who never held public office and who seldom had a remark quoted in the local weekly paper.

Empirically, communication researchers identify opinion leaders through self-reports and nominations from others and then triangulate the results. What they find in general is that opinion leaders tend to be perceived by their followers as personifying values held in high regard by the group, competent and knowledgeable in the subject matter, and accessible to the group yet with valuable outside contacts, including specialized media.

Usually an opinion leader is homogenous with his or her group. But in the so-called "technology transfer model," new ideas often come from "change agents," such as small business owners or agricultural extension faculty who are quite dissimilar from those receiving the information or advice (clients or farmers) in that they don't necessarily share attributes such as educational level, social status, or beliefs. But the "change agent" has credibility with the group.

Opinion leaders will very likely emerge as you begin to research public attitudes. Many times, common-sense insights will reveal them.

For example, Midland's engineering dean wants to involve his college in Industrial Education for Foreign Students, Inc., a program that arranges internships in U.S. businesses and industries for graduate students from foreign countries.

His draft list of potential opinion leaders might look like this:
- Business and industrial leaders, particularly board chairs, CEOs, personnel, and PR directors

- Government officials, particularly in the state development office, and state and federal commerce and education departments

- Leaders of national, state, and local manufacturing and commerce associations

- College and university administrators, particularly deans of graduate schools, foreign student advisors, PR directors, and engineering/business outreach personnel

- Foundation directors, national and institutional

- Leaders of service agencies such as the Institute of International Education and Rotary International

- News media, particularly business and education editors

- Members of his own faculty and staff who are interested in this area and tend to be drawn to new ideas ("early adapters")

- Foreign alumni who have benefited from their U.S. education and experience

The next step would be for the dean to plug proper names into that initial screening list, through information networking. The longer he has been in a position to be in contact with these key audiences, the more names will pop out of his files. No matter how refined his methods, it's likely that some opinion leaders will emerge that will surprise him and he'll discover that some old contacts won't be appropriate in this case. Whomever he identifies, he'll know that they may or may not be helpful at another time in another situation.

Faculty — A crucial "invisible" audience

Faculty and staff should not be the last to hear about key issues — nor the last consulted for their opinions on issues to which they are often closest. These include personnel matters, budget policies, and fund-raising campaign needs. Yet, based on a countrywide study of successes and failures in college presidencies, Robert Birnbaum, professor of higher education at the University of Maryland at College Park, concludes (1992) that perhaps the biggest weakness of college presidents is their inability to communicate candidly and listen carefully to faculty. The end results of such alienation include declines in faculty morale, in the ability to recruit top faculty, and in the unit's or institution's ability to compete for resources.

In many fund-raising campaigns, for example, the donors are in as much control as campus leaders. In fact, the "wish lists" of faculty who have the best sense of their program's needs often take a back seat to the donor's wishes when it comes to decisions about which projects will proceed.

At least three explanations — none of them completely satisfactory — have been offered for the lack of communication between administrators and faculty. First, so focused are academic leaders on communicating with external audiences from whom all blessings flow — legislatures, foundations, donors, denominational bodies, and so on — that they have too little time and pay too little attention to their internal constituencies. Second, faculty members are so involved in their professional pursuits or so instinctively distrustful of administrators that they don't heed communications that come their way. For example, instead of framing the fund-raising proposal in a way most acceptable to the donor, the faculty member may plunge ahead with his or her own uncompromising vision and thus destine the proposal for the reject pile. Third, in their desire to keep their faculties from being distracted by "the real world," administrators may simply refrain from communicating the harsh facts of life to their colleagues.

Another explanation is that decision-makers know how difficult it can be to get group consensus. Often it is easier simply to make "executive decisions" and avoid the discomfort and inconvenience of communicating. Certainly it can be challenging to communicate with faculty — as complex a group as ever you will meet. In fact, often the qualities that advance a faculty member in his or her profession go against the grain of group consensus. Being a successful faculty member at many institutions requires an entrepreneurial spirit, a willingness — if not eagerness — to go one's own way, and a large dose of self-confidence and strength of opinion on a wide range of subjects, within and beyond the discipline.

But if you don't consult your faculty when you make important decisions that directly affect them, then sooner or later you will have trouble.

If you are a campus leader, should you look for opinion leaders among your faculty? Absolutely. Your department or division likely has a few strong, outspoken personalities. Certainly, your unit is full of distinctive individuals who value their academic freedoms in different ways and who hold important opinions. You would be wise to know what those opinions are and to find ways to involve each individual in constructive communication.

Students — An even more "invisible" audience

On any college campus, the overwhelming majority of the population is composed of the students. And yet, how many of the communications that emanate from your unit are aimed at current students? Not many, we'll wager. There is great attention given to communicating with prospective students and to communicating academic information — schedules, timetables, course offerings — to enrolled students. But beyond that, institutions generally rely on the student press to get information to this important constituency.

Students, however, are increasingly important as opinion molders and image-builders — especially in this age of consumerism. And they can be surprisingly receptive to your attention and excellent sounding boards for your ideas and messages.

At the University of California, Berkeley, Linda Weimer has formed a student advisory committee for public affairs. The group meets once a month over an elegant pizza dinner to consider issues as varied as which speakers to invite to campus and how students are using computers to do their classwork and communicate with each other. The students on the committee represent a spectrum of campus organizations, including student government, student activity groups, returning adult students, athletics, the band, the student newspaper, and government internship programs. There also are students recruited at random, to ensure a range of ages, interests, ethnic backgrounds, majors, perspectives, and experiences.

The effort has been exceedingly productive on several counts. At a meeting in early 1995 to consider how students get their information, the editor and publisher of the *Daily Californian*, the student newspaper, were guests. Both found the feedback from the students on the committee exceedingly helpful. As an example, a woman representing re-entry students criticized the paper for not running more news of interest to older students, such as features on students with children. The editor, who is of a more traditional college age, said she had never thought about that point of view. As a result, she not only solicited opinion pieces from students in the re-entry program, but made it a point to run several stories related to the interests of older students.

Two other interesting sidelights came from that particular meeting. First, it was surprising to find that most of the students at the meeting read the *Berkeleyan*, the faculty/staff newspaper, even though it is not distributed to students. The *Berkeleyan* had, by the way, run stories about re-entry students, a fact that was noted in the meeting. The other surprising fact that emerged was that none of the 30 or so students in attendance, with the exception of the *Daily Cal* editor, read the local daily paper, the *Oakland Tribune*. At the same time, nearly all the students said they regularly read the *San Francisco Chronicle*. This information was very useful to the public information director, who factored that knowledge into his approach to getting news through the media to students.

A by-product of getting student input in this way is discovering the hidden gems in your midst who can be fantastic ambassadors for the institution. Often the best way to woo a donor or placate an angry legislator is to put him or her into direct contact with students. Often the students' personal experiences will be enough to sell the program to a wealthy alum who feels that "the place just hasn't been the same" since he graduated or to convince a legislator that a student *can* get good teachers and graduate in four years.

The "invisible" community

The community surrounding a college or university is all too often an audience invisible to the academic leader. What can happen when an institution neglects two-way communications with its community was illustrated when Marquette University proposed to sponsor a massive urban renewal program in its Milwaukee neighborhood. The plan came under a barrage of criticism from area residents, business people, and city planners when they learned that it called for closing long blocks of city arterial streets that bisected the sprawling campus.

On the other hand, there are abundant examples of what happens when a campus combines a strong community relations program with an equally strong communications program aimed at local constituents:

The University of Alabama at Birmingham, once a monolith of segregation, now actively supports the area's black residents and has become the city's largest public employer. So it speaks often to receptive citizens of its role as a cultural and economic asset.

Since 1985, the University of Pennsylvania has engaged in a model campus-community connection called the West Philadelphia Improvement Corps, a school-based, neighborhood revitalization movement involving faculty and students in hands-on projects in public schools.

In the District of Columbia, it is a rare week in which Washington newspapers fail to carry stories about George Washington University's array of community outreach programs, from Adopt-a-Family to a Washington Area Junior Academy of Sciences, that are helping public school students succeed, nurturing senior citizens, and lending legal assistance to the poor.

If any experiences testify to the value of caring about the community, they are those of the University of Southern California. Built more than one hundred years ago in what was then a garden suburb of Los Angeles, USC was by the 1960s right in the middle of one of America's poorest and most distressed neighborhoods — Watts and Vermont-Normandy. Yet during the terrible Watts riots of 1965 and the reactions to the Rodney King verdict in 1992, USC suffered nothing worse than a broken window at a parking kiosk.

That USC came through unscathed was no coincidence. It was due in large part to the hard work and dedication of thousands of individuals. USC's insurance policy is a communications program that constantly alerts its urban audiences to long-time, wide-ranging civic and community relations activities.

Campus leaders on the lower rungs of an institution shouldn't assume that reaching out to a community audience has no relevance to them or is exclusively the responsibility of a president or vice president. Every academic department has its own potential community constituency. For example:

- The University of Colorado's fine arts departments run a series of art and museum exhibits in Boulder, Denver, and beyond.

- The Monroe (NY) Community College English department raises money for adult literacy programs by sponsoring spelling bees five times a year, in which teams of business executives pay to compete for the title of "Best Corporate Speller in Rochester."

- A Johns Hopkins Peabody Conservatory of Music reaches out to Baltimore area music lovers by distributing 35,000 copies of a tabloid containing previews, interviews, and an events calendar.

In fashioning a community communications/relations program, it is well to heed this word of advice from Ira Harkavy, director of the Penn Program for Public Service (1993): "Work and study *with* the community; never treat them as mere patients, subjects, or unredeemable persons to collect data about."

And add this from Peter H. Hollister, vice president of Northern Kentucky University (1992): "None of us can deal with town-gown relations in an ad hoc manner. We must develop comprehensive strategic and tactical plans to deal with this important constituency."

Many of these observations on community audiences can be broadened to include other important external constituencies — whether they are state lawmakers who decide the budgetary fate of state-supported colleges and universities, business leaders who recruit and employ graduates, or fans of the athletic program who may drive hours across the state just to attend a game. The general principles of keeping all important audiences in mind and communicating with them regularly, in some way, are critical to the success of your program.

For further consideration ...

"Strange bedfellows"

As leaders, "you have a great opportunity to seek public support for your interests, not only from your traditional stakeholders, but from the third-party advocacy or constituency groups I call *strange-bedfellow allies*." So says Sheila Raviv, vice president of

Burston-Marsteller, a major public affairs consulting agency in Washington, DC.

She suggests that "you seek relationships with groups that at first glance may not appear to be related to your interests." Depending on your discipline or division, Raviv specifies, "I'm talking about associations, for example, of business and professional women, black lawyers, civic clubs; about public interest, public health, consumer and environmental watchdogs, advocacy groups for women, the elderly, health and safety concerns, and various groups of elected officials, just to name a few." Such groups play an important role in how public agendas and perceptions are set.

Developing relationships with such special-interest groups *before* you need their help is an important and necessary investment, as is getting to know all about them so that you can tailor your message to each group in terms of *its* reasons for caring about your interest and issues, Raviv says, rather than *your* reasons for communicating.

"Target the young"

Robert S. Topor says colleges and universities should "re-think their marketing strategies to involve outreach and targeting directed to younger and younger audiences."

Topor contends that decisions about higher education are becoming more and more influenced by college-bound students and their peers and they have emerged as a powerful force for marketing attention.

Topor goes on to urge that practitioners at all levels of education "begin to think about marketing in ways that go far beyond application in admissions and 'enrollment management.' "

chapter four

How It'll Play in Peoria
Researching audience attitudes

Public opinion about higher education continues to rank among the top concerns of higher education leaders across the United States. But what is "public opinion about higher education"?

That's a misleading question, because the public doesn't have a single opinion about higher education. The "public" actually consists of many segments of the population, with different opinions about higher education, according to sociological and economic factors and to their particular beliefs and interests.

So we find media reports of rising expectations and growing skepticism and mistrust, while public opinion polls show that colleges and universities enjoy extremely strong public support. Indeed, retired Speaker of the House of Representatives Thomas Foley recently stated that he strongly believes that colleges and universities still enjoy an almost unique blend of respect and admiration in Congress. A common refrain in academia is that the public doesn't appreciate research, yet poll data consistently show that Americans actually regard scientific research (and especially medical research) very highly.

Does this difference between perceptions and poll results indicate cognitive dissonance? No. There are legitimate concerns on the part of the public about the academic enterprise. But it is dangerous to make generalizations about public opinion and there are good reasons for taking a quantitative approach to assessing audience attitudes.

Unless we accurately identify and analyze the strains of opinion among the many publics, we cannot shape our messages and select media to reach and influence those who influence us. This is where audience research and analysis comes into play. Indeed, we cannot overemphasize its importance. We would be wealthy if we had a nickel for every brochure or video that is languishing on a shelf because it was developed for an audience of one — its producer — with no attention to addressing the needs of a real audience.

What determines attitudes

Why do people adopt certain attitudes? To borrow the classic definition of social psychologists, an attitude is a relatively enduring organization of beliefs that finds its expression — knowingly or unknowingly — in an opinion about a particular object or situation. That expressed opinion, in turn, can become an ingredient in a constant, gradual reformation of attitudes.

Each of us, for better or worse, is a bundle of fears, loves, hates, habits, peculiarities, prides, and prejudices. These proclivities all stem, at least in part, from four primary determinants — although none of us has to be an absolute prisoner of any but the most obstinate of roots!

One determinant of attitudes and opinions is, of course, *biology and heredity*. Amanda Perkins, for instance, will forever be a white, Anglo-Saxon female, with whatever innate traits her inheritance bequeaths. Her Welsh blood has made her slight of build and stature and partially determines her susceptibility to heart trouble, all of which might affect her personality. Her inherited brain power certainly set the stage for her present role in life.

A second broad determinant is *environment or culture* — nationality, family, religion, ethnicity, education, community, and so on. Perkins is an American Protestant from a close-knit family. She has had advanced educational training and has lived all of her adult life in college towns. All of this helps influence her attitudes, her interests, her mind-set, her view of the world.

Third is *role or group membership*. Perkins is inevitably influenced by her economic and social class, her gender identification, her age, her status as a single parent, her political affiliation, and her profession.

Often the most powerful determinant of all is *experience*. The minor events of our lives are profound wellsprings of our opinions and attitudes. We are emotional and intellectual chameleons who frequently reflect the color of our surroundings and the patterns of our accumulated experiences. For Perkins' parents, the Depression was a defining moment; the difficult years they experienced as children of the Depression forever influenced their attitudes toward money and security. A defining experience for Perkins was losing her husband in Vietnam; a defining situation was the challenge of becoming head of her department.

You can detect comparable roots in your present attitudes and opinions. Yet you also know that your attitudes change and evolve, that you are not totally locked in by those primary determinants. We are the products of our cumulative experience, our changing environment, and our shifting group memberships. Our attitudes and perceptions about certain things change — glacially perhaps, but surely.

Engines of attitude change

When our attitudes or opinions change, there is usually some predisposing motivation that makes us ready to respond. These motivations can be *personal* or *biological*, such as physiological drives for self-preservation, security, or sex, and emotional needs for trust, affection, and personal significance. Motivation also can arise through *group pressures* or norms exerted in the workplace, the organizations to which we belong, the friends with whom we associate, or the people whom we admire.

A recent Kettering Foundation study reported that Americans depend largely on the opinions of fellow citizens and on their own sense of "what rings true" in forming judgments on political issues. People get involved when an issue is relevant to their lives, but they don't rush to make a decision. Rather, they first ask questions, discuss the issue, and test ideas as they interact with others in churches, libraries, and community centers. "The public teaches itself through an interactive, exploratory dialogue, not a debate," said Kettering President David Matthews.

Most of us are naturally drawn to conform to the standards of the groups in which we find ourselves. Even the eccentric professor is expressing in his eccentricity an accepted "norm" for the academic. But while our groups influence us, so too do we influence our groups.

Perkins, for example, has an inherited and acquired drive for personal significance that, in turn, is tempered by her allegiance to the tenets of the American Association of University Professors (AAUP). Yet now that she's a department chair, she may be constrained to challenge the AAUP's prescribed tenure-review procedures.

Personal and group motivations play out in an environment in which we are constantly pummeled by forces that would change our opinions, such as political parties; professional, interest, or pressure groups; propagandists for partisan causes; the mass media; church groups; and the communication programs of industry, government, and education.

These generators of opinion change operate in an environment of censorship, filtering out elements of communication that don't conform to their basic premises. Sometimes that censorship is imposed at the source; sometimes it is imposed by the receiver through his or her unconscious desire to know just what he or she wishes to know and believe what he or she wishes to believe.

Nearly every communication problem has its basis in differences in perception — two or more people assessing the same set of information or the same situation in different ways.

Scott Cutlip, Allen H. Center, and Glen Broom (1994) have compressed most of the foregoing into *four guiding principles of persuasion*:

1. *Identification.* Unless their interests are involved — their desires, fears, feelings, or aspirations — members of the intended audience will tend to dismiss your message. They must identify with the message in some way.

2. *Action.* People are more receptive to messages that are connected to action — either action that those spreading the message are taking or about to take, or action that people receiving the message can take.

3. *Trust.* We buy ideas that are put forward by people or institutions with whom we are familiar and that we regard as credible.

4. *Clarity.* Most people — young people in particular — tend to see things in black and white and will discount or disregard messages that are ambiguous or ambivalent. Effective communication means a clear message that expresses an opinion and uses words, symbols, and allusions that are familiar to those receiving the message.

Listening well

Critical to successfully understanding your audiences and their attitudes is listening well. Take care not to tune out what you don't want to hear. Assessing attitudes is largely a matter of empathetic communication and common sense.

As you pick up on how a particular group feels about your unit, you are better able to assess the likely barriers that your message must overcome to reach that audience. You are also better able to adjust your unit's functions and policies to meet audience needs and expectations. This process does not mean that you try to follow every constituent whim. Rather, in your operational planning, you take into account the legitimate needs and expectations of your primary constituents.

Listening doesn't necessarily come easily to academic types. Many of us tend to assume that our rational thought processes will automatically produce the ideal answer to all questions, particularly those associated with higher education. We tend to discount opinions of our constituents. After all, what do they know?

Admittedly, constituency opinions are often ill-defined, vagarious, inconsistent. Sometimes our constituents have no opinions at all. It is easy, then, to adopt a patronizing air. Yet without an honest attempt to appreciate audience attitudes, an academic leader is shooting at targets in the dark. As Thomas Jefferson advised leaders of the infant University of Virginia: "We must lead our fellow citizens where we can, follow where we must, and still go with them."

Listening, for many of us, is an acquired skill. And yet, if we think of those who have led us effectively in our professional lives, we will find that they had that skill. They took our needs and motivations into account and turned our will to helping shape their vision for the unit, department, or institution.

If, for example, Perkins wants to start her master's program in biological conservation and sustainable development, she will need to listen to the interests both of her pool of potential students and of her pool of potential employers of graduates. If she and her colleagues create a curriculum that students don't wish to study or that trains students who are then unemployable, their best ideas and efforts will fail.

To take the pulse of these important constituencies, Perkins must use one or more of the many tools available for measuring attitudes and opinions. Some take a lot of time and money; others are fairly cheap and fast. Whatever the method, and whether you are department chair, a car manufacturer, or the president of the United States, it's important to do audience research before going forward with a message, product, or campaign.

Polling research is now a dominant feature of our political landscape and its techniques are moving rapidly into other arenas of the public sector. The only danger is that an organization might succumb to telling people what they want to hear, rather than telling them what is real or what they need to know.

Today, public opinion polling has become a sophisticated business that calls for specialized training and skills. If you don't have the money for a professional, full-scale public opinion poll, you can use inexpensive ways to survey your audience and get a sense of their attitudes.

Informal survey methods

Opinion polling by walking around

Linda Weimer has known several high-level university administrators who have sometimes exasperated their staff when it comes to certain issues. Why? Because the boss seemed to form his or her opinion about a subject based on what "the last person they talked to had to say about it."

This can be frustrating when that "last person" doesn't know anything about the subject. But what was actually going on, in most instances, was very positive. The campus leader was out talking to the folks — faculty, alumni, students, donors, voters, legislators — whose opinions really counted and was bringing those perceptions and ideas back to the staff who were far behind the front lines.

Anecdotal experience is one of the strongest — and perhaps most prevalent — means of testing attitudes. One doesn't have to be gregarious to develop a talent for picking up on how people feel about an issue. In fact, the most retiring academic leader can informally measure attitudes and opinions about his or her unit. These techniques lack the precision of more scientific opinion research, but unless the subject is totally obscure or the audience completely unknown, these informal methods of assessing attitudes may give you all the information you need. There is nothing like just getting out and rubbing elbows with your colleagues, students, and alumni, and putting yourself in their shoes.

You could use your lunch break to get out and around your department. Some of the most successful college leaders are those who make a practice of walking around the campus every day and talking to their colleagues and the students. Brown bag lunches with colleagues can be revealing. Join a table at the faculty club. Get in a cafeteria line with students. Attend a downtown service club luncheon. Slide onto a stool at the corner bar or coffee shop. The key is to get out of the office and take the pulse of your constituents simply by getting around, talking with people, and seeing the campus.

Of course, once you are out there, you need to strike up conversations and listen to what people have to say. Find something in common with the folks around you and then let them do most of the talking. A casual question or observation from you can yield a wealth of insight and information on a particular subject or issue.

If you want to know what your external audiences are thinking, go to them. If you are interested in what parents think of the campus, go to an event for parents, or talk to them as they are moving their children into the residence halls. If you are curious about alumni attitudes, attend an alumni board meeting and chat with the members during the break. In these situations, it is important to empathize with your audience and perceive the campus or unit as they do.

For example, a popular vice chancellor at the University of California, Berkeley left to take a very good job elsewhere. The rumor among some of his employees was that he left because he didn't get the better job of vice chancellor for academic affairs that was then vacant. From the viewpoint of the non-academic employees, any talented and dedicated person should be able to work his or her way up through the hierarchy of the university. Thus, the employees concluded that this able and charismatic man had been passed over for this "plum" position, although the reality was that he was not a viable candidate because he wasn't a tenured faculty member.

The moral of this story is that, if campus officials hadn't listened to the employee rumor mill, it never would have occurred to them to explain the situation, because they would have simply assumed that all employees were knowledgeable about the university hierarchy and the difference in leadership qualifications between the academic and business sides of the house. Even "insiders" can misconstrue actions and events. Attention to reactions, beliefs, perceptions, and attitudes around you can help minimize misunderstandings and image problems.

As an exercise in "walking a mile in someone else's shoes," you could try speculating about how different audiences might define an excellent college or university. Your list might look something like this:

- *A student* — I can get into all of the classes I want to take, my professors are accessible, the lectures are interesting, I am getting good grades and learning a lot, I like my roommates, and there are many fun things to do on campus.

- *A professor* — I am pretty much left alone to do my teaching and research as I see fit, the library is very good, my colleagues and students are smart and motivated, and the bureaucracy isn't too overburdening.

- *A parent* — My son or daughter is getting a good education, the campus is relatively safe, the college is affordable, my child is likely to get a good job upon graduation, and I am getting good information and service from the institution.

- *An alumnus* — The school is high-quality, so people are impressed when they learn that I went to school there, the athletic teams are winning, and the campus is in touch with me without bothering me too much for donations.

- *An employee* — The campus is clean and safe, my bosses treat me with respect and pay me what I'm worth, I am working for a good cause, I have a decent office, and I can park near where I work.

- *A federal agency* — The institution is doing great research with our support, handling our funds very responsibly, and giving us credit for our support.

- *The mayor* — The school is a good neighbor. It is paying for city services and working with us to solve community problems.

Common sense might have supplied you with some of those answers, but personal contacts can reinforce them and can sometimes supply you with perceptions that would have never occurred to you. Remember: the more varied your contacts, the richer your feedback and the more reliable your assessment.

For example, for many years, Clay Schoenfeld has maintained a cabin on a woodlot in a rural township an hour's drive from the campus. There he studiously fades into the countryside and becomes one with its residents. He hunts and fishes with the locals, plays poker with farmer neighbors, eats breakfast regularly at a crossroads kitchen, mends shared fences, and keeps his ears more open than his mouth. The perspectives he has gained have lent a valuable balance to otherwise campus-bound viewpoints — and have kept his prose colloquial.

Perkins uses several similar stratagems: conversations with the students who rent her studio apartments and with neighbors at her upstate summer retreat.

Opinion panels

A step beyond mingling at random is to form an "idea jury" — a panel of selected people who will give you candid viewpoints on any variety of subjects.

The panel's members can be broadly representative or narrowly focused, depending on your objective. For example, to get a sense of the efficacy of a particular curriculum, you might invite not only students but also peers and potential employers. On the other hand, to get a feel only for the quality of teaching, you might simply assemble a panel of students.

Panel feedback is only as sound as the character of its members and their willingness to speak candidly. To encourage free and honest exchanges, you may opt to appoint a panel chair and absent yourself from the discussion. On the other hand, you may choose to stay and stimulate discussion — but avoid steering it. You often will be surprised at what you learn in such discussions and how they might reinforce impressions for which you otherwise have no solid basis.

Advisory committees

A variation of the opinion panel is an advisory committee, temporary or permanent. Examples of the latter are your regular departmental faculty and executive committee meetings. Indeed, if you come from a campus on which faculty governance is very strong, such bodies may be more than simply advisory.

But apart from such "constitutional" committees, we find that academic programs, departments, and divisions are relying increasingly on advisory committees for guidance and support. These are committees to which you, as the unit head, can appoint colleagues, friends, critics, students, and experts, depending on the role you want them to play. Some committees may be short-lived — intended to advise only on a particular project or event. Others may be continuing.

An advisory committee can play a dual role. Not only can one give you a sensitive response to a proposition, but its members may become ambassadors for you among the constituencies from which they are drawn. A group frequently overlooked in this regard is the students. An advisory committee of students not only will give you good advice and insights from their unique perspective, but also will constitute a cadre of ambassadors who understand your objectives and will represent your point of view to their peers.

But there's one catch in employing advisory committees. There's no fury like an advisory committee scorned or a member feeling merely "used." You must sincerely seek advice and honestly take actions that reflect that input. Otherwise, you may contaminate the wellsprings of good will that you are seeking to tap. Committee members who feel well-connected and appropriately acknowledged develop a sense of "ownership" and pride in the program; those who do not may actually develop an antipathy to your efforts and undermine your attempts to gain access to key audiences or implement your agenda.

In developing her plan for a new master's program in biological conservation and sustainable development, Perkins sought counsel from many committees — in-house, on-campus, and off-campus. Members provided useful input, and some of them became key players in selling the concept to Midland University's academic planning councils and administrators.

Ombudspersons

Many of today's enterprises have an ombudsperson, who is responsible for fielding confidentially all complaints, concerns, and other feedback from customers, employees, and others. Such a person is particularly valuable in large institutions that may seem impenetrable and hopelessly bureaucratic to outsiders. Even in small units, there is usually an employee who functions as an ombudsperson. You may have one or more. An administrative assistant, unit manager, secretary, or student advisor may be a willing ear to students and colleagues. A senior faculty member or assistant to the chair or director might have the confidence of colleagues, young and old. A janitor, though not empowered to resolve issues, still may be privy to a surprising amount of frank feedback from students and colleagues.

Be sure your close constituents have access to a "friend in court," who can, in turn, pass on to you information about incipient problems or negative perceptions. Keeping posted on the attitudes and opinions of your colleagues and students is vital to your success.

Perkins inherited two ombudspersons: a veteran administrative assistant known as a friendly soul to generations of students and a middle-aged professor blessed with great rapport with faculty colleagues in two distinctly different camps of the department. Though their roles are unofficial, they play them well, keeping confidences but providing Perkins with much needed feedback on departmental sentiments.

Calls and letters

External constituencies need campus ombudspersons as well. Many colleges and universities have set up 800-number telephone "hot lines" or "query lines." Others do so for particular constituencies, like parents or alumni. If the operators of these lines are encouraged to keep diaries or notes on their calls, deans and department chairs will undoubtedly find them valuable sources of feedback.

A word of caution: do not read too much into telephone feedback. By the very nature of the process, calls tend to be long on complaints and short on constructive suggestions or compliments. They may not be a valid reflection of attitudes and opinions out there.

A few years ago, the state of California set up a hot line for the public to call with suggestions on how the University of California System could save money. Only a handful of useful ideas came out of the hundreds of calls. The most frequent suggestion was simply to fire all the university's leaders!

The California experience raises two useful points: don't establish a hot line in a crisis unless you are serious about using the information you receive, and don't subject the employees who are answering the line to the insults of an outraged public. Yet don't simply dismiss angry phone calls to your office — they can reveal widespread misperceptions or problems with your public relations program.

A periodic analysis of your incoming mail also can reveal areas of favor, disfavor, or misinformation. Letters can hoist warning flags, provide surprising kudos, and indicate information vacuums. Here again, the mail is not necessarily a valid sample. Like the letters to the editor of your local newspaper, the mail you receive comes from highly motivated constituents, not from a professional poll.

Electronic mail is a relatively new development that allows communication that is simpler and more instantaneous than a letter or even a phone call. Email provides a wonderful means of seeking feedback from people who are sometimes hard to reach otherwise. However, it does not afford one important safeguard of written mail: the "cooling off" period before a letter is actually stamped and posted. Sentiments are fired off through cyberspace by people who might never have put them on paper or, at least, would never have mailed them. Opinions expressed via email, therefore, should get somewhat less credence than those arriving via "snail mail."

Perkins has the department secretary make photocopies of pertinent correspondence and collate them in "opinion" files labeled according to the audiences to which they pertain. She learned this practice while working in the private sector. She tries to answer every reasonable letter and memo in a timely fashion. That takes time, but it's "good PR."

News media analysis

Newspapers, magazines, radio news broadcasts, and television news are essential means of keeping track of what is being said about your institution, unit, program, area of study, and education in general.

Your campus public information office may subscribe to press clipping and broadcast monitoring services and may distribute periodic summaries to deans and departments. You may want to assign a staff member, colleague, or student the task of keeping track of items in the news that pertain to your division or unit. Cutlip, Center, and Broom (1994) have this pithy advice about how to analyze the news media you assemble:

> The press, when used with caution, can be a fairly reliable guide to current opinions, particularly those of protest and criticism. Still, the wide disparity between the voting opinions of the people and the editorial opinions of newspapers, as demonstrated in elections, should warn against uncritical acceptance of newspaper editorial opinion. The same is true of radio and TV news communicators; interpretive reporting may or may not reflect public opinion. *Mass media can be used as indicators, not as yardsticks.*

Professional sources —
Colleagues in the field

Many colleges and universities have personnel "in the field" — student recruiters, outreach specialists, fund-raisers, researchers, extension agents, and the like. These representatives have been trained to listen to their constituencies and report on the opinions and attitudes they encounter. The feedback of these professionals can be especially valuable if you know them personally and trust their judgment and reliability.

For example, Perkins puts a good deal of faith in the intelligence-gathering of her neighbor — Midland's director of admissions, who has trained a squad of career counselors to bring back reports from the parents, guidance counselors, and students they meet at college nights and high school visits throughout the region.

Academic and professional peers, too, are an excellent source of feedback. Again, the better you know them, the more able you are to appreciate their input. Conferences and programs are useful places to gather information and informal feedback. Journals and newsletters also contain excellent reports of public attitudes and how other departments and institutions are dealing with them. The *Chronicle of Higher Education, Academic Leader, Change Magazine, Academe,* and *Higher Education Record* are a few of the most fruitful interdisciplinary sources of such information. Most academic professionals and disciplines have their own specialized periodicals. Perkins, for example, follows *Science* magazine regularly.

Data on public opinion and attitudes about issues in higher education may be available at the touch of a computer keyboard. Already, publications like the *Chronicle of Higher Education* are available online and World Wide Web sites provide more and more information that may answer at least some of your questions.

Instincts and sense

Never underestimate the power of your instincts and common sense in assessing the attitudes of your constituents. This is particularly true in situations in which you don't have the time or resources to use other means of gathering information. Of course, the more your judgment has some basis in either formal or informal surveying of attitudes, the sounder it will be.

For example, the Midland admissions director told Perkins that he used to mail promotional literature first-class on the assumption that a first-class stamp enhanced receptivity. But he interviewed a representative sample of prospective students and learned that they typically will open *anything* with a university address in the corner of the card. Now he mails at a much cheaper rate, saving Midland thousands of dollars in postage.

Perkins took that information and used her judgment to apply it to her mailings to departmental alumni, figuring that her alumni would be intrigued enough to open a mailing from their alma mater, whether it had first-class postage or not. On the other hand, for special fund-raising letters, she continued to use a first-class stamp. She found through anecdotal feedback and good response to her solicitation letter that her hunch was right.

Formal survey methods and audience research

Social scientists and market researchers have developed sophisticated methods of determining public attitudes and opinions. In fact, many institutions offer graduate courses in opinion research in departments of business, public policy, sociology, political science, and communication.

If your campus offers such courses, you may be able to get a course instructor to work with you or you may engage a student to do some opinion research for you as a seminar or class project. Many institutions, in fact, have survey research laboratories, which are in-house opinion research centers. They may let you piggy-back questions on a project already being conducted. A number of colleges and universities have been able to get data on public opinions about higher education in this way. You may get intrigued enough to learn something about these techniques and take a crack at some opinion polling of your own with a little help from your colleagues.

Focus groups

A focus group is a scientifically constituted opinion panel or idea jury, convened by a trained investigator to gather opinions on a given subject, sometimes at several time intervals. Some results can affirm your intuitive approaches to communicating with certain audiences; others can be quite surprising.

Not too long ago, the development office at the University of California, Berkeley, assembled a group of alumni of different ages living only a few miles from the campus to assess their awareness of the university and to find out how they were getting their information. Members of the group regularly received a variety of materials — most of which touted a specific program or college. Yet focus group leaders found that the audience *did not distinguish among the publications originating from various units of the university,* including those from the alumni association, the development office, the university public information office, and, in some cases, the University of California System President's Office, located in nearby Oakland. Some members of the focus group also were surprisingly ill-informed on many issues, despite the bombardment of information from the campus. These findings led the university to develop a new presentation that could be delivered in person to gatherings of area alumni groups.

The interactive discussions that occur in focus groups are especially valuable in gauging audience reactions to specific issues. The limitations of such forums stem from the small size of the group. If the members are not chosen carefully, the group can yield perspectives that do not represent the audience in question.

Gary L. Kramer, associate dean of admissions and records at Brigham Young University, is a fan of focus groups (1992). He periodically forms a "council" of randomly selected students to give him feedback on the effectiveness of his communications materials. For example, when his council reviewed a mailing for new students and a related videotape script, they were in consensus that the script covered more material than a new student could grasp and that it would be more appealing to have a student narrate the presentation.

In-depth interviews

A trained interviewer or skilled analytical team can probe attitudes through long, candid interviews with representative individuals. In such settings, subjects are encouraged to talk freely and candidly to interviewers, who often are consultants with no direct responsibility for the area covered in the interview. In planning fund-raising campaigns, for example, such interviews are a good way to assess potential donors' interests in the various needs of the institution.

Billiee Pendleton-Parker of Georgia Institute of Technology and Sammy Parker of the University of Georgia conducted in-depth interviews of faculty colleagues to find out what department chairs should be doing to improve faculty motivation. They learned that faculty wanted the chair, from the very start, to communicate to new faculty fully and clearly about unit and institutional standards and expectations as well as about such items as fringe benefits and spousal employment. Thereafter, they were told, nothing is as important as receiving recognition from the chair, publicly and privately, for their significant accomplishments.

Questionnaires

A more economical approach than the in-depth interview is the questionnaire, which can either be given out at an event or mailed to the pool of individuals to be sampled. The questionnaire, however, has two major flaws. First, a sheet of paper lacks the flexibility of an interview. Second, it's very difficult to get enough responses — even when you are personally collecting them from an audience at the end of a meeting session — to render the sample representative of the population you are surveying. Also, with this technique, you often get a disproportionately high number of critical responses. Yet, used carefully, questionnaires can provide a very useful, quick, and relatively cheap means of assessment.

Polls

Based on the laws of mathematical probability, a survey asking precise, understandable questions of a truly representative sampling of the whole can measure public opinion quite accurately. Done properly, polls cost money. Indeed, their accuracy probably correlates directly to the money invested in them, since it is important not only to properly select the survey sample and construct the survey instrument, but also to use trained pollsters. On the other hand, if done properly, a poll doesn't require a large sample.

If you are wondering how you might best judge the caliber of whatever agent or agency you might employ to poll your constituents, analysts Barbara C. Burrell of the University of Wisconsin-Madison and Theresa A. Neil of the University of Minnesota-Duluth have developed this checklist:

Checklist for Questionnaire Construction

1. Have you decided what information you need and how you'll use it?

2. Does each question solicit a specific piece of information that you need?

3. Are the response categories worded well? Are they comprehensive?

4. Does the questionnaire begin with interesting, easy questions and end with demographics?

5. Are your questions grouped by topic, proceeding from general to specific?

6. Are the questions conversational without being slangy?

7. Is the wording clear and unambiguous, so that questions have a single, common meaning for respondents?

8. Do you use vocabulary familiar to the respondents?

9. Do you alternate long and short questions, with the longer questions requiring the most thought on the part of the respondents?

10. Does each question ask only one thing?

11. Are questions free from assuming too much respondent knowledge or opinion?

12. Do you avoid loaded phrases that might suggest a certain response?

13. Do you, in most cases, offer a "don't know" alternative?

14. Are the questions substantively balanced, offering equal-weight answers?

15. Do you vary "agree/disagree" questions to avoid acquiescence bias?

Constructing a questionnaire is a complicated business best left to professionals. Even then, it's difficult to avoid bias. Many factors can influence how respondents answer questions, including the order in which the questions are asked, the ways in which the questions are phrased, the age and gender of those polled, even the region of the country in which the poll takes place.

If you rely on poll results "from the outside," it's important to remember that most polls are sponsored by organizations that are often seeking particular answers to particular questions, so bias is not uncommon or even unanticipated. There are even times when pollsters try to bias their results. For example, political pollsters may use a relatively new phenomenon called the "push poll." The purpose of such a poll is not to assess opinions about candidates, but rather to push respondents toward the candidate sponsoring the poll or, at least, away from the opponent.

Polls can provide knowledge; knowledge can be power, if it can influence people in power. Those are basic facts of life. When higher education institutions commission polls, for example, it is to gauge public opinion, of course, but it is also to use any positive results to sway key decision-makers, be they donors, legislators, or community leaders. If you pay attention to the results of any such outside polls, bear that pragmatism in mind.

In short, opinion polls can be as destructive as they are constructive, if they are used without scruples or simply to boost ratings. If done well and honestly, polls can provide a complex view of how citizens reason, separately and together, about public problems.

Pre-testing

There is one form of relatively scientific opinion research that even an amateur can use with reasonable care. It's called "pre-testing."

Let's say that Perkins and her intern have an idea for a poster. They want to distribute it around the country to alert potential students to Midland's new master's program in biological conservation and sustainable development. However, they aren't sure what design and wording would most appeal to their audience. To find out, they draft three variations on the theme and send small numbers of each version (which will carry a code) to a variety of departments in selected colleges, chosen randomly. Then they count the responses by the attached codes to gauge the relative effectiveness of their poster versions. The results may just surprise them and save them money. A glitzy presentation may be less effective than one that is straightforward and substantive or one that takes a very creative approach.

Putting it all together

Researching public attitudes is essentially a five-step process:

Collection of data is the phase that has been the focus of this chapter, illustrating that there are many ways to collect information about your audience's knowledge and attitudes.

The next step is *collation*, the process of organizing what you have gathered in some systematic way. You might organize survey results according to topics covered, chronology, or key audiences.

After the results are collated, you begin the process of *evaluation*. This means you assess the data in terms of the credibility of its source, perhaps rating it from A to D; for example, an editorial in a campus daily paper with a good record of reflecting student opinion will usually be more reliable than a chance conversation with an individual student. Also consider in your ranking how relevant the information is to you and your unit; for example, a Midland development officer's report on results from a questionnaire focusing on donor support for environmental issues will be much more important to Perkins and her colleagues than a *New York Times* opinion piece on national prospects for private support to public universities.

The fourth step is *interpretation* of your research results. What does it all mean? To answer that question, state concisely what each component of the data seems to say about attitudes and opinions. Then, from this collection of summary statements you should be able to put together a pretty fair assessment of a particular audience's positions on a range of topics or the positions of a range of audiences on a particular topic.

The last, and critical, step is *dissemination* of your findings. The memo you draft will become a guide in formulating your communications plan, but you should do more with it. Key colleagues in your unit or institution and people in your campus public affairs office may find your opinion research informative and useful.

Also, sending your memo around may refine the assessment, as others contribute their own findings or add valuable insights about particular audiences or issues.

The experience of Cuyahoga Community College (Tri-C) in Ohio demonstrates the importance of surveying your audience (Carter 1993). And it anticipates the message of chapters to come: by putting that market research to work as you pick your medium and craft your message, you will succeed in reaching your targeted audience.

Tri-C's market research indicated that its students tended to be older, work full-time, and serious about advancing their careers, but that they previously had not considered college. Sandra Golden, associate vice president at the time, and her staff decided that their most important message was that Tri-C was affordable, accessible, and a smart choice for people wanting to move up.

Tri-C was recruiting its students from the metropolitan Cleveland area and wanted to reach a broad audience and age range. Additional audience research indicated, therefore, that advertising, especially TV ads, would likely be effective. So the college developed a recruiting campaign around the theme "You'll Come Out Ahead," and developed animated ads showing an eagle learning to fly and a lion learning to roar. From this theme, they developed direct mail pieces, radio jingles, print ads, and a free career guide. The print ads listed phone numbers for information on courses in particular career areas. The campaign worked splendidly.

In summary, the value of knowing your audience's knowledge, attitudes, desires, interests, biases, and receptivity to new ideas and products cannot be overestimated. Warehouses could be filled with the thousands of posters and publications that have been produced without regard to audience interest.

Not long ago, a university system, to commemorate its anniversary, invested major funding in a hard-bound book that showcased all of the system's campuses. But it turned out that there was no audience for the product, because the alumni for which it was intended held their allegiances to specific campuses and didn't want to spend big bucks for a book with only a few pages and pictures of their alma mater. A little preliminary market research could have avoided the subsequent massive book give-away and financial loss.

If you are under pressure from trustees, the president, or the alumni board to develop a special project or communication product, learn from that experience. If the project or product suggests, "Let's tell them what we want them to know, not what they want to know," then recommend some survey research in advance. It is well worth the investment.

For further consideration ...

Differing views

College and university administrators must work harder to com-municate the strengths and goals of higher education to their constituencies, a 1995 opinion poll commissioned by the Ameri-can Council on Education has revealed.

Complicating that task is the fact that public perceptions of higher education differ vastly depending on the segment of the population, says pollster James Harvey, a Villanova University (PA) professor, in *Higher Education & National Affairs* (1995). Community leaders have a "sophisticated understanding" of higher education issues and problems, but they decry the "lack of basic skills and poor business skills" of recent college gradu-ates, believe campuses need restructuring, think matters of race on campus are "poorly handled," and have "little sympathy" for the financial problems of higher education institutions.

Among the general public, on the other hand, there is practically no knowledge of higher education issues. Those people with an opinion think "too many people go to college because there is nowhere else to go" and that "more vocational offerings —

apprentice programs — should be available," yet strongly support student assistance programs.

Paradoxically, historical patterns of support for higher education seem to be reversed, Harvey notes:

> The rank-and-file used to complain about higher education while community leaders defended it; now the general public is relatively quiescent, but "leaders criticize higher education's inflexibility and arrogance."

Putting advisory committees to work

Too many administrators in higher education think advisory committees "just get in the way," when actually "they can provide mechanisms to help improve communication with the outside world," says Lee Teitel, professor and director of the educational administration program at the University of Massachusetts at Boston.

Teitel is the author of *The Advisory Committee Advantage: Creating an Effective Strategy for Programmatic Improvement* (1994). In this handbook, Teitel explains exactly how advisory committees — groups of volunteers that meet to guide or advance an institution — can help connect colleges and universities to their environments — when academic leaders learn "how to use and manage them."

To help administrators do just that, Teitel examines the purposes and advantages of an advisory committee, discusses the determinants of an effective committee, and draws upon a score of sources for various recommendations for starting and sustaining an effective committee.

chapter five

A Picture or a Thousand Words
Surveying your media options

You may be tempted to skip this chapter if you already have some notions about the best medium for your needs. Please don't do it! In communications, operating on notions can be extremely costly. The authors have seen too many excellent publications, feature articles, slide shows, press conferences, and the like fail to reach the intended audiences — largely because notions about how to deliver the message were vague and unrealistic. Objectivity is essential in matching medium and audience.

Selection of media begins with understanding the message to be delivered and recognizing *all* the options available for reaching your target audience. An important first question is whether one medium will do the job appropriately.

This question is pertinent even if your audience is a familiar group, close to home. Should you, for example, reach your faculty by sending an announcement by electronic mail, by making a pitch at the departmental staff meeting, by putting a flier in their mailboxes, or through some combination of the three approaches? What about faculty who bury their mail or skip meetings? Or, if you want to promote your unit's interactions with industry, should you use only a brochure or should you also use a videotape?

The answer: it depends. Part of the answer will lie in the nature of your message. How important, difficult, or complicated is it? Can it be simplified or subdivided? Do you have time, space, or budget limitations?

Another part of the answer will lie in the nature of your audience, as we have explored in previous chapters. To what channel(s) is the audience tuned? Is it close by or far away? Will one means of communication do it? Or do you need several different approaches? These and other factors will weigh heavily in your selection of media.

Reviewing your options

To jog your thinking about the channels of communication on your campus, in your community, or beyond, here is a partial list of media categories. Others may come to mind as you read it.

The Printed Word	*The Spoken Word*	*The Image*
advertising	assemblies	art
agendas	faculty meetings	cable television
annual reports	forums	charts
billboards	grapevine	closed circuit TV
booklets	information booths	computer multimedia
books	news releases to radio	cybercations
brochures	paid adverisements	displays
budget documents	panel discussions	exhibits
bulletins	press conferences	film clips
bulletin boards	public addresses	films
conventional	public announcements	graphic posters
electronic	radio	open houses
Internet	television	photographs
direct mail	radio programs	community access TV
electronic mail	speakers' bureaus	news releases on TV
editorials	speeches	signs

The Printed Word

Facsimiles
   individual
   broadcast
feature stories
house organs
handbooks
information racks
inserts and enclosures
letters
letters-to-the-editor
magazines
manuals
memos
minutes
newsletters
   internal audience
   external audience
news releases to mass media
news tipsheet for media
pamphlets
photocopies
position papers
posters
progress reports
proposals
reprints
tabloids

The Spoken Word

internal audience
external audience
talk show on radio
talk show on television
telephone news lines
videocassettes
World Wide Web

The Image

slide shows
souvenirs
special events
television clips
tours

Selecting the medium for your message

Assuming that several message carriers on this list show potential
to reach all or some of your specific audience, the next step is to
mentally screen them, selecting a few categories, such as "re-

gional magazines" or "radio," that seem especially appropriate to your situation.

Next, examine *specific media within each selected category*. For example, of the two regional magazines and four radio talk shows that you have identified, which are truly suitable outlets for your message? To find answers you will have to gather information on the following characteristics for each medium:

Audience and circulation.   Do the people you want to reach pay attention to this medium in sufficient numbers? Where do they live, what do they do, what are their levels of education and income, and what is their cultural background? What is their interest in this particular medium? Any commercial enterprise such as a newspaper, magazine, or television network will have extensive demographic information about its audience and may be willing to share it with you.

Content.   What is the subject focus of this medium? Do you have the information *and the resources* to reasonably tailor a message to the content requirements of this medium?

Dispersion. Does the medium reach a lot of people in a kind of unfocused spray or does it take direct aim at a smaller, more defined group?

Geographic scope.   Does this medium focus only on people in a particular region? Depending on your message and target audience, a limited geographic scope can be to your advantage or disadvantage.

Receptivity.   Is this a medium to which people eagerly pay attention (e.g., their pay statement or the movie guide)? Or is it one they tend to ignore (e.g., mailings from fund-raising groups)? If it's basically a good medium, but has become too boring or mundane, can you overcome that hurdle?

Periodicity.   How often does the vehicle reach out to its audience? How long in advance must you get information to the editor or program director in order to be included in the publication or program? This factor will affect the utility of that carrier for your messages in obvious ways. A daily newspaper is ideal for calling attention to tomorrow night's event; an information rack suits a message whose time frame is longer-term, such as next spring's special extension courses.

Prerogative.   Is this a medium you are encouraged to use freely and directly? Or are you expected to approach it through another unit, such as your news service, development, or alumni office?

Prestige, credibility, and character.   The esteem in which any medium is held is largely in the eye of the beholder. If it's a reliable source of information and its contributors are skilled reporters or respected technicians in that field, then it garners esteem, whether it's *Rolling Stone*, *Fine Woodworking*, *Wired* magazine, or the *Journal of Physiology*. Of course, within any field, some information sources are more prestigious than others. In academic circles, journals in which articles are reviewed for publication are more highly respected than semi-professional journals or conference proceedings, largely because it is harder to gain entry into their pages. The same holds true for more popular media.

So ask yourself: Does information that appears in *this* medium carry more weight than if it appeared somewhere else? With *whom* does it carry weight? What about credibility? Is it an accurate and reputable source of information? Or is its treatment of material uneven and questionable? Bear in mind that reports about your unit or institution may be perceived as more credible if they come through media not within your control or the control of your institution.

Appropriateness.   This is an extremely subjective characteristic. Depending on the mores and culture of your campus and unit, it may be "acceptable" for you to use some media but not others. For example, it might be OK to send a glossy recruiting brochure to potential undergraduate students, but something more subdued and substantive may be required in recruiting graduate students. It may be desirable to have a story about one of your star professors in the *Boston Globe* but not in the *National Inquirer*. Personally, we feel hang-ups about "appropriateness" too often stymie the effectiveness of academic communicators.

It's never appropriate, especially for a public institution, to indulge in expensive publications or media when budgets are tight or when other avenues work just as well. But in other areas, it may be time to experiment with more varied media and more styles. A mention on David Letterman's television show may get you more interested student recruits than a fancy poster mailed to a thousand high schools.

Proximity. When an outsider or a stranger says you are doing a good job, it carries more weight than when your best friend says it. For the same reason, people pay more attention to local accomplishments when they are recognized or lauded by a regional or national publication. This is one reason why college PR offices spend so much energy garnering the attention of national media, even when the target audience is largely local and the local media are already providing good coverage. Of course, the authors also know of many instances where the local media have picked up an excellent news story only after it has been carried in national newspapers and broadcasts!

Cost. The bottom line, ultimately, in selecting the media to use may be cost — direct and indirect. You may have the funds to buy a full-page advertisement in the alumni magazine, but can you afford the graphic designer to prepare it? You may have money to produce a newsletter, but what about the sizable costs of postage, mailing, and mailing-list management? Even a product of modest cost is questionable if it's going to reach only a tiny fraction of your audience. Some items that are exciting to produce — such as films or exhibits — are not only expensive to produce initially, but also costly in terms of the human resources required constantly to find new venues for their showing.

The most economical medium for communicating about forthcoming events and opportunities to people outside the institution is usually not the "free" story sprayed out through a mass news medium. It is the message of modest cost carried directly to a chosen audience, either through the mail or through an advertisement in a publication exclusively targeted at that particular audience.

Control. When you are seeking as many outlets as possible for your message, it may seem inconsequential to consider who is in control of each medium — that is, who decides which stories are used and how they are presented. You may care only about the visibility. But control is an important consideration.

You are in charge when it's your own *in-house medium,* such as a departmental newsletter, poster, or event. These are products, venues, and facilities that you and your colleagues control or that are there to serve you. Using such media is fairly simple. It involves preparing information in the appropriate style and format and meeting your own editorial and production deadlines. You decide the content and distribution. New electronic networks also fall into this category. The Internet, theoretically, allows anyone to become a publisher. Similarly, *you are in charge* with a *purchased service,* such as advertising space or air time on a radio station, since you are buying the right to determine content, style, and timing — within the guidelines of good taste.

You may have influence when it's a *medium within your institution* (such as a campus newspaper or radio program), one with a *high affinity* to your institution (alumni or trade magazine), or an *academic publication.* You do not have total control, but through your contacts and status you can influence the choice of content and the manner of presenting your message, to some extent.

You are not in control when you are appealing to a *commercial news or trade medium* (including television and newspapers). Whether you are the subject of breaking news, a feature story, or a video feature, you have no control over how the reporters, editors, and producers will use your information. Your task as a communicator, therefore, becomes more complex. For one thing, you are competing with many other news sources that may have equally attractive messages. For another, you may pitch a story one way, but the reporter may find a different angle, not to your liking. For example, you may want to show how your department is helping a local business, but the reporter may be more interested in how your faculty are using their time outside the classroom or the consulting fees they're collecting for their work.

It is worth noting that by developing personal relationships with reporters and editors — the "gatekeepers" who select and shape the news — you can be more successful. The reporter is not only more likely to take a tip from someone he or she knows and trusts, but also is more inclined to present the information in a way that satisfies your aims.

To use the news media as vehicles for your message, you must not only persuade the gatekeepers (reporters, editors, producers) of the merits of your information, but also play by their rules. That includes respecting their decisions on content (what makes for an interesting story), style, format, and presentation. A little thanks to the media for their thoughtful coverage of your unit never hurts either.

It is a source of constant wonder to the authors that, when a newspaper or television show runs an excellent feature on a faculty member, for example, the subject will want to write an angry letter to the editor because he or she feels some small item in the story was wrong or taken out of context. This behavior calls to mind something about not seeing the forest for the trees! Appreciate the coverage and don't sweat the small stuff. Of course, when serious errors are made in coverage, you should correct them. But do it judiciously if you want to be on good terms with the media.

You also must become adept, or find someone who is adept, at the modes of communication that fit your selected media's needs: news releases, media advisories, tipsheets, and so on. Your campus news and information service can be of great assistance, since dealing with the mass media is their daily business. They generally know many radio, television, and print editors and reporters. They know those reporters' and editors' likes and dislikes, their interests and biases.

Considering the time and energy that goes into persuading mass media to carry your message, it is clearly wiser to first exploit to the fullest every medium over which you have control or influence. Most of your communications probably will be produced and distributed close to home and geared toward familiar audiences. The challenges of wooing larger and more remote markets can be left largely to the experts.

Other considerations in selecting media

- What is the major aim of the medium — to instruct, entertain, interpret, persuade, or a combination of all of these?

- Do people use this medium consciously or unconsciously (for learning — that is) as a source of information?

- What is competing with this medium for time, interest, and response?

- Has its effectiveness been measured in terms of the audience you have in mind?

- Can an audience member control his or her own exposure? (A newspaper reader, for example, sets his or her own pace, selecting which news to read, while a radio listener will hear all of a news broadcast.)

- Is the media's treatment limited? Does it deliver only the gist of messages (radio news) or also the details (magazine features)?

- Is it likely that people have an emotional attachment to one medium over another?

Scoring your selections

To simplify your ranking of media characteristics, especially if you are developing a plan for a wide-ranging publicity effort, you might try putting your "wish list" of media in a column down one side of a page and pertinent characteristics across the top of the page. Then assign a number score (1 — most desirable to you, 3 — least desirable) at each intersection.

For example, Amanda Perkins, in planning the open house for her department at Midland, might make the following list.

Publicity for Annual Department Open House

Wish List	Pertinence to my audience	Costs (direct & indirect)	Likelihood of access	Appropriateness?	Total score
video segment for regional TV	low (3)	high (1)	low (3)	low (3)	(10)
local radio talk show	medium (2)	low(3)	medium (2)	medium (2)	(9)
item in student newspaper	high(1)	low (3)	medium (2)	high (1)	(9)
feature in student newspaper	High (1)	low (3)	high (1)	high (1)	(6)

Perkins could add email, departmental newsletter, fliers, the alumni magazine, and other means of communication to her list. By tallying the numbers, she can readily see that trying to promote her open house with a video clip on regional TV would be a mismatch, while aiming for the student newspaper will give her high impact for low cost. These media would be of limited use, however, if her goal were to attract attention to a research discovery. Then it might be acceptable to put more time and energy into less accessible media (e.g., regional television, metropolitan newspapers).

How to assess the medium

How do you determine if a potential vehicle for your message — including a campus medium of communication — is going to meet your needs, reach your audience, and offer reasonable access?

If it's a *publication*, check out several recent issues:

Pay attention to the title. If it's called *Financial Affairs Today*, you can be 99.9% sure the editors are not interested in an article on educational methods, unless it has to do with new training methods for bankers or teaching about investment strategies.

Skim the articles to get a sense of the topics covered. If the medium's mission and focus are such that you have to bend your message into a pretzel to make it fit, then this is not the publication for you. The chances are high that the readers are not paying attention to this particular vehicle for the kind of message you want to deliver. (If they have an interest in your topic, they are likely to look for it in other media.) If something along the lines of your message doesn't show up within five or six issues, best forget it.

Check on periodicity. Examine the masthead for statements regarding circulation and frequency of publication. If the medium is to your liking but appears only twice a year, it won't be the best carrier for a dated message.

Check the table of contents. The table of contents (and the article bylines or footnotes) will give you the names of the writers and their credentials. If articles are written by academics, you may have reasonable access to the publication. If they are written by the publication's own staff or by freelance writers, access may be harder. The table of contents also will point you to various departments within a publication, some of which may be markedly different in tone and content from the rest of the publication.

Look at advertisements. Advertising agencies invest heavily in market research. Ads can tell you a lot about the readers — for example, age, gender, income, and educational background. Are the advertisers heavily into messages about cosmetics or cellular phones? BMWs or Fords? Classical music or frozen dinners? The ads will give you clues to the interests and lifestyles of the readers. Airline magazines are a good case in point. The next time you fly, note the ads in the in-flight magazine, then notice how the ads relate to the magazine's stories.

If it's *a radio panel or TV show* that you are considering as a medium, watch or listen to a number of programs. Note the topics, the kinds of guests, and their professions or credentials. Also pay attention to the kinds of questions asked, the presence of a bias or focus in the conversations, and how often the guests' affiliations are mentioned. (After all, you're seeking recognition for your institution.) And, as with print media, pay close attention to the commercials. What do they reveal about the audience?

If it's *one of many other media* you are exploring — exhibits, open houses, videotapes, Web sites, films, and posters, to name a few — ask the experts what they think. Find out which colleagues on campus have recently produced a video or held an open house and talk to them. Find out what kinds of resources and budgets were required, how audiences responded, what unexpected (pleasant and unpleasant) discoveries they made. If you're considering a speech, talk with colleagues who have addressed the same group and ask for pointers. As you gather data and learn from others' experiences, you'll feel more comfortable. But remember that selecting media will always involve a certain amount of guesswork.

Is this *a medium for which you have an especially high affinity or "comfort level"?* Perhaps you're more at home with a speech than with a direct-mail brochure, with a display than with a news release, or with an informal memo than with a stylized position paper. Such affinities may guide you in selecting a medium, provided that it's a good match for your message and your means. Any communication will be successful if the messenger is adept and enthusiastic.

If a medium meets your criteria of appropriateness, credibility, cost, reach, and comfort, then begin working to gain access and begin tailoring your message to meet the requirements of *that medium.*

Coming back to the control issue

If the media you have chosen are among those over which you have no direct control, you must consider how you will approach the gatekeepers — the editors, writers, producers, talk show hosts, publications officers, "bulletin board editors," and any others who have the authority to decide whether or not to convey your message.

If you need an in-house service that requires cooperation — someone to let you use a hall for a photo exhibit, an editor in another unit to run an announcement in his newsletter, a campus daily reporter to cover a special departmental lecture — you should use your influence carefully to get what you want. If you encounter resistance, talk to a colleague who has supervision over the individual or activity, explain what you want, and ask if he or she will intercede for you. Do this judiciously, though, if you want to keep coming back to the same source of service.

Stress that you are willing to be flexible: you will be happy to give that other department space in your newsletter in the future, you can provide the reporter with background that will add considerable interest to the lecture notice, your staff will clean up the exhibit hall, or whatever. This kind of bargaining shouldn't be necessary, but it's pragmatic to build trust and cooperative relationships with people on campus with whom you will work again.

A caveat: even if you have influence, don't ask people to deliver your message if its content or style obviously does not fit their vehicle or their stated policies of access.

Media outside the campus are a different story. Let's say you have studied the kinds of academic topics a metropolitan newspaper likes to include in its special Sunday feature section. You are confident that your unit's activities are of interest to the paper's readers. But when you call with your proposal, the editor is indifferent or negative. Why? What can you do?

The editor may appear cold to your ideas for very practical reasons: he or she may be under deadline pressures, or may be highlighting special issues for a readership promotion and your subject just doesn't fit.

Suffice it to say that people who control mass media are running a business. They must sell a minimum quantity of newspapers or magazines or ads to stay in the black. They have a keen sense of what kind of news "sells" and what kind of things people want to read or hear about. They also know that their credibility as a news source depends on their relative objectivity in covering the news. These factors, along with their sense of community responsibility, drive their decisions on whether to cover your press conference announcing a new administrative appointment or to report on your colleague's studies of a Romantic poet. Chapter eleven deals with understanding this important industry and how to approach these professionals with your news.

Clearly, analyzing media to determine what's appropriate for your messages can take time. You certainly should try to delegate this task. You will find useful suggestions on how to get help on this score in chapter seven.

For further consideration ...

Public forums

In a survey of faculty members at liberal arts colleges (*CASE Currents*, June 1993), Mason M. Smith found that 83% reported they had communicated through some form of popular media during the last five years — 65% through quotes in a newspaper or magazine, 54% through one or more popular articles, 41% through appearances on television or radio. The median number of communications per respondent was about 3.5, but some claimed to have published as many as 15 articles and done more than 100 broadcast interviews.

Admittedly, few of those communications involved major national media, and there was considerable variation in communications activity from field to field, as 75% of economists and political scientists appeared "active," in contrast with 38% of biologists and 32% of English professors. The higher the professorial rank, the more likely the faculty member was to engage in popular communication.

Why did they do it? The leading answers: "To communicate with the public ... To communicate with non-academic decision-makers ... To enhance my college's visibility."

"We have no scientifically proven method to compute the value of 'popular communication' by faculty members," says Smith. "There's no formula that says one 'MacNeil-Lehrer' expert opinion plus two *El Paso Sun-Times* book reviews equals a *Wall Street Journal* article plus a 'Good Morning America' sound bite. But we all have a sense that a campus's reputation benefits every time our faculty members demonstrate their keen intellect in a public forum."

Consumer media

To improve your skills at selecting optimum communications media, it's good to "become a voracious media consumer," says university publicist Robert S. Topor (1993):

Be on the lookout for publications that are new to you. Read magazines and newspapers carefully to determine their themes and styles. Study radio and television listings and listen and watch broadcasts. Effective communication is a constant learning practice.

Then test your ideas for "newsworthiness," he recommends, asking yourself these questions: Is it timely? Of interest to someone? A first or unusual in any way? True, accurate, honest, confirmable? Does it involve some sort of conflict? Is there a local angle? National significance?

Newsworthy communications won't necessarily meet all these criteria, Topor says, but they had better meet at least some of them.

chapter six

Know Where You're Going, So You Know When You Get There
Planning your communications program

In their many travels, evaluating communications programs on college campuses, at military installations, and in businesses across the country, the authors have seen one common key to success: *planning*. You seldom, if ever, find an effective communications program without an overarching plan; the most effective programs are invariably the result of a comprehensive written plan.

To quote Scott Cutlip (1993):

> The importance of long-range planning to achieve specific strategic goals and tactical objectives can't be overestimated. Without a plan, a communication program seldom results in a definite lasting impression on public opinions and attitudes. And only planning permits a fully coordinated program.

It can be added that only a plan enables you to make the most efficient and effective use of your resources — human and financial. So far in this guide, we have been laying the groundwork for the planning process: assessing the mission of your institution, the environment in which you live and work, the audiences that are important to you, how those key audiences get their information, and what media options are open to you. Now is the time to weave all of this information together into the tapestry of a plan. You could delay crafting your plan until you've investigated the options for assistance and funding (See chapters seven and eight), but now is the best time to plan, because your plan will dictate the kinds of help and resources you will need.

Planning is the process by which you essentially distinguish yourself as a manager. Planning is a means by which we can feel safe *and still take calculated risks*. By laying out our objectives and the strategies by which we plan to achieve them, we can gain support from our bosses, our colleagues, and our employees for the ways in which we choose to reinvent or reinvigorate our organizations. Ideally, everyone involved will come to endorse, if not "own," our plan, enabling us to move forward without worry that our actions will be undermined or derailed. This may be one reason why "strategic planning" has become the modern mantra in business and higher education circles.

Developing a communications plan has many direct and indirect benefits to your program. Although not its primary purpose, one of the most important benefits is a certain *clarification of thinking*. Planning forces you to focus on the things that are most important. The sheer task of framing a communications program in support of a particular activity will force you to ask some basic questions:

- What is the purpose of this activity?

- Why are we doing this rather than doing something else?

- How will we evaluate the results of what we are doing?

Framing a communications plan not only helps you set goals and objectives, but also forces you to *recognize the distinction* between *strategic goals* and *tactical objectives*. Supporting the unit's goals in the context of its mission — that is the *strategic goal* of any communications plan. Stated simply, "Where do we want to go?" *Tactical objectives* constitute the means by which we get there. Amanda Perkins' mission, as the head of her department, is to maintain and enhance the department's excellence in the field of plant ecology. Given that mission, her strategic goal is to attract the very best faculty and students. To do that, she will use various means of communication. Her tactical objectives are the means by which she accomplishes this task. In terms of communications, her tactical objectives focus on the vehicles and methods she develops for recruitment and retention, along with a detailed accounting of how and when she will deploy these resources.

A plan can help you to program and track both long-term and short-term communications activities. Long-term plans usually aim to cause or to prevent something over months or years. Short-term plans aim to take advantage of or remedy an immediate situation.

The communications plan serves several important functions. Among other things, it will:

- Outline the organizational framework

- Clarify the roles of all program participants and coordinate their activities

- Establish a timetable for accomplishing tasks

- Define material, staff, and facility needs for the duration of the activity

- Provide the unit leader with a checklist for measuring progress

Elements of a sound plan

A sound communications plan consists of many elements.

- *It exists in context*. As such, it reflects and supports the overall strategic needs and plans of the academic unit.

- *It is tuned to its constituencies*, internal and external, and their needs.

- *It is simple*, eliminating possibilities for misunderstandings and allowing for direct communication "up, down, and sideways" among all parties involved.

- *It is indigenous*. Its tone, style, and strategies fit the situation and are "at home" in the institution of which they are an expression.

- *It stays focused on solid public relations* and is not diverted into the mere seeking of publicity.

- *It strikes a balance in assigning responsibility*. It delegates as much freedom and initiative to others as possible, while making them accountable to the group leader for achieving the stated objectives and meeting the timetable and budget.

- *It is timely*. It is carried out with thoughtfulness but also dispatch, capitalizing on opportunities as they arise. An effective communicator must be sensitive to the consequences of indecision. At times, crucial factors cannot be measured precisely and you must be willing to take risks and try unusual approaches.

- *It is continuous and flexible*. Although based on specific conditions and assumptions, and aimed at carrying out a particular proposal in a specific area, a good communications plan can be changed, refined, and updated as a result of unforeseen opportunities and continuous assessment and course correction.

One of Perkins' goals is to communicate with key donors in an effort to raise funds for an endowed chair in plant ecology. Suddenly, a local oil spill affecting a lake and streams focuses public attention on habitat restoration. Perkins finds a way to capitalize on that event and take advantage of the climate of support it creates for ecological research, to achieve the goal of raising funds for the faculty endowment.

Flexibility will also prevent you from sticking to a losing strategy. Although her fund-raising plan calls for three mass mailings, the first such mailing yields less than the cost of paper and postage, so Perkins rethinks the strategy and revises the plan rather than throwing good money after bad.

Setting your goals — The first step in planning

There are dozens of ways to articulate goals and shape plans. The best involve group dynamics. It is critical to have those who will help you pursue the goals also help you define them. You might seek input from your dean or president, your colleagues in the department or division, or campus administrators. Whoever they are, they will understand your goals better and will work harder to help you achieve them if they are involved in setting them.

At this point, you may be thinking, "My so-called communications program consists of my secretary and me. Do I really need a written plan for such a small operation?" Absolutely. In fact, we could argue that the more limited your time and resources, the more important to have a focused and realistic plan.

We recognize that our readers come from a myriad of backgrounds and situations. Your communications programs will vary tremendously in scope and methods, as will your goals. Your goal may be to improve your rapport with your faculty through regular meetings, memoranda, electronic mail, and quarterly newsletters. Or your goal might be to raise money for your department via better communication with your wealthy alumni. Or you might be trying to increase your enrollment, in which case your communications program will focus on prospective students. Whether big or small, your program will have the best chance of success if you take time to define and articulate your goals, and then plot a course to achieve them — in short, if you take the time to plan.

True, it doesn't take much planning to write a regular memo or send an email update to faculty, if that's what's needed. On the other hand, the memo requires that you regularly schedule time to compose and distribute it. And it needs someone — you or an assistant — to collect news items to be included. Also, someone must do research on the format and experiment with it. Are they more likely to read a written communication or to scan their email? What is easiest to read — a chatty letter or short bullets of information? Who cares, you ask? Well, your readers care. If it's too ponderous, they may not read it; if it's too cute, they may not believe what they read.

If you don't take time to plan and assess how your plan is working, your effort to improve communications may flounder, even as you zealously spend hours churning out your weekly memo. By the same token, if you find your regular communiqués are simply riling up your colleagues, you may be creating dissension when your goal was to increase harmony. Revisiting your written goals and objectives will help you decide when, if, and how you need to change your tactics.

With a written plan — and a planning calendar — you will stay on track and remember all the things you set out to do when the communications fervor initially struck you. A plan helps you to accomplish more with greater efficiency.

Plans also provide a vehicle for sharing information, which is a healthy way to run your organization. For example, some of your colleagues may have unrealistic notions of what a communications program entails. Perhaps your unit has no history of public relations efforts and abhors anything that smacks of self-promotion. Here your written plan can be invaluable in persuading a skeptical faculty why intensified communications with constituents would be a good idea, explaining whom you plan to reach, how you will reach them, what your plans will cost, and how you intend to measure your success. Generally, the more details people are given, the less hostile they are to new approaches.

Conversely, you may be head of a unit inclined to aggressively demand more public visibility than resources allow. Your written plan can help persuade colleagues that, given the existing budget, their expectations are not realistic. You can show them what expectations would be more reasonable in terms of your budget. In these cases, your written plan is a means of inviting feedback and greater participation from faculty, to solve the problems of the unit cohesively and creatively. In examining a draft plan, your colleagues begin to take some ownership and interest in its outcome.

Degrees of planning

We might actually think of the planning process as simultaneously occurring at different levels, each level of planning nested in the plan above it. For example, Level 1 might be a unit's strategic three-year plan, Level 2 might be its annual plan, and Level 3 might be the series of detailed tactical objectives.

Strategic planning

The strategic plan is the Level 1 process when you realize that you must persuade certain groups of people to adopt your way of thinking or to adopt your goals as their own, in order to make your unit or institution successful. It is a calculated kind of planning — and it's essential.

The "calculating" aspect suggests that you seek relationships not only with obvious supporters of your unit, but with what Sheila Raviv, vice president of the Burston-Marstellar public affairs consulting agency, calls "strange-bedfellow allies" (1993) — "groups that at first glance may not appear to be related to your interests." These may include other departments or units, civic clubs, business and professional groups, ethnic associations, watchdog or advocacy groups, and various opinion leaders or elected officials. Developing relationships with these groups *before* you need their help is a necessary investment, says Raviv. By getting to know about them, she says, you can tailor your message to each group in terms of *its* reasons for caring about your interests, not *your* reasons.

Yes, these are calculated relationships — most human relationships are, to some degree. But without the calculation that enables lines of communication to open up, neither you nor your audience will reach the desired ends.

Strategic planning lets you define your many audiences and allies, fix on communication goals and objectives that are consonant with your unit's mission, prioritize your elements, and select the appropriate medium and message.

Here's how Carol Halstead and John Ross, communications professionals, describe strategic communications planning (1992):

> To thrive, colleges and universities and their academic units need sustaining internal and external environments, and audiences that know and support them. ... Strategic communication builds long-term relationships with key audiences. It begins with an identification of the resource inputs most important to the institution or academic unit and of the nature of internal and external environments. Next is the identification of the individuals and groups who make or influence decisions that control the flow of those resources to the institution and who set the tone for those environments. Finally, strategic communication provides information to decision makers with the goal of eliciting behaviors more favorable to the institution or academic unit. It sounds manipulative, almost nefarious, but it isn't. What is a proposal to a foundation or government agency if not a strategic communication?

When you are writing a proposal, you may be more concerned with how to present your data and credentials than with how the proposal fits into a strategic plan. But if you have done your strategic planning in advance, you *know* that this proposal is taking you a step closer to your goals.

But, as we acknowledged above, keeping all the pieces of a plan in our heads for a long period of time is almost impossible. Hence the value of a written plan.

Plan formats

What format should the written plan take? Depending on its scope, it can range from a to-do list and a series of calendar dates to a formal document of several pages. In general, preparing a plan is very similar to preparing a proposal, a process quite familiar to most academics.

Here is an example of how you might arrange a plan, whether it's a general outline of long-range activities, or the rationale and assignments for a particular activity.

- *A general introductory statement*, perhaps outlining the situation and/or a particular problem

- *A statement of purpose*, indicating the goals and objectives of the unit or program/project that the plan proposes to support

- *A description of the plan's scope*, clarifying the time frame and characteristics of the plan

- *A statement of assumptions* on which the plan is based, supplementing assured facts of the case

- *Objectives and guidelines*, broken down into general strategic and specific tactical components, and laying out philosophical policies or major operational themes

- *A discussion of alternate courses of action*, if appropriate and necessary

- *A statement of particular tasks, audiences, and media* to be encompassed by the program

- *A discussion of budget* and/or access to existing communication resources

- *A description of organizational structure*, defining participating personnel, their relationships, and their responsibilities

- *A schedule*, laying out a timetable as tightly as possible

- *Pertinent references*, such as executive directives or constituent surveys, that provide a rationale for the plan

- *Summary*, a brief recapitulation of key points

The situation or your own proclivities may suggest other major components.

The time frame

In drafting a strategic plan, no matter how you organize it, it is very important to keep the time frame in mind, to keep your focus over the months and years that your plan is in effect. Newcomers to our colleges and universities frequently tell us that it takes two years just to learn the culture of a particular institution and to get a feel for the rhythm of the place. For the same reason, your plan will take time to develop, implement, and bear fruit. It is important, therefore, to craft your strategic plan for the long haul and stick to it. Focus and consistency will serve you well. At those moments when you feel things are moving at a frustrating snail's pace, look back. Often you will be amazed at how far you've actually come in a relatively short time.

Annual planning

This is the form of planning with which many of us are most familiar. Colleges and universities are programmed in annual cycles: summer session, fall semester, exams, winter holiday break, spring semester, spring break, exams, commencement, intersession, and back to summer session again. The annual cycle is tied to the institution's budget cycle, which is, in effect, an

annual plan. When your department or division requests resources for the coming year, it is presenting its plan.

It is important to get ahead of the budget-building curve. If you
develop your communications plan and then factor your needs
into your budget request, you obviously will be better off than if
you let whatever free funds that might be available (fewer and
fewer, it seems) dictate whatever communications plans you can
make. It has been the authors' experience that campus administrators generally are quite supportive of communication activities, especially outreach efforts that will raise the tide and buoy
up all the institution's ships. But the budgeteers like to know
precisely what the institution will get for its money. A vague
request for $20,000 for a special student recruiting campaign will
not garner the same support as a tight proposal, spelling out
audiences, methods, and projected expenses in some detail *and*
describing how a rival institution executed a similar program with
tremendous success!

The development of the annual plan is the best vantage point from
which to involve your staff, friends, and colleagues. Linda Weimer has made it a practice to hold a planning retreat at least once
a year with all of the unit's staff. She has found this to result in
some lasting program innovations over the past decade. On the
Berkeley campus, this annual planning effort involves everyone
from the elevator operator of the famous Berkeley bell tower —
the Campanile — and the editor of the campus staff/faculty
newspaper to the artist who designs the campus recruitment
materials and the chancellor's speech writer. All are equally
important contributors to the process. The overall mission and
objectives of the public affairs program are renewed and
amended as necessary, and the program takes its cues from the
priorities and objectives of campus leaders. But within that broad
mission, the staff collaborates on developing the tactical plan and
sets its priorities as a group.

Without a plan, a communications unit is particularly prone to
spending all of its time responding solely to external cues — a

media crisis, a research discovery, publication deadlines, or the business school's anniversary. With a plan, those same demands for service can be met, but the plan provides an overall context and direction, such that the whole becomes greater than the sum of its parts. The plan also highlights important audiences and gives rise to new vehicles with which to reach those audiences.

At a planning retreat in 1992, the UC Berkeley public affairs staff identified its most important audiences and rated itself (and the university as a whole) on how it was reaching those audiences. The results of those deliberations were as follows:

Top Ten Audiences	Quality of Communication
Students	Thumbs down
Political Leaders/Legislators	Thumbs down
Voters/Taxpayers	Room for improvement
Media	Good work!
Prospective Students	Good work!
Faculty/Staff	Good work!
Alumni	Room for improvement
Donors	Good work!
Parents	Thumbs down
Multilingual Audiences	Room for improvement

The staff ranked the students as the university's most important audience by far, but gave the institution a "thumbs down" rating in communications with that group. Now, four years later, as a result of this and other planning efforts, the Berkeley public affairs office has a student advisory committee that works with the unit on student communication issues.

In terms of other key audiences listed, there is a new parents program, with a regular newsletter that goes out three times a year; a new alumni magazine that goes to 200,000 alums twice a year; and a key advocates program consisting of influential alumni and friends who can reach out to the state legislature and U.S. Congress when it comes to issues affecting higher education. Also under development are maps and guides in a variety of languages for visitors. In other words, planning works and it pays off in many ways.

As one example, the public affairs office has been staffing the new Cal Parents Program for three years. Services and information (including a parents' hotline) are geared toward parents of new students. In early 1995, the development office conducted a telefund campaign, targeted to parents of first-year students. While telefund campaigns are considered successful if they get pledges from one in four donor contacts, almost 50% of the parents contacted pledged money to Cal, with the average gift being almost $200. When one considers that 20% of Cal's incoming students come from families making less than $25,000 annually, that is indeed a successful campaign — and not coincidental to a greater emphasis on communicating with Cal parents.

Reaching consensus

In conducting a planning session with staff and colleagues, one problem can be reaching a consensus on priorities. This is especially true if you have a few colleagues or staff members who are extremely outspoken and other colleagues who may be very creative, but quite shy.

One strategy that Weimer has used to great advantage has been a process by which priorities can be assigned to planning elements in a systematic way that allows for equal access to the process. After background discussion and a brainstorming session, she asks each participant in the planning session to list the five or ten items that he or she feels represent the highest priority for the unit. Then, going around the room and asking each person in turn for his or her input, she puts all the items up on the board in a numbered list. Many participants will have the same items and these are combined on the list, so she usually ends up with about 25 items on the board.

Then she hands out six index cards to each participant. On the first card, each participant lists by number and item the five ideas of the 25 or more listed that he or she believes are the highest priority. In a public affairs planning retreat, one employee's index card, copying his top items from the board, might look something like this: #4 - more visibility in the East Coast media, #7 -campus open house, #14 - radio spots on university teaching and research, #22 - more internal coordination with other units on campus, and #24 - media training for deans and administrators.

Then Weimer asks each participant to number the remaining five index cards with Roman numerals, I through V. Taking card V, they each put down the item from their list of five that they think is most important. If, for example, our staffer thinks visibility in the *New York Times* is most important, he would put #4 on card V. Then he is asked which of the remaining four items is least important and to list that item number on card I. So, if media training is least important, #24 would go on card I. Then, of the remaining three items, the most important — say #22 — goes on card IV. The least important of the remaining items — say #7 — goes on card II. Finally the middle-ranked item, #14, goes on card III. These cards are then collected and the points (I = 1 up to V = 5) are tallied up for each item (#1 – #25) on the list.

Weimer has done this exercise many times, yet is always impressed by how much consensus emerges from a group vote like this. Most often, the votes will center on five or ten items that can then form the basis for the plan. Everyone has voted and all are prepared to work hard on executing the plan. The plan is then incorporated into each subunit and each employee's annual work plans.

If you are embarking on a communications plan for your unit, you might want to consider asking your campus public relations or news staff to help out. They may have experience with communications planning that could help you. They certainly know the local media scene and have good ideas about the relative time, effort, and resources required by the activities you and your colleagues may be considering.

Activity planning

There is another level of planning to be considered in our "nest" of plans. Within the strategic and annual plans will lie specific activities or items to be done, such as a specific publication, a lecture series, or a special event. Each of these may require their own planning efforts, and these then form the detailed plans or tactical objectives that constitute, in total, your overall plan.

This level of planning is, in some ways, the most critical, because this is the level of detail that will dictate your resource and staff needs, or vice versa. Too often, plans fail because big visions and lofty goals are never translated into details — Who is doing what? How much will it cost? What are the deadlines? Developing a plan is not all that difficult, but success lies in the execution — and that is the more challenging task.

Below is the partial list that Gilbert E. Gilbert, Midland University's director of outreach and continuing education, put together as he began preparing for his unit's 50th anniversary banquet:

- *Staff Meetings.* Key people alerted? Anyone omitted? Regularly scheduled?

- *Topics for First Staff Meeting.* Name and theme of event? Purpose? Location? Budget?

- *Program.* Banquet emcee decided upon? Speakers selected and confirmed? Instructions and assignments to participants clear? Program approved?

- *Invitation List.* Who is to suggest names? Who approves list? Which invitees are "musts"?

- *Invitations.* What kind? When to be mailed? Follow-up mailing?

- *Publicity.* Scheduled? Any tie-in promotions? Any special features?

- *Weather.* Forecast? Alternate plan in case of inclement weather?

- *Services for Guests and Speakers.* Hotel reservations? Transportation? Guides?

- *Printed Materials.* Official programs? Guest list? Map of location? Name badges? Souvenir folders? Signs?

- *Media Coverage.* Invitations? Copies of speeches and photos of speakers available? Fact sheets and biographies prepared? Platform for photographers and camera operators? Telephones? Press room? Post-program interviews and pictures?

- *At the Scene.* Adequate parking? Registration desk? Receptionist? Seating arrangements? Decorations? Backdrop? Exhibits? Coat checking? First aid facilities? Distribution of programs and other materials? Facilities for children? Central information desk?

- *Food and Beverage Arrangements.* Adequate facilities? Menu selected? Alternative items?

- *Platform Arrangements.* Rostrum or speaker's stand? Sound systems? Projection equipment? Seating of speakers? Special lighting?

- *Supplemental Events.* Campus tours? Reception for dignitaries?

- *Controls.* Firm deadlines for completion of all preparations? System for tracking responses to invitations? Rehearsal of program?

- *Aftermath.* Arrangements for returning any borrowed equipment? Accounting of expenditures?

Final report to sponsors, trustees, or others? Letters to guests and press? Review by participating staff of planning and execution?

The above may seem like pretty tedious business, but anyone who has staged such an event knows well that an ounce of preparation is worth a pound of fixing the foul-ups.

Just so, each element of any communications program — whether it's arranging an institutional celebration, coordinating student registration activities, or producing a quarterly campus research report — merits detailed planning.

Amanda Perkins and the Midland Plan

At Midland University, Amanda Perkins has had several meetings with campus public relations experts to discuss what she can do to increase visibility for her unit, the Department of Botany and Applied Ecology, given her very restricted budget and resources. She has reported back to her faculty and has their approval to prepare a communications plan that will depend in part on their active participation.

Let's look over Perkins' shoulder as she gathers her thoughts to draft a three-year strategic communications plan for her unit. Her dreams are ambitious but she must be realistic. Her resources consist of a journalism student intern working 20 hours a week, an energetic secretary, a basically good-hearted group of faculty who have expressed a willingness to do their part, and the periodic assistance of the campus news service.

Her goals are:

To garner more visibility for the department in order to enhance the unit's effectiveness: (a) in recruiting students for the baccalaureate and the new masters' program, (b) in soliciting funds for research and teaching, and (c) in retaining faculty with strong commitments to teaching, research, and public service. The emphasis is on establishing, or affirming, a working knowledge of our unit among those constituents who should know us best but may not — among them, students, alumni, local and regional business and industry, and the immediate community.

To simultaneously initiate modest actions that will enhance the real quality of teaching, research, and outreach.

Her three-year plan includes the following objectives, each with some sample specific tasks:

To increase the visibility of the department's research activities.

- Chair will develop working relationship with campus news service reporter and will call/meet every three months with reporter to provide update on research activities.

- Student intern and news service writers will write and place stories and will "tip" other regional and national news writers to the research work of professors.

- Department will send out a two-sided news sheet (also via email) every other month summarizing in short, plain-English paragraphs the unit's recent grants and research outcomes. This will be distributed to all students, faculty, and staff in the unit, any campus personnel with expressed interest in the department, selected members of state government and industry in related fields, and media.

- Profs will be encouraged to accept *public* as well as professional speaking engagements regarding their work.

To have a departmental presence at all campus public events.

- Secretary will check the campus master calendar weekly and note the specifics of public campuswide events to which the department might send faculty or student representatives or present an exhibit.

- Chair will recruit and prepare volunteer faculty and students to be spokespersons for such events.

To seek out opportunities to highlight the department's unique teaching strategies and successes.

- Chair will seek out speaking engagements that offer opportunities to discuss the department's emphasis on teaching and its especially successful teaching strategies.

- Chair will ask faculty to make a point of discussing teaching when they make professional presentations.

- Department will emphasize examples of teaching in all brochures, exhibits, or other unit materials.

- Chair will meet with faculty to determine if the unit can expand its offering of "unique" experiences to undergraduates, to include more independent studies, intersession field trips, or other activities.

To pursue outreach activities that focus on the local community and that will provide practical experiences for students while also expanding the unit's network of contacts in the community.

- Chair will ask profs and selected community/industry leaders to help identify conservation- or botanical-based class projects (with real academic merit) that would contribute to meeting the needs of the local community. Use these projects as opportunities for media coverage and for furthering future community-department interactions. (This might also be part of expanded educational opportunity above.)

- Chair will set up faculty committee to look into junior/senior student internships with local businesses, particularly those that are potential employers of graduates.

To promote awareness of the new graduate degree.

- Increase on-campus awareness by using public events, promotional posters, and feature articles in student and campus newspapers. Produce and distribute descriptive brochure, prepared by chair and intern, to faculty/advisors in related departments. Include same information on email.

- Increase off-campus awareness through mailing and/or email distribution of descriptive brochure to pertinent faculty/advisors at other colleges/campuses and to local media, including radio/TV talk shows. If possible, intern will place articles in conservation magazines. Explore cost of paid advertising in same publications.

- Have faculty use public and professional appearances to slip in a mention of new program. Have them carry brochures with them when they travel to give lectures.

To use various communications activities/opportunities to help raise funds to update the biology library and upgrade laboratory equipment.

- Use basically the first three strategies described above for promoting the new degree program.

- Chair will submit proposals for funding to Midland University research committee and other promising funding agencies.

- Prepare article on this and other new developments in the department for *Midlandite* alumni magazine.

- Deliver short speech at alumni picnic and follow up with a mailing requesting contribution.

To improve contacts with department alumni and gather more data on their successes in the job market.

- Student intern will produce a simple two-page alumni newsletter three times per year.

- Department secretary will obtain mailing list of department's grads from campus alumni association. Will work with intern on a short, return-mail questionnaire to determine grads' success in finding jobs in the conservation field and the usefulness of their degree.

- Will invite alumni to first annual department picnic, to be held in conjunction with campus-wide alumni open house. Will work with campus alumni organization to determine what features/activities are most appealing to returning alums. Will try to increase departmental presence at other alumni events.

To better prepare all department staff to respond to media queries.

- Ask each faculty/staff member to prepare a succinct, plain-English summary of his/her research interests, current projects, and a statement of the work's significance. Bind and distribute the collection of summaries, along with current facts/statistics about the department, to the unit's faculty/staff members and students, and to campus and local reporters.

- Ask news service to provide guidelines or to prepare a workshop for department faculty/staff on how to interact with the news media and respond to queries.

To regularly review quality of staff/student interactions.

- Schedule quarterly non-optional reviews with clerical and teaching staff to identify services that could be improved. Require profs/TAs to solicit written assessments of courses from students at end of each semester.

To increase personal communications and networking among fellow chairs, deans, and other administrators.

- Through email, lunches, and other informal encounters, chair will find out what others are doing and let them know what she is doing, looking for opportunities to cooperate and coordinate efforts.

From plan to execution

As she has developed her list of objectives and specific tasks, Perkins has noticed that some of her objectives are more directly academic and only indirectly "communications." Her communications planning exercise has made Perkins aware that she had never before considered opportunities for advancing the department and made her realize that every advance that focuses on serving constituents is, ultimately, good public relations.

Perkins also is keenly aware that this plan is *tentative*; she really must have the input of key faculty and others who can give her guidance, help her avoid pitfalls, and help her "sell" the plan to other key players. She can take it to a faculty meeting and see who takes a real interest in it. She might sign up not only those with enthusiasm and creative ideas, but also some of the complaining curmudgeons. She needs to form an advisory committee to whom she can take ideas and from whom she can draw help. She must also establish regular mechanisms for keeping her faculty informed of the plan's evolution and for getting their feedback and input.

With this set of objectives before her, Perkins must now do some research to get a better idea of her audiences and of which combinations of media and message will appeal to particular groups. She also must develop a time frame for the various activities, coordinate the proper sequence of events, sort out the responsibilities of her key players, total the number of printed products or other special materials, and roughly estimate her costs. For example, her intern has quite a lot of work. Each of the intern's assignments will have to be broken out and further defined. Some will be one-time tasks; others will be ongoing or regularly scheduled. Perkins will have to draw up a list of duties for the intern, specify her priorities for their accomplishment, and then have the intern draw up his/her own schedule for the year. Perkins will have these documents handy in a file for referral when she meets with her intern every other week to discuss progress. In fact, Perkins purchases a large calendar on which she can schedule all her communications-related meetings and deadlines over the next semester.

Looking over her list, Perkins totals up the materials that her unit will have to produce: (a) an alumni newsletter three times per year; (b) a department newsletter every two months; (c) a yet undetermined number of news stories on research, teaching, and outreach; (d) a traveling exhibit for public events; (e) a brochure for the degree programs; (f) posters for the degree programs; (g) a questionnaire for alumni and a course evaluation questionnaire for students; and (h) a bound annual summary of faculty research interests. In addition, plans will have to be laid for an annual alumni picnic.

Perkins immediately sees that her department will have to purchase or borrow the services of a good graphic designer to set up the format for newsletters, design the posters and brochure, and help prepare a simple traveling exhibit. She also sees that this program requires a good deal of writing and editing, but that many of the written materials can do double duty; for example, items from the departmental newsletter can be used in the alumni newsletter. She senses that one intern may be overwhelmed by the amount of work and that, even as she searches for additional help, she will have to be clear in her priorities as to which products are most important.

As she prioritizes the activities, she sets tentative target dates, to be further defined as she meets with her faculty and staff and as timetables are matched with semester schedules, professional meetings, campuswide activities, and the publication dates of magazines and other periodicals in which they hope to get coverage. She also begins noting names of individuals and other offices/agencies with whom she will want to coordinate particular activities.

When she has roughed out all of these elements, Perkins will prepare a neat, written plan, like that described earlier, that she will submit to her advisory committee and then, after revisions, to her faculty.

For those of our readers with fully staffed communications operations, Perkins' plan may seem modest, even though there are substantial costs, particularly for printing and mailing. But she has made a good beginning toward achieving greater recognition for her unit among targeted audiences.

Hallmarks of an effective communications program

The plan developed by Perkins generally follows the hallmarks of an effective communications program, as we shall see below.

Effective communications are proactive

By this popular term, "proactive," we simply mean that effective communicators don't wait for something to happen or for someone else to get things started. Instead, they take the initiative and get out in front. They set their own agenda and act on it. They make good things happen and also anticipate problems and trends well enough in advance that they can head them off or minimize their damage. They are planners.

Effective communications are planned

We already have discussed at length the importance of planning at all levels of operation. Here is another good example of how planning can pay off.

Cuyahoga Community College (Tri-C) in Cleveland, Ohio, needed to convince local voters to double a .6 mill tax levy. College officials planned an aggressive media strategy with the theme "Tri-C: Where Futures Begin." In the early stages of the campaign, the upcoming levy vote wasn't mentioned. Instead, the emphasis was on the college's role in providing accessible, quality education and on the importance of keeping Tri-C programs up-to-date in order to retrain the local work force.

For instance, students visited twelve area radio stations on Valentine's Day with heart-shaped cookies, baked in the ovens of the school's hospitality management program. The students also gave on-air testimonials to the school's importance in their career preparation. These actions prepared the public for a subsequent message about the levy vote.

In stage two, college administrators visited media editorial boards, which resulted in endorsements for the tax increase from all area newspapers and TV stations. TV stations also carried public service announcements produced in-house, featuring successful Tri-C grads and the ending, "Thank you, Greater Cleveland, for making Tri-C possible." Then followed a luncheon in a downtown restaurant with a Tri-C grad as the head chef, a student walk with the marching band, and a forum featuring the college president, political figures, and religious leaders discussing the role of the community college. The final media event was a press conference on Public Square with Tri-C's many successful alums dressed in their caps and gowns — planned just in time for live, remote coverage by noon news programs on area TV stations.

The levy passed by a 57% margin, and the college won an American Association of Community Colleges award for its campaign. The next year, Tri-C repeated the campaign in support of a request for a second levy — which passed by a 70% margin. Those are the benefits of planning!

Effective communications are coordinated

As we have seen, communication plans are connected to the mission and goals of the institution and unit, and coordinated with a variety of parties within and beyond the division or the campus. In this way, effective programs garner maximum visibility, while taking advantage of all the help they can get.

Effective communications are creative

If ever a routine communications program could work, those times are past. Society is "media rich" and we are bombarded with materials and messages that compete for our attention. Only a creative plan, with fresh ideas and approaches, will really make its mark — creative events, creative messages, and creative dissemination all contribute to success.

Kankakee Community College (IL) won a major award for its Literacy Fest. The modern languages faculty won public and media attention by making Minnie Mouse and Bugs Bunny their literacy spokespersons at the weekend fest in a shopping mall. They persuaded a local book publisher to donate more than 20,000 children's books to be given away at the event.

To demonstrate KCC's top-to-bottom commitment, two vice presidents dressed up as Bugs Bunny and Minnie Mouse, and the president performed in the "reading corner" dressed as a friendly dragon. A faculty member/ventriloquist wrote and performed a piece on the importance of reading, a magician proved "Reading Is Magic," and a drama student performed an eight-minute version of *The Wizard of Oz* — all to the delight of the public and the media.

But an event doesn't have to be out of the ordinary to serve a strategic purpose. Sometimes it just needs to be a bit more eye-catching or ear-catching. A speech, for example, can be more engaging if supplemented by striking visuals — be they charts or video clips — or salted with a few good jokes.

There also is a role in the effective communications program for creative dissemination. Valparaiso University (IN), a Lutheran college, designates one Sunday each year to put its case before 4,000 Lutheran congregations across the country. Aside from presentations from the pulpit, the effort includes the distribution of 960,000 church bulletin inserts, several hundred thousand offering envelopes, posters, publicity kits, children's leaflets, and sermon and prayer suggestions.

If your institution fosters a creative climate, you will find it easier to get creative ideas accepted, and to find the funding and help to take creative advantage of unexpected opportunities.

For example, Quincy College (MA) invested $40,000 in a long-term account to pay the tuition of 53 fifth-grade students at a local elementary school. Through "Project 2000" the college will develop support services for those students — including tutoring and academic assistance — and then offer them paid admission when they graduate from high school. Not only does this project exemplify a wonderful commitment to public and community service, it also generates tremendous goodwill and continuing, positive press coverage.

Effective communications are aimed

Effective communications are aimed — at persons and at the media. Imagine a specific individual to whom you are talking or for whom you are writing. Associated Press reporters, for example, have long been told to "write for a milkman in Omaha." *New Yorker* writers are reminded that the magazine is *not* aimed at "a little old lady in Dubuque." Select a particular individual out of your intended audience and speak to him or to her as if you were conversing over the back fence.

Effective communicators also aim their messages by tailoring them to the requirements and formats of the particular medium selected — especially if the medium is not under their control. A good example is aiming a message at the press.

To get support for an adequate tax base, Lane County Community College (OR) had to get the attention of the media. LCC was up against anti-tax sentiment that had defeated five such levy requests in 10 years.

LCC's strategy was to hit the media repeatedly with examples of the college's strategic role in retraining laid-off wood products workers. The key was customized news releases to area papers, featuring hometown people. Campus communications specialists arranged photo opportunities, coached spokespersons in interview techniques, and made them directly available to reporters.

The result was dozens of human interest stories and photos of individuals with headlines like "Program Retrains Displaced Workers," and "Underfunded LCC Program for Dislocated Mill Workers." Despite an unfavorable climate, this carefully aimed media campaign contributed to a victory.

Effective communications are timed

Good communications are timed — to meet the deadlines of the media, to appeal to audience interest, to suit the needs of the institution, and to accommodate the limitations of your resources.

Dealing with the timing factor in its various forms forces you to recognize two important principles. First, no matter how many times it may have to be revised, sooner or later you have to settle on a timetable. The dates on your planning chart are just as important as the assignment of tasks. Second, take the high ground if a crisis looms. Act fast and decisively. Many an institution might have avoided bitter public attack if it had timed its communications to give constituents, including its own employees, the facts first.

If you expect the news media to carry your messages, you must plan your communications to meet media needs. Newspapers, radio stations, TV stations, magazines, and newsletters all have deadlines. It's your job to know what they are and to plan around them. Your campus news director can help in that regard.

Good timing also means capitalizing on serendipitous events as they happen. Less than 24 hours after Bill Clinton's victory in the 1992 presidential election, Georgetown University, his alma mater, delivered a press packet to 40 writers in Washington DC. Included were a statement from Georgetown's president ("We at Georgetown are immensely proud that our alumnus, Gov. Bill Clinton, has been chosen ..."), the president-elect's yearbook picture, examples of his writings as class president, and a digest of his days on campus. Betting on the outcome of the election, Georgetown's leaders had begun preparing that press packet months in advance. Their success was the result of great planning — and some luck.

Effective communications are continuous

Like several other program characteristics we have described, "continuous communications" operates on several levels.

It is the effort you make to keep the lines open with particular constituencies — to make contact with them on a regular basis and say, "Don't forget us and what we're about," or "We thought you might be interested in this." The department chair who regularly sends a page or two of "what's new" notes to the campus news service or to alumni leaders is practicing a form of continuous communications. Alumni magazines, quarterly newsletters, and similar vehicles are other forms.

"Continuous communications" refers, as well, to an information flow intended to keep people focused on a particular event occurring over a certain time, such as a capital campaign or a building project. Continuous communications is also critical to programs and institutions when they are facing major crises, such as drastic budget cuts, downsizing, or major restructuring. At such times, the usual communication vehicles must be supplemented and intensive effort must go into allaying the anxiety and stress of faculty, staff, and students; preparing people for rough times; boosting morale and generating esprit de corps; and enlisting everyone in finding solutions to the problems ahead. Communications must be constant and must run up, down, and sideways in the organization to ensure a smooth transition.

Effective communications are constantly evaluated

Effective communications programs are built with regular feedback and evaluation in mind. It is critical to incorporate these elements into your plans. Audience surveys, focus groups, eavesdropping around the departmental coffee pot — feedback, whether official or unofficial, will help you refine your strategies and messages to more surely hit their mark.

All of these elements for effective communications should be considered as you craft your communications plan. How will you know if you are successful?

We offer the example of Dorothy Durkin, associate dean of public affairs and student services at New York University (Santovec 1992). Durkin has increased her institution's enrollments in continuing education by 50% in less than a decade, to more than 60,000 students.

Durkin launched a marketing program that was carefully planned, proactive, coordinated, aimed, and continuous. Its success reflects Durkin's understanding of her audiences:

> First, we position the school as a leader in continuing education through the general quality of our advertising. We make sure the image that's projected is one of quality. Second, we use a sampling approach in our ads. ... Students think, "If they have this course in real estate, let's order the bulletin to see what else might be available."

Durkin also uses direct mail — six million pieces per year — targeted to specific audiences. While she finds that former students are the best audience, Durkin also purchases mailing lists of people going through a life transition:

> Most people are interested in taking courses during their transition points. For example, moving is a change and it precipitates other changes. So we send a letter to someone who's moved. People who start a new business are candidates for continuing education. They need to learn how to operate machines, to get some information about sales and marketing.

Durkin also buys lists of people who have purchased magazines or books on a certain subject — a good clue to their interests. She buys her lists from brokers who help her identify appropriate audiences. Geodemographic information on current students can also provide clues to the geodemography of future students.

By watching the courses for which students register, Durkin and her staff constantly monitor the market for emerging trends that suggest which courses the institution should offer. Durkin also appreciates the advice of industry leaders who serve on her advisory boards and provide insight on where careers are heading and where jobs are available.

Durkin counsels those who are interested in improving communications programs to build an overall plan, rather than just respond to individual problems. This, in essence, sums up the overall message of this chapter.

When we find a very productive, high-quality unit or department, we will inevitably find a game plan that has guided its development. Quality doesn't evolve by accident and success doesn't usually result without the discipline of a plan.

For further consideration ...

Planning and the environmental scan

"Trying to figure out what lies ahead" has long been a role for academic leaders. The process is now called "environmental scanning." This is a means of identifying and evaluating trends, events, and emerging issues of import to the institution.

All campus administrators should engage in environmental scanning, says James H. Banning of Colorado State University (1995). He uses the director of student housing as an example:

> His or her scanning process may reveal that nationwide the number of incoming college students with private bedrooms in their family homes is reaching nearly 90%, and a third indicate they did not share a bathroom in their home. Other scanning reveals that, as a result of new federal legislation, more students with disabilities will be coming to the campus and seeking accessible accommodations.

Such data have significant implications for the housing director's marketing, space allocation, and future construction plans.

Whether you're planning housing or scheduling courses or plotting communications strategies, Banning recommends that more than one person in an office or unit "scan," because a single scanner's interests, attitudes, and experiences can introduce "interpretation bias" and "systematic distortion" of the raw data discovered.

"The environmental scanning process will not insure the future success of any operation," Banning says, "but should provide an early warning system to identify the future challenges and opportunities."

chapter seven

You're Not Alone
Marshaling communications assistance

The theme of this chapter is "You are not alone!!"

All colleges and universities — large and small — have communications professionals whose job it is to serve you, as advisors and, at times, as extra members of your staff. You should tap them for service as you organize and execute your communications program.

They may come looking for *you* if your department has a hot story or is in the news. But hot story or not, if you have communications questions or needs, you shouldn't feel shy about finding your campus professionals and enlisting their help. We will cover their services in detail later in this chapter.

In the meantime, there are many other places to look for assistance, and this chapter is a guide to the roles that various staff, scholars, students, and others can play in the communications process on campus.

It is unlikely that there will be one person with the time and talent to help with all your communications needs. So look in a variety of places to take advantage of the range of expertise at your disposal — in your own department or division, in the campus public affairs or communications offices, in the printing or publications division, in the media services department, in the development office, in the academic departments that teach in these areas, and — on occasion — in the local community.

By searching out these experts, you can not only stretch your often meager resources much further, but also use them with far more impact and effect.

Help from those who know you best —Intradepartmental aid

While intradepartmental personnel won't necessarily be your best source of help in communications, you may be surprised at what you might find in your midst. People with a knack for communications are found in every field, in every department, and in every type of job around the campus.

Seeking support staff

You can frequently find among support staff — clerks, typists, analysts, administrative assistants, managers, and others — people who, by nature and/or by training, have a knack for communicating well and/or gathering information. Two examples can show how good ideas and approaches — and, most important, good feedback — may come from unexpected places.

When Clay Schoenfeld was a department chair, one of his very best sources on gaps in the flow of unit information was a building janitor. Schoenfeld got to the office just as the janitor was leaving his night shift and they would grab a cup of coffee — and gossip. Whether the janitor was reading wastebaskets or what, Schoenfeld never knew, but his sense of what was known and unknown among department personnel was encyclopedic. His tips helped Schoenfeld bridge chasms in unit communications.

Linda Weimer makes it a point to meet regularly with groups of staff and faculty from across the UC Berkeley campus to hear what information is spreading via the campus grapevines and to get advice on how to better tailor the information that is flowing to the employees via more formal communication channels.

Some support staff may welcome occasional tasks that involve assembling data for an annual report; developing a departmental calendar; compiling news briefs about the faculty and staff for an internal newsletter, a campuswide publication, or alumni periodical; or even drafting an orientation brochure for the department's incoming students, staff, or faculty.

Once tuned into the communications needs of the department, these employees often come up with imaginative ideas on their own that will contribute to your objectives.

At UW-Madison, an employee in the university relations office came up with the idea of sending CARE packages to the campus' students, faculty, and staff who were called up in the reserve forces for the Gulf War. The chancellor adopted the idea and many vendors contributed items to be sent. Not only did the men and women serving overseas appreciate the gifts, the university got positive publicity and goodwill from the project. Of course, the CARE packages all included T-shirts with the school logo for the soldiers to wear.

There may be people in your department who have training in communications or who have experience through their personal lives. For example:

- The chief secretary of a major department of limnology prepared a periodic public information bulletin for the department — she was the daughter of a rural weekly newspaper editor.

- In a chemistry department, the man in charge of instrumentation was an Army Reserve intelligence officer with academic and active duty experience in developing periodic intelligence reports. His chair drafted him to write portions of the department's annual budget proposals. The college dean was so impressed that she used the proposals as a model for her own reports.

The only caveat in employing this kind of talent within your unit is to make sure that you don't run into problems with the unions or with employees who enjoy doing your communications projects to the detriment of their other work.

Seeking students

Undergraduate students are another wonderful source of help and talent. There are likely unpolished gems among your students who can help make your program shine. Ask your faculty colleagues to be alert for good writers among their students. (For example, Weimer was a biology major who was steered into communications by her major professor, who noticed the quality of the author's essay responses on biology exams.) There may be students in your department who work on the student newspaper or have other experience in publishing.

Of course, school comes first and your deadlines might not mesh with their class schedules and assignments. Also, those students will leave within a few years. So, ask them to do the smaller, stand-alone projects, like writing newsletter articles or setting up a department electronic bulletin board.

If you find a match and can use students, wonderful! You need the help and they need the experience. If you can pay them as student hourly workers, all the better. Students can usually use the money.

Graduate students offer an even richer pool of communications talent and their tenure is longer, especially in doctoral programs. Be especially alert for graduate students with natural communication and leadership skills or experienced journalists and communications professionals who have returned to school for a graduate degree. If you can afford to offer a graduate student stipend or arrange a fee remission, you are bound to get some good part-time help. If your department or college is large enough, you might even work out a cost-sharing or talent-sharing arrangement with the campus public information office.

Finding faculty

Faculty members may be great communicators in their particular disciplines, because they need to communicate with their students and colleagues. Whatever their specialty, they are likely to be skilled in the art of collecting, evaluating, interpreting, and disseminating information. You may be able to identify such talent in your midst and turn it to your advantage.

Two words of caution. First, if you are preparing information for a general audience, enlist faculty members who can communicate in "plain talk," without jargon or ponderous phrasing. Second, don't distract the willing assistant professor from his or her primary mission of getting tenure. Senior faculty may be your best bet, especially if they have experience in reaching out to varied constituencies or an interest in getting into something new, such as writing something for alumni or making the local talk show circuit on a hot issue. Again, you must be careful that those whom you tap for a particular task are not only willing but also able.

Faculty members can be particularly helpful in formulating departmental policy statements, since they are most familiar with the institution and the roles of its various departments and governing bodies. They should recognize that it is to their benefit to participate directly and personally in the communications program of your division and institution, though each will undoubtedly contribute in his or her own unique way.

Faculty also can have a powerful impact on advancing the institution's mission when, in the course of a media interview or profile, they express their commitment to their vocation and their loyalty to the institution and its students. Reporters, like the rest of us, respond to these straight-from-the-heart statements and generally quote them in their stories.

Foraging in other fields — Interdepartmental aid

Beyond the resources you can find in your department or division, you should seek out the communications specialists on your campus. If your institution is large, you may have professionals close at hand who can help you.

There are eleven colleges on the Norman campus of Oklahoma University; seven employ in-house "external relations" specialists independent of the all-university news service, albeit with a "mutually supportive" relationship. This is a trend that has grown in recent years, spurred primarily by the decline in state support for public education and the rising dependence on fund-raising — through private gifts and federal, state, and industry grants. Many of those grants come, in fact, with an explicit charge that the findings of the supported research must be communicated not only within the discipline but to the public at large.

Colleges of agriculture, born of the land grant model, have long had outreach programs that began with the mandate to convey the results of research to the nation's farmers and food producers. Many of these have evolved into highly sophisticated communications operations. In fact, several lead the academic community in using communications technologies and techniques. The University of Florida's Institute for Food and Agricultural Research, for example, is using compact discs to convey information to Florida's agricultural businesses and produces an excellent and entertaining half-hour weekly TV show broadcast on cable stations throughout the state.

Schools of engineering often employ "technology transfer" specialists to interpret research findings that may find applications in industry. Schools of education do outreach to the public schools in their states, business colleges work with local and regional businesses, and so on. Another highly sophisticated operation is often to be found in schools or colleges of medicine, especially if they are associated with teaching hospitals.

In short, there is communications expertise available across the campus that you may find ways to tap, perhaps through some mutually supportive project. But such a communications specialist won't necessarily be available to help as much as you would like. His or her primary mission is undoubtedly to help the dean and campus administrators meet their goals.

Whatever the situation, consider approaching the specialist as a client would approach an advertising agency. You might benefit from the advice that advertising executive Fred R. Messner (1992) offers to those considering an agency:

- *Learn as much as you can about each other*. Make sure the agency knows your communication objectives and strategies, your functions and policies.

- *Share all pertinent information*. Take the agency into your confidence.

- *Agree on specific, measurable goals.*

- *Do your homework*, to help reduce the number and length of meetings.

- *Conduct informal evaluations of each other's performance* once a year. For deans and directors, this same advice applies to your interactions and relations with the campuswide communications operation.

Students in communications

Your institution undoubtedly has some department of communications, journalism, art, business marketing, or public relations. These departments can be a real gold mine for you. There are almost always interns to be placed or courses that give credit for doing practical communications projects. Get to know the faculty teaching such courses, make your needs known to them, and you can get free help in the form of energetic students.

For example, Weimer had students look at how the University of California, Berkeley represented itself in its communications to students and the public, and how that image squared with the students' own experiences and image of the institution. (It didn't!) The university got valuable insights for planning future publications and the students who did the study got academic credit for it — a win-win situation.

Student communications talent resides in other departments as well. Research, writing, editing, and illustrating talent can be anywhere on campus.

For instance, Schoenfeld enlisted a history Ph.D. candidate to write the division's centennial monograph, which the student parlayed into a thesis. Schoenfeld also got an education graduate student to help write a book on year-round education patterns, which the student adapted into a seminar paper. As a law student, the current Dean of the School of Law at Maine University worked with Schoenfeld on a national assessment of college and university summer session policies and practices.

How do you locate such talent? The campus grapevine is one good way. There also are student job offices or electronic bulletin boards where you can put out the word that you are looking for help. If the task is interesting, students will come to you.

Campus communicators

We have mentioned the communications professionals employed by the institution. How do you locate these folks and find out if what they do is relevant to your needs?

To start, "let your fingers do the walking" — check your campus phone directory for resources. Because each campus is organized somewhat differently and uses different titles, search for these key titles. First, look at the top of the pyramid for a Vice President, Vice Chancellor, or Assistant or Associate President or Chancellor with the titles University Relations, Public Affairs, Development, External Relations, or Communications. Normally these individuals are responsible for the public relations and communications functions of the institution — often including fund-raising, alumni relations, news and media relations, publications, government relations, and other related areas.

In addition, the directory may list specific offices, such as Public Information, News and Information, Communications, Public Affairs, Community Relations, Publications, Periodicals, Marketing, Public Ceremonies, and Special Events — any one of which can guide you into the infrastructure of campus communications support. If you receive a campus newsletter, magazine, or newspaper, look at which office or division publishes it — another guide to the key units.

Actual production facilities — copy offices, printing shops, media support services, radio and TV studios, mailing services — may well lie within other administrative areas. Sometimes such operational units are under the Administrative Vice President or Vice Chancellor, sometimes within other departments or divisions, such as extension, library, intercollegiate athletics, or journalism.

The point is to become familiar with how your institution is organized in this respect and find out who bears the prime responsibility for communicating about your institution with the general public. These colleagues will invariably be your best guides to finding your way through the maze. Also, ask faculty and staff associates who have been around the institution for a long time. Many will undoubtedly know something about these units and resources.

At the top of the structure is the campus' chief public relations officer, whatever his or her title. It is this person's job to worry about all of the outreach functions of the institution and to help build a climate of support and understanding for the institution among many constituencies, including students, faculty, and staff.

This person may have a very small staff or may have a number of large units that report to him or her. It depends on the size of the institution, the availability of resources, the evolution of the program, and the inclination of the campus CEO, to whom this person most likely reports directly.

The chief public relations officer is also responsible for supporting the communications and outreach efforts of others on the campus — and that includes you. Although it may take some energy to find out what resources are available, the results should be worth the effort.

What follows are some thumbnail sketches of "generic" campus units that can help you in particular areas.

The news office

Whether it's called the news bureau, the public information office, or media relations, there is usually a unit at larger colleges and universities that plays the role of intermediary between the institution and the media.

If your department or division has news that is worthy of media coverage, this is the unit that is ready and eager to help you get the word out. It may notify media contacts through telephone calls, faxes, and/or press releases. It may work to get relevant campus experts interviewed on radio and television. It may find yet other ways to publicize your news.

Time and again, these activities have paid off handsomely for an institution. It is not uncommon for information from a press release to find its way into a newscast several states away or a newspaper overseas. If the story is good, it will have "legs" and the media will pick it up and run with it, sometimes getting it not from your institution's press release but from coverage in another newspaper or by a wire service.

This dynamic requires that you be realistic about how your story may be covered — by the time it reaches the newspaper in another state, it may take on a life of its own. It might not include information that you consider vital, such as the most important research result or the source of funding for the project. Reporters and academics are worlds apart in their ways of reporting news. Just remember that the average person doesn't absorb as much information from a newspaper as a scholar obtains from a professional journal. If people get a sense of the finding and its importance and the institution that did the work, that is enough to be very beneficial.

A key service that the news unit can provide is in matching the expertise of faculty in your department or unit with the interests of the media. Radio, TV, and newspapers all have an insatiable appetite for experts close to home who can comment on a current issue or breaking news story — even if it is half a world away. Many campus news offices, in fact, publish experts lists for the media. Your faculty should be in it. If you have experts who can discuss a timely event or an issue of current interest, they're likely to be pursued by the local and regional media. The news office can help get you out there and set priorities on how you can best use your time in fielding media requests.

Consider, for example, the following chain of events. On Oct. 8, 1992, Ripon College (WI) professor of politics and government, Kim Shankman, got up at 6:30 a.m. to write an opinion piece about a negative element in the Bush-Clinton campaign. At 8 a.m., she sent it via email to the associate college relations director, Jean Grant. Grant reviewed it and faxed it to Ripon's public relations consultant in New Hampshire, who liked it so much that he faxed it to *The New York Times*. When the *Times* rejected it, he faxed it to *The Los Angeles Times*, which published it. Less than 24 hours after Shankman wrote down her thoughts about the presidential campaign, people on the West Coast were consuming them along with their eggs, toast, and coffee.

Your news office can also help you out with news relations in a crisis or controversy. There will inevitably be some unfortunate situation that will crop up during your time as dean, unit head, or department chair — whether it be a public fight over a faculty tenure case, an explosion in the chemistry lab, a distraught student who runs amok, or an accusation of research fraud. Your campus news professionals are the folks whom you will want by your side at such moments. With experience in such crises, they have an excellent sense of how the media will approach and cover such situations — and their advice may be invaluable. We strongly urge you to get to know them before such a situation throws you together. We also urge you to read Chapter 12 for more on crisis situations.

The publications office

Traditionally, these offices produce campus-wide publications such as the catalogue, student recruitment materials, campus brochures, alumni periodicals, and campus newsletters. They have editors and designers on the staff and may even have in-house production facilities. In some cases, these professionals may be available to help you with your unit or departmental publications — sometimes for a fee. In other cases, they may not have the capacity to do this work but can guide you to others, on or off campus, who can do it.

Many of these operations are in a state of transition, due to the dramatic changes in communications technology and the changing habits of consumers of information, particularly students. Some campuses have even eliminated their publications offices — incorporating their writers and editors into the public information or public affairs office and using desktop publishing technology to send materials directly to off-campus printers or to outside design vendors. On other campuses, these publications programs are being transformed into what are essentially marketing offices that use a broad range of media and materials to craft and deliver the institution's messages and to "market" the institution to potential students, alumni, and supporters.

If your own unit has at least some capacity to do desktop publishing, you may find the campus publications office eager to help you with editing, formatting, and designing your materials. They may even lean on you to accept their help.

Why? Because PR directors are increasingly frustrated by the amateur desktop publishers all over campus who, in the name of economy, control, or convenience put out publications that, in the opinion of Robert S. Topor (1992), "look like ransom notes."

Topor, a former communications staffer at Stanford and now a California consultant, notes that such materials hurt the institution's image because they are so poorly done. Many campus designers these days are working with departments and programs to design standard formats for brochures, catalogues, and recruitment materials. These "prefab" publication templates are very cost-effective: units can simply flow their information, graphics, and pictures into the form to produce what Topor calls a "thrifty-pub."

You may seek out the publications unit on your campus for help with a newsletter or special report, but be aware that they often have much more to offer. Because of the changes in this field, many publications directors have become attuned to more effective and cheaper ways to get your message across. They can be an invaluable source of advice on how to market your message, as mentioned earlier in this book. Instead of a printed report, maybe you'll produce a videotape. Instead of a newsletter to reach students in your department, maybe you'll set up an electronic bulletin board.

In short, these professionals are experts in matching media, audiences, and messages. They can be of enormous help to you in developing your communications strategy.

Government relations offices

Every institution of higher education has many interlocking relationships with government entities — city, county, state, regional, and federal. In fact, every institution depends on government entities for support, whether it be federal government grants for research, state funding for public colleges, or fire protection from the local municipality.

Somewhere on your campus, there will be a person or a group of people whose job it is to facilitate interactions with various branches of government. In large universities, such contacts are spread throughout the institution. At the University of California, Berkeley, for example, there is a community relations office under one Vice Chancellor, a government relations unit under another Vice Chancellor, an assistant to the Chancellor who works closely with elected officials, and a federal relations component to the Provost for Research office. Several academic units, including the School of Public Policy and Institute for Governmental Studies, have close government ties. There also are a myriad of research units and faculty projects that are closely allied with individual government agencies. This may seem a tangled web, but it is born of pragmatism.

Make it a point to know a few key people in this web; when a problem or an opportunity arises that involves a funding agency or community group, these contacts can invariably be helpful. Be aware, however, that college presidents are very dependent on government funding and sensitive to the concerns of public officials. You would be ill-advised to go off on your own to lobby for funding or to surprise your campus CEO with a community relations initiative or problem that came from your unit — another reason to keep in close contact with those in your administration who work on these issues. Though Schoenfeld knows of a dean who ultimately won high praise for lobbying a legislature for a new building over the head of his provost and is now the institution's vice president, he also knows of another dean who did the same thing and was stripped of his rank. These days — with funding competition so fierce — you are more likely to end up like the latter.

The alumni office

After office or lab space and parking, alumni are probably becoming the commodity most in demand on campus. Colleges and universities are finding alumni a critical constituency for several reasons.

First, in this age of accountability and outcomes assessments, your alumni are evidence of the quality of your enterprise, especially as measured by what they achieve through their education. Second, individually and collectively, your alumni can be a powerful lobbying voice, whether the target is the state legislature, key opinion leaders in your area, or a private funding source. Third, your alumni can help mentor and sometimes even find employment for your current students. And fourth, they can, of course, be a direct source of gifts, pledges, and bequests to support your programs.

As a consequence, at many institutions, deans and department chairs actively communicate with their alumni, jealously guard their mailing lists, and fend off attempts by other departments — and sometimes even the president's fund-raisers — to contact and cultivate those alumni that they consider "their property."

Your institution's alumni officer — or alumni office — can be a valuable ally in communicating with this critical group. The staff have the infrastructure, experience, and contacts to help you track, reach, and cultivate your alumni. They can help you maintain alumni mailing lists; in fact, you may be able to piggy-back on their lists and mailings. They also can help in the sophisticated, and sometimes sensitive, task of rounding up alumni to intervene on your behalf politically and to generate gifts from graduates.

In turn, the alumni office will rely on you to give them names and keep them up to date on what your graduates are doing and what's happening in your department or division. The better the alumni relations at all levels of the institution, the better the institution will be for it.

Alumni office operations are becoming increasingly sophisticated and professional. Many use the latest technology and marketing techniques, including targeting their communications to subgroups of alumni by region, interests, ethnicity, age, and gender. They are also very active with the student body, generating new alumni association members among the students before they even shed their caps and gowns.

Barbara Tipsord Todd, assistant director of alumni services at Illinois State University (1992), asks department chairs to identify juniors and seniors to become student members of the alumni association and carry on such activities as career exploration workshops, represent the students at class reunions and alumni meetings, host campus tours for alumni, and plan other programs for fellow students. Her personal support for students led some of them a few years ago to give her a charm reading "#1 Mom."

There is another important aspect to Todd's kind of program. Nothing impresses alumni more than bright, articulate, poised undergraduates. Their enthusiasm for the institution is often infectious and they show the alumni that their alma mater is continuing to uphold its tradition of quality. Find opportunities to bring your students into contact with your alumni; it can be a mutually rewarding experience.

In reaching across the campus to tap resources for your communications effort, the alumni office is one of the first places you'll want to explore. Because they almost always publish a newsletter or magazine that goes to members, alumni office staff can offer you advice on techniques for marketing your unit and you may get news of your department or program into their periodical. This is free publicity — and one of the most cost-effective ways of reaching out with your message and accomplishments. If the alumni office mailing operation is sophisticated enough, you may be able to insert four pages of news from your department or division into the alumni publication and send those special issues just to your alumni mailing list. That technology is growing more prevalent — just look at the many "personal" sweepstakes mailings you get. Soon, colleges and universities will use those same methods to tailor mailings.

It is important to solicit the help of the alumni office for yet another reason: to identify volunteers. Alumni can serve as advisors, advocates, and sometimes critics. Whenever you go looking for assistance, be prepared to be receptive to suggestions that challenge unit practices and goals. The alumni are your major link to the "outside world" and those who are active are naturally likely to be supportive of you. If the alumni have ideas with merit, heed them; if not, educate them.

The development office

Rare is the academic department or division that couldn't use more money — for scholarships, fellowships, program initiatives, equipment, faculty support, even buildings. This is where your campus development or fund-raising operation comes in. Not only can it give you help in raising funds — from writing a case statement to identifying potential donors — but it also can advise you on how to target your message such that the response from alumni and friends is positive.

Development and alumni cultivation go hand in hand. The alumni association and public affairs programs of your campus do the friend-raising; the development operation then taps those friends for hard cash. Often, the alumni and fund-raising functions are in the same department or under the same administrator. Sometimes they share communications staff. Other times, they are quite independent.

Though this is a book about communications and not fund-raising, it is very likely that one reason you have reached this chapter is because you are interested in communicating with donors in a compelling way. Again, seek out the professionals on your campus — or in your community. (We'll come to that next.) Get their advice and direction, and look for ways to plug into their programs that will benefit you both. Also, be sure to read the discussion on capital campaigns in Chapter 12.

Community programs, summer sessions, and outreach

Whatever the size of your institution, you undoubtedly have some programs in community relations or service. Perhaps you have an outreach or extension office or a continuing education unit. All of these provide the surrounding community with access to your college or university. The responsibility for these three birds of a feather, in fact, is often vested in one person or unit. And quite often, that person or unit has some of the most sophisticated marketing communications to be found on the campus. The reason? These programs live and die by the income generated through fees for their courses, programs, and other offerings. And it is here that you are likely to find the most sophisticated "marketers" on your campus.

They may be eager to support your unit's summer term offerings, community programs, or outreach courses, for example, with public information and marketing activities designed to attract students and attendees. Often, they will encourage curriculum development that is attuned to the needs of nontraditional students — increasing the reach and visibility of your department or division.

Let's visit Amanda Perkins for an example. When she proposed to offer a field course in "Identification of Spring Flora" in the three-week session between the close of the spring quarter and the beginning of the school's eight-week summer term, she enlisted the aid of Summer Session Director Gertrude A. Cowles. Cowles developed and mailed special promotional fliers to garden club members, nursery and flower shop owners, and biology teachers in the area, using her departmental budget. The result was an overflow crowd of students that benefited both Cowles and Perkins.

In some strait-laced academic circles, the marketing approach that summer sessions and extension/outreach programs employ may seem too "Madison Avenue" to be comfortable. But more and more, colleges and universities are turning to these techniques in their mainstream programs — to attract students, faculty, funding, and public support. A department chair or dean would be wise to welcome such communications assistance.

Other sources of assistance

In addition to the units we've already covered, there are other sources of communications support around the campus. One that is becoming increasingly important is your computer guru — sometimes known as the director of information technology or computing and information management.

Computers are transforming the way we communicate. Those who keep abreast of this technology and its application to academia can offer you a wealth of ideas, information, and technical assistance. They can help you and your colleagues wend your way through the labyrinth of electronic mail, bulletin boards, and publishing, as well as the Internet.

Not only can this technology save you money and time, it may be the best way to reach some of your constituencies, particularly students. Today's students have grown up with computers and, when they want information, they may turn first to the information highways, not the traditional rivers of ink. To be effective, you need to find ways to get into their computers.

Assistance also may be available in the educational media office, which develops teaching materials such as slides, films, videotapes, audiotapes, and other multi-media aids. These units, too, are getting much more deeply involved in new communications technologies, such as interactive video and computers to facilitate distance learning. (You can read chapter thirteen for more insight into these trends.) Such expertise undoubtedly exists on your campus and can be your guide to these new tools as well as more traditional media uses, beyond the printed word.

Likewise, there may be good contacts in your business office. Here you may find communications support entities such as copy centers, photography labs, mailing services, perhaps even a print shop if you're on a large campus. Business office contacts also can help you through the maze of purchasing and requisition procedures that govern your acquisition of communications support, whether it be a freelance writer or the bulk mailing of an alumni newsletter.

The list of people and programs on your campus that relate in some way to communications may seem overwhelming. Certainly, you don't have time to seek out all of these people. The key points are, first, to be aware of what resources exist on your campus, and second, to identify a couple of people who can be your guides to other services. Your best bet is probably the chief public relations officer, who typically has the best overview of this area.

Foraging further afield — Help on the outside

We have already mentioned alumni as members of the "campus family" who, though off campus, still can be very helpful in your communications program. Apart from enlisting them to help generate public and financial support for your program, you can prevail on them and other friends of the campus for professional advice in communications.

You may already have a general purpose advisory council of people from beyond your academic unit, perhaps beyond your campus borders, who meet regularly to keep abreast of what is going on and help you in various ways. It may be redundant to create another council to provide communications advice, but it is worth considering the possibility of having some members of that council recruit volunteer *professional* communicators — within and beyond the campus — and provide you with specific and strategic advice in this area.

Perhaps among your alumni is a business or industry CEO who would be willing to tap one of his or her lieutenants for such service. Perhaps you have a student whose parents are in the communications field. Certainly in your community — perhaps in your own circle of friends outside the institution — there are accomplished professionals willing to serve on such a group.

A few caveats are in order, however. Make sure you have some explicit tasks for this group or the committee will end up generating more work for you. The goal is to get them to work on *your* behalf. If you energize such a group solely for the purpose of fund-raising, the members will see the hidden agenda a mile off and find excuses not to participate. If you seek their counsel, be prepared to heed it. If you think the group is going to want to get into more fundamental issues of policy (Why don't the faculty teach more? Why aren't your students able to graduate faster? Why are the tuition bills so hard to decipher? and so on), you're right. Be prepared with answers to such questions — and be prepared to keep the group focused on your needs. Finally, be ready to recognize and reward them for their efforts. An invitation to the president's house for brunch, special seating for an athletic event, or a framed certificate of appreciation will help them feel better about their work for you and redouble their commitment to your agenda.

Now that you've formed a council or subcommittee, what do you ask it to do? One of the best and most useful opening gambits is to have them audit your existing communication plans, programs, and personnel. (If you can't pull a current communication plan out of your desk drawer, that will tell them something right away.) This will lead to a discussion of the strengths and weaknesses of your effort, and one or two committee members may well volunteer to help plug the gaps.

While these advisory group members can't be expected to be intimately familiar with your academic unit's missions, messages, and media, they will bring expertise and instincts based on their experiences that will help you develop an effective program. They also serve to build bridges of information and support back into the community.

Through these connections, you may even come across somebody who would be happy and willing to offer assistance, either to gain professional experience or to take on a project, *pro bono*. For example, a faculty spouse with a writing and editing background may offer to work with you on your case statement, or a local public relations firm may assign an intern to help promote a community event that involves your department. It's unlikely, however, that members of the media will volunteer to help — newspapers and TV stations, in particular, jealously guard their editorial objectivity and strongly discourage (sometimes prohibit) their reporters and editors from getting involved in any activity that smacks of advocacy.

You may consider hiring outside experts to help in some specific communications project — a practice that is becoming more widely accepted. And the size of your unit or institution is not necessarily an issue. While retaining outside professional public relations counsel is relatively common among four-year-colleges, now two community colleges are known to be doing the same thing — Hocking College in rural Ohio and Robert Morris College in Chicago.

Hocking, which features unique programs with an environmental bent, has signed up with Sumner Rider & Associates of New York and Washington DC. As a result of the firm's efforts, when the college held a press conference in October 1995 to announce its new eco-tourism associate degree program, the event drew reporters from four national environmental magazines. When students from the college's fire science program went to the Northeast last summer to fight wildfires, CNN went along to report.

Robert Morris, a private not-for-profit institution, has retained McCann and Associates of Chicago to attract coverage in metropolitan dailies and on TV. Vince Norton, vice president for enrollment management, says the arrangement costs less than the average cost for a middle manager's salary and fringe benefits. He calls the heightened media exposure a "major coup." He added, "Colleges think nothing of having auditors and CPA firms work with them on financial matter, but then they try to do their PR on a 'home brew.' Hiring the experts is worth it."

National networks/associations

Schoenfeld has childhood memories of watching his country-preacher father poring over a magazine called *The Expositor*. It was only in later years that he came to know the magazine as a monthly compendium of draft sermons, each complete with Biblical text, appropriate parables, and a "message of the day."

Campus leaders need *Expositors* and they have them, in a wide array of national academic media, each with a particular type of communication aid.

The most scholarly of disciplinary journals aren't apt to be of much help — they are devoted to peer-reviewed research reports. But each discipline is apt to have a more plebeian journal in which thoughtful commentaries on disciplinary issues can be found. These can become fodder for articles and speeches and even some "how to" suggestions on communication strategies.

For example, while the *Journalism Quarterly* is the repository for cutting-edge research in the field of mass communication and the recorder of what's going on in departments or schools of journalism, it is not as utilitarian as *Journalism Educator*. The latter discusses teaching and outreach strategies, and even carries occasional reports on the communications programs of academic units.

Among the many general periodicals for academics that can stimulate ideas are *Change* magazine, ACE's *Educational Record*, the AAHE's *Bulletin*, *Academic Leader*, *Administrator*, AAUP's *Academe*, and *Lingua Franca*. Perhaps the most widely read of all is *The Chronicle of Higher Education*, a weekly publication whose circulation has exploded over the past decade. It offers the most comprehensive news of higher education, as well as thoughtful opinion pieces on a host of issues, written by guest columnists from an array of disciplines and institutions.

If you really want to delve into the world of communications and get practical tips aimed directly at the university environment, you can subscribe to *Currents*, the magazine of the Council for the Advancement and Support of Education (CASE). Your campus' chief public affairs officer will know how you can get access to the magazine. Another highly specialized periodical that could be of assistance is *Radio/TV Interview Report*. This is the magazine that talk-show producers use to find guests. CNN producer Betsy Goldman calls it "the *Cliff Notes* of the industry." It is probably too specialized for your use, but make sure your campus news bureau or public information office gets a copy.

The national professional association to which you belong may also be able to render communications assistance on occasion. For example, the North American Association of Summer Sessions invariably devotes a portion of its annual conference to a roundtable discussion of marketing, as does the National Association of State Universities and Land Grant Colleges (NASULGC). Two premier support networks of this kind are the National Council for Marketing and Public Relations, an affiliate of the American Association of Community Colleges, and the Council for the Advancement and Support of Education.

Both organizations annually conduct awards competitions for college and university communications programs. They hold conferences and workshops, publish "how to" reports, and provide a wealth of resource information that could be very useful to your porgrams.

Finally, in casting your net for assistance, look to your colleagues at other institutions. If they have come up with a good communications idea or vehicle, consider copying it. Conversely, if they copy you, take it as flattery: it means you're doing something right, something that's proving effective. Within the academic communications field, the greatest source of good ideas is one's counterparts on other campuses. Take advantage of the hits and misses of others as you approach your communications agenda.

It has taken many pages to cover the topic of marshaling communications assistance and yet it can be summarized in one word "networking" — and in one phrase — "get others to do your work for you." The effectiveness of your communications program often hinges as much on what you can get others to do for you as on what you do for yourself. You don't have the time to become an expert in communications and you don't need to. It's enough to know who those experts are — and they are all around you. Tap into them. They will be flattered and you will be successful.

For further consideration ...

Ready help

Andrea Barbalich, managing editor of CASE *Currents*, offers these examples of campus leaders enlisting the help of their campus news service people to communicate in imaginative and effective ways (*Case Currents*, 1994):

- At the University of Maryland at College Park, chemistry Professor Tom O'Haver's CHEM-CONF, held in mid-1993, was an email-only convention. "Some 450 chemists from 33 countries traded research papers, contemplated statistics, and discussed developments in the field — all on the Internet."

  Tom's chair thought that novel event merited some publicity, so she got John Fritz, campus public affairs officer, to send a press release by — how else? — email to *Wired*, a monthly magazine about computer culture. The result: a story about the online chemistry conference, titled "A New Formula for Conferences."

- At University Preparatory Academy in Seattle, the start of the school's first capital campaign wouldn't be exactly big news in a big-media market. After all, the eighteen-year-old institution has only 333 students. But the development officer_challenged Kimberly Hill, the Prep communications director, to come up the some-thing novel. She did.

Hill bought six Mylar balloons, wrote "Good News in Education" on them, and delivered one to each of four TV station and two news-papers. The result: that night three local news anchors gave their broadcasts with a balloon floating in the background. The next day a news crew came to the campus to do a story on the two-year $1.2 million goal, which ended up as a five-minute tape on the evening news. The daily Seattle *Post-Intelli-gencer* also ran a feature.

- At Chapman University in Orange, California, the provost thought Professor Fred Caporaso worthy of an appearance in *The Chronicle of Higher Education*'s "Portraits" column, which profiles academics, usually ones whose stories are quirky in some way. Ruth Wardell of the campus news service got the drift right away. In her pitch to *The Chronicle*, she played up the professor's specialties, which appeared "seem-ingly unrelated" — food science and herpetol-ogy.

Sure enough, *Chronicle* reporter Christopher Shea asked for more. The result: a full-page feature explaining the link between Caporaso's two interests — certain chemical compounds give animal meats their flavor, and some reptiles, particularly turtles, secrete similar compounds to help them find their way back to where they've been before.

The *Chronicle* story contributed to several of Provost Harry Hamilton's goals — helping to build the university's national profile and focusing on the link between teaching and research.

chapter eight

Putting Your Money Where Your Message Is

Finding and budgeting funds

If there is a universal truth in higher education in the mid-1990s, it is that financial resources are tighter than they have been for decades, at public and private institutions alike. Funds are short for instruction, research, and service activities. And yet, investment in communications is a "must" for everyone — from the individual faculty member and department head to the dean, program director, and president.

Without strategic communication approaches, which cost money to develop and execute, it is difficult to communicate effectively with your constituencies — be they research grantors, donors, students, parents, or taxpayers. You will want to tell them about what you are doing to carry out your part of the "contract" to educate students or to push forward the frontiers of knowledge and scholarship. Communications also are vital in recruiting resources — students, faculty and staff, state and federal dollars, and donations.

This is a tough chapter to write because campus leaders operate under different fiscal conditions. Some already have staff and funds available for communications projects and programs, while others have to hunt for help. Some campus leaders have great latitude in how they can move money around in their budgets to cover such needs, while others have none.

Once you have determined your communications needs, the next logical step is to conduct an audit of sorts. This exercise is beneficial whether or not you are new to your position and responsibilities.

The fiscal/talent audit

The audit process is simple.

First, identify what fiscal resources are available within your budget — and within your control — to devote to communications programs. This would include the budgets for any existing materials, such as departmental or divisional newsletters, campus magazines, alumni mailings, and the like. Include as well any flexible money that you are willing to commit to this activity.

Second, survey your staff resources to see what, if any, personnel are presently available to devote to communications activity. This listing would include any people — part- or full-time, professional staff, and students, who are writing, editing, designing, or producing communications materials of any sort. You might also identify people within your unit who have an aptitude for communication — verbal or written — and might be drafted to help out with your communications efforts.

Next, using surveying techniques and anecdotal information, ask yourself how effective your existing communications strategies really are. Are people reading your publications? Watching your videotapes? Paying attention to your electronic bulletin board? Is the impact of these projects measurable? If your communications are effective, is the amount of money (as determined by your fiscal audit) appropriate to the need being met? Would a less expensive newsletter serve your purpose just as well, for example?

If so, tally up what might be saved and put it in your "dollars found" column.

The fourth step in this audit follows a basic principle of this book — look for others to do your work for you. Although we discussed this topic in depth in chapter 7, for the purposes of your audit, you should make a list of other resources (personnel, services, facilities, products) that are available to you. You are probably surrounded by communications resources in the form of campus news operations, alumni publications, electronic mail networks, student newspapers, college or university catalogues and publications, video services, campus-produced TV and radio programs, and so on. Making use of those outlets will save you money.

If you can get the alumni magazine, for example, to publish an article on your department, not only will the information reach a much broader audience than you can afford to reach, but also you can buy reprints of the article at a fraction of the cost you would incur in publishing the article yourself. If your unit's researchers work with a particular sponsor or company, don't overlook their communications resources. An article in the Department of Commerce magazine or the Bank of America's employee newsletter can pay considerable dividends.

Once you have completed this audit, you will be better able to identify where resources can be redirected to your communications plans. You also will be in a much better position to make your request for any additional resources necessary.

A concrete example of the benefits of such an audit can be found in the experience of a new dean of international studies at a major public university.

Upon arriving on the scene, he and a top aide immediately conducted an audit of the sort described above. He found that his program was devoting one-and-a-half positions and some $15,000 per year to produce a newsletter to carry news of the campus to faculty and friends overseas. He asked, "Why not just distribute the campus employee newspaper to faculty and friends abroad?" Because, he was told, when the project started there had been no such newspaper; after one was launched, no one in his unit questioned continuing the international newsletter and the duplication of effort. The new dean promptly replaced his newsletter with the campus publication and thereby freed up substantial funds and personnel that he could apply to other communication needs of the unit.

Each reader will undoubtedly find similar situations in his or her own environment — most not quite so dramatic perhaps, but there are almost always resources to be found. Whether you initially search for funds and personnel and then construct a budget or you first draft a "what if" budget and then go looking for money and talent, the audit is an important first step in the process.

Finding funds through reallocation

Whatever your situation, it's probably safe to assume that you would not be reading this book if you did not see the need for a more aggressive communications program than whatever you have. And, no doubt, you want to identify funds for such a program. Where might you look for pots of gold?

Charity begins at home and so does scrounging for communications money. Actually, given the lean times in academia, these strategies may also be useful in freeing up funds for any number of important unit priorities.

Interviewing academic administrators around the country, Ellen Ryan (1991), Wendy Ann Larson (1991), Andrea Barbalich (1991), and Catherine L. O'Shea (1991) collected some great tips on ways to dig for dollars. For instance:

- Bring back in-house those services that you can do that are now performed by outside vendors. Reopen bids on functions you can't absorb. Look for ways to collaborate with other units, so that you can make the most of your limited resources to acquire services.

- Take advantage of any seminars (and expertise) on campus or in your community on "waste not, want not" fiscal management.

- Review travel guidelines. When business requires several faculty members and/or staff to travel regionally, encourage them to go together in a campus vehicle rather than traveling individually. This can have the added benefit of improving camaraderie and communication.

- Do not approve fancy lodging and expensive meals. Ask employees to make air travel plans early, to take advantage of discount rates and to consider a Saturday night stay, which can often save hundreds of dollars and more than pay for an extra night or two in a hotel.

- Train and employ students for jobs in your unit. They're smart. They're energetic. They don't cost a lot. And the experience they get working with you will help them later in their job searches.

- When faculty and staff do outside projects on college or university time, ask them to consider donating a portion of the honoraria they receive to the unit's kitty.

- Look at mailing and telephone costs. Frequently there is money to be saved in postage, phone, and overnight delivery service budgets. In large mailings, make sure your department is taking advantage of first-class bulk postage discounts. Are people sending materials via overnight carriers when they could be faxing? Are they faxing when they could be mailing? More to the point, are they mailing, faxing, and sending materials via overnight carriers, when they could be sending material electronically? New communication technologies and delivery services have afforded us great convenience, but not without cost — and those costs should be examined.

- Sell rather than give away any marketable publications and services. Deciding what's basic service and what's a "market" product deserves careful thought.

- Eliminate or scale back on personnel positions that are no longer necessary to the unit and recapture those funds.

Those "for instance" tips may help you unearth money here and there in your unit that could be diverted to meeting communication needs. It may be productive to involve your staff and/or senior aides in this hunt for resources. They often are closest to program expenditures and you may be surprised at the thoughtful suggestions they contribute.

For those who already have communications programs or units, there are other money-yielding possibilities:

- Slim down external publications or scale back their frequency to trim mailing costs.

- Look for cheaper formats for publications that will not make them less effective.

- Send camera-ready copy or computer disks to printers, instead of raw text.

- Try to make some publications serve more than one audience through reformatting or judicious editing.

Those with communications programs also will want to examine the resources that are going into personnel rather than products. As our case of the international studies newsletter suggested, you can have mismatches: you might have too many people with not enough funds to produce and distribute what's needed, or you might have an overworked employee with lots of supply money but not enough support staff to adequately use it.

Communications professionals disagree on which end of the equation to prioritize — funding people or funding products. The truth is that the balance differs depending on the situation. Only through the kind of careful auditing we have described, and through the careful crafting of a communications plan, can the right formula be derived.

Asking for resources to meet your needs

Now you've done your audit and you've got your plan, but the bottom lines don't match. You need more resources to get the job done and you need help acquiring them. Wherever you are in a campus hierarchy, you report to a superior whom you picture as Mr. or Ms. Money Bags. Although these are tough times, it can't hurt to hit him or her up for communications funding, especially if you have a solid, detailed plan.

Writing from her perspective as the chair of the English department at Eastern Michigan University, Marcia A. Dalbey (1993) has this suggestion on how to proceed:

> Establish a good relationship with your dean. Make a point of talking with him or her at times other than when you're asking for money. Help the dean become aware of what your department is doing, and establish your-self as someone the dean can call on for advice or assistance. This strategy isn't necessarily artful decep-tion; it's simply forming good professional relations. A dean who knows and respects you and your department is more likely to consider seriously your requests for resources.

Sooner or later, of course, you'll probably want to make a direct pitch. Whether it encompasses an annual budget or just a specific project, April Harris (1992) notes that "making a formal proposal enables you to bring activities to the attention of decision makers as they select programs and plan funding." So, think of it not only as a request for resources, but an opportunity to communicate about your unit.

In making these proposals, be sure to analyze and address what's in it for your boss — what will it do for the unit and the college or university? If you clearly address those benefits, you are more likely to get support. If, however, you bring in plans for a departmental newsletter in which the name of your umbrella organization appears in tiny type, don't be surprised at a flat rejection of the proposal. Look for ways to mesh your needs with those of the unit or institution and you will have a better chance of success.

As Leslie Brill, English chair at Wayne State University (MI), notes (1993):

> When seeking support of any kind, chairs should set out with a quid for the desired quo. We need to set out, in brief, with something besides our hats in our out-stretched hands. If the problem is clearly defined and limited, and if the solution appears reasonably cost-effective — and especially if the solution promises to have some potential to attract a scrap or two of commendation beyond the department — then assistance may well be available.

Finding funds outside your unit

Given the constraints on higher education funding, your chair, dean, or provost may not have the money to fund your communication proposal. But don't despair. You may find support through collaboration with other college units or organizations outside the institution.

In your audit, you will have identified other campus entities that already have the dollars to spend on communicating with important audiences. Involve them in your planning and ideas and, more often than not, they will help you execute those plans. The campus development office may be willing to help fund department or division publications aimed at alumni and other potential donors; campus public information offices will prepare and distribute department or school news releases. In fact, if those unit heads endorse your proposal with the dean or vice president, it might have a better chance for successful funding.

Collaboration is all the more critical when resources are tight. Larson (1991) gives us these other examples:

- The Fairfield University (CT) alumni relations office provides seed money for student class councils.

- The University of Miami School of Business cosponsors programs with the School of Marine and Atmospheric Sciences.

- Butler County Community College's Registrar's Office (PA) lets departments include materials in the registrar's mailings to students.

Dalbey (1993) offers another example. Eastern Michigan's Continuing Education Division cosponsors, with the department of English, a highly successful annual conference on children's literature. The division provides facilities, promotion, and funding, and the department makes arrangements for speakers and teaches a credit course in which registrants can enroll. Again, a "win-win" situation, with each group getting positive publicity.

If your college or university has an English, communications, journalism, computer science, and/or business department, you might also find some free or low-cost assistance. (See also chapter seven.) To cite just a few examples:

- At the University of Wisconsin-Madison, a journalism class did an excellent readership survey for *Wisconsin Week*, the campus employee newspaper.

- A UW-Madison business marketing class did a project assessing the number of visitors to the campus annually and their information needs.

- At Austin Peay State University (TN), a television-studies intern created a 10-minute video for a division.

- At Eastern Michigan, members of the student English club members write articles for the departmental newsletter.

- At the University of California, Berkeley, seniors in business are helping local non-profit agencies, including the California Alumni Association, develop new strategic plans that include communications goals and objectives.

Use of "for credit" student power represents a low-cost answer to varying types of communications needs. It has the added advantages of giving the students "real-world" experience and perhaps also involving their professors, as consultants.

Looking outside the college or university for financial and in-kind support for your projects and programs can also be productive. A cautionary note here, however: the competition for this support is growing keener and you should check with the dean and campus development officers before going off on your own to chase these dollars. If a business is considering making a major gift to the President's Scholarship Fund, but then decides instead to underwrite your (less expensive) anniversary banquet, you may find yourself worrying over whether your unit will live to see its next anniversary!

Nevertheless, local businesses and companies with some relationship to your college and/or department are frequently happy to help out by providing expertise, cosponsoring events, helping to fund special projects, and, perhaps, even making direct contributions that can be used to carry out your communications plans.

You might also consider carrying paid advertisements or getting company underwriting for specific communication vehicles, like newsletters or magazines, depending on institutional policies. Amanda Perkins, for example, got the local Sierra Club to co-sponsor her departmental open house at Midland University. Not only did the organization pay for half the program printing in exchange for space, but members also promoted the event in their own newsletters, handed out programs through their offices regionally, and staffed a table for interested visitors at the event.

Other examples of symbiotic relationships that help stretch dollars

- The Faculty Club at UC-Berkeley underwrote a reception for parents in return for advertising in the campus' parents newsletter.

- Collin County Community College (TX) approaches corporations, small businesses, and individuals to donate items for an annual auction. The businesses, in turn, get visibility.

- Simmons College (MA) uses alumni volunteers to stuff envelopes and staff booths at college fairs. The alumni feel good volunteering and the campus gets free person power.

- Montgomery College (MD) found a printer who would print event programs free of charge in exchange for a credit line in the program and other college business.

- The College of William and Mary (VA) rents facilities in its alumni house. The community, in turn, gets use of a lovely low-cost facility.

One place to seek advice on these extramural support opportunities is your athletic department, if you have one. The staff has likely been in this business a long time. These departments usually have the strongest marketing and community relations programs on campus and you can, no doubt, learn from their experience — and maybe, in the process, link up with them on a project to benefit your unit.

Budgeting funds

"Preparing a budget," says Anita Webb-Lupo (1992), "is like a religious experience — part faith, part hope, part charity. Planning informs budgeting and budgeting limits planning. At its heart, budgeting reveals priorities, because budgeting is the making of decisions that distribute resources to enable action." Budgeting is not the same as accounting, she goes on: "Budgeting is the resource allocation process; accounting is the process of measuring the actual use of resources."

As a document, a budget is at once a record of the past, a statement of future expectations, and a contract. As a process, a budget is a means of communication, a decision-making procedure, and a method of converting rhetoric into an action plan.

Ways of budgeting

There are a variety of approaches to budgeting, and the type you use at any one time is likely determined or strongly suggested by your campus business office. Most of you have budget officers at the department or division level to help you prepare and audit budgets. Nevertheless, if you are interested in the different methods of budgeting, we highly recommend *College and University Budgeting: An Introduction for Faculty and Academic Administrators* (Washington, DC: National Association of College and University Business Officers, 1992).

In this very readable book, Richard J. Meisinger, Jr. and Leroy W. Dubeck describe several general approaches to budgeting funds, which we summarize here:

Incremental budgeting. This is how most individuals, departments, and institutions tend to manage resources. They assume last year's budget as their platform and figure up or down from there. Very often, a unit's pattern of spending does not change radically from year to year, so this is a sound approach. However, it doesn't encourage a healthy examination of the rationale for spending patterns, nor does it foster new initiatives or reallocation.

PPBS. Planning, programming, and budgeting systems (PPBS) link the planning process to the allocation of resources. This practice calls for focus on the macro level, with strong, central management and a consensus on goals and objectives. It also generally involves a longer-range view of budgets and lengthy analysis of alternative plans and options.

Zero-based budgeting. This, in contrast with PPBS approaches, focuses on the micro level and is initiated at the lower levels of the organization. Each budget cycle begins with a clean slate and budgets are built to fit the programs being executed. For practical purposes, institutions like colleges and universities, in which services and activities remain relatively fixed from year to year, can best benefit from this approach if they assume some fixed base of support (say 80%), and then do a zero-based budget exercise with the remainder.

Performance budgeting. With this approach, resources (inputs) are related directly to activities (structure) and results (outcomes). Accounting structures relate expenditures of resources directly to results. Desired input/output measures or ratios are defined and resources are allocated on that basis. Performance budgeting works well in companies where manufacturing or service is the focus; in academia, where outputs are more difficult to quantify and responsibilities are diffuse, this is a more complex (if not impossible) approach to budgeting resources.

Formula budgeting. In this process, resource requirements are estimated by looking at program demand related to cost. These relationships are typically expressed as mathematical formulations. The instructional budget of a public institution, for example, might be driven by a faculty-student ratio or by the costs per credit hour, calculated for each discipline individually. In general, budget formulas are used on a system- or state-wide basis for state-supported institutions, because they represent a simplified model of the institution's projected financial needs, which is both the appeal and the weakness of formula budgeting. Institutions are not alike, even those in the same systems of higher education, and enrollment-driven formulas cannot fully handle their diverse financial needs.

Cost center budgeting. This approach could be characterized as "every tub on its own bottom." It treats every unit in an institution as if it were self-supporting. The approach can work well for institutional auxiliaries, like the bookstore or student housing program, or academic units that are relatively self-contained in their teaching, research, and service, such as professional schools and colleges or the summer sessions program. It works less well when applied across the institution.

In reality, unit heads and budget officers will use several of these budgeting approaches. In a public college or university, for example, the formula by which the state determines how much to allocate to the institution will be different from the way in which a unit head will budget his or her funds. Applying this to your communications planning, you may find performance-based or cost center budgeting useful for certain projects, while folding the staple communications program into the incremental budgeting process. Whatever you decide, the important point is to keep close track of your expenditures in order to inform your future plans and make a better case for needed communications resources, in future budget cycles.

The publish and perish environment

When we refer to your unit's communications budget, what's the first thing that pops into your head? The departmental newsletter? The campus magazine? The course catalogue? Traditionally, our communications programs at colleges and universities have been dominated by the printed word.

But our world is changing dramatically. We are in a world of TV, radio, telephones, fax machines, on-line computer services, multi-media, email ....

Even with these changes, the printed word continues to grow, in volume if not in importance. We need only to look in campus mailboxes to realize how inundated we all are with information. How much of what's in your mailbox do you actually have time to read? If we are to budget resources effectively, therefore, we must consider not only how to get our message out, but how to get it through the clutter of other messages bombarding our audiences.

Other chapters in this book go into this issue in more detail, but it is important to note it again here because your budget will reflect your strategies. Sometimes the most effective ways to communicate are also the cheapest. Also, while the printed word may be losing impact among certain audiences, the costs of printing and postage are climbing dramatically. All of these factors contribute to the importance of a multi-dimensional communications plan.

Getting bang for the buck

In designing a budget for communications, it is important to understand the relative costs of the various communication options to be employed. For example, an inexpensive 30-second public service TV announcement costs about $20,000 to produce (airtime not included). For that same price, you could print 7,500 copies of a high-quality, 16-page full-color booklet. Or you could print 80,000 copies of an eight-page tabloid. (Costs vary depending on your geographical location and institutional arrangements with vendors.)

The content and impact of these three projects will differ greatly, but from a budgeting perspective, it is important to view them as competing for your money. Resist the temptation, however, to go automatically for options that give you the most for the least. Three million people might see your television spot and be persuaded to support your program, while 80,000 tabloids could follow the weekly shopper into the recycling bin.

We are not recommending specific approaches in this chapter, but emphasizing that you need some idea of the relative costs of various approaches and products when formulating your communications plan so you can make wise decisions about using your resources.

To give you an idea of what publications cost these days, for example, and how they can vary from campus to campus depending on quality and circulation, the following data from the Council for the Advancement and Support of Education (Barbalich 1991) illustrates alumni magazine costs (per copy, excluding salaries) at eight representative institutions:

Brown University	$0.60
Bryn Mawr	1.04
Eastern Michigan University	
limited mailing	2.53
mass mailing	.43
Iowas State University	2.00
Northern Virginia Community College	.55
Texas Tech University	1.15
University of Alberta (US)	.56
University of Portland	1.30

A second important factor in getting the most for your money is to build funds into the budget for project evaluation. There should be "up-front" funding to make sure that proposed activities are likely to achieve desired results, and there should be funds at the end or midpoint to test the project's effectiveness. Few of us would buy a car without a test drive, and yet an unnerving amount of communications activity is funded without testing. When you consider the costs of producing, printing, and distributing a color brochure or magazine, this seems imprudent indeed.

Your tests need not be expensive. For just the cost of refreshments at a late afternoon get-together, you can meet with groups that represent the intended audience *before* you produce a brochure or develop a slide presentation. Such focus groups can be enormously helpful, as we saw in chapter four. It is also relatively inexpensive to build a readership survey into a publication or to use the telephone to informally survey readers of your alumni magazine. By building these "reality checks" into the budget, you are reinforcing your "contract" to keep your program cost-effective.

There are also budgeting "rules of thumb" used in various disciplines. Trevor Fisk, Thomas Jefferson University (PA) vice president for external relations, says (Carter 1993): "If you work out the value of one new student or hospital patient, then the unit cost [of the piece of mail] must be less than one-hundredth of that amount. That's assuming a 1-percent response rate, which is reasonable to expect."

The rule of thumb at New York University's School of Continuing Education is that all the public information and marketing staff, agency fees, and office and marketing expenses (from postage to telephone) come to about 15% of the school's income from tuition and fees (Ryan 1993).

Personal interaction

A final factor to consider is what can be done with little or no money. Because we are often seeking to reach a broad audience, we must rely on mass production and distribution of information. But study after study have shown that the most influential and effective communication is one on one, or one with a small group. In other words, don't underestimate the power of personal communication. If you want to tell something to a colleague down the hall, don't write a letter or send an email; walk down and talk to him or her. If you need to convey information to your immediate staff, gether them and discuss it. If you have important information for a few key alumni, give them a call.

Use the same strategies with outside audiences. If you can send a colleague out to a local alumni chapter meeting, it will make a much greater impression on members than a written newsletter. If you have a complaint about the local newspaper coverage of your research, call and politely discuss it with the reporter or editor. If appropriate, follow the phone call with a letter to the editor that can be printed.

The point of these examples is that, even in this age of wondrous and instantaneous communication technology, the personal touch remains the most effective and persuasive means of conveying information. Furthermore, it is frequently one of the cheapest and easiest strategies. A thank-you note to a donor will go far beyond an annual report in which his or her name is printed with 100 others.

These gestures take time, of course. But if you get in the habit of sending out just two or three notes a day, your communication with key audiences, including your colleagues and staff, will improve dramatically with very little material investment.

What to spend your money on — And what not to

There are clearly situations that call for some means of communicating information to a broad audience and, in those cases, you will want to get the most for your precious dollars.

One strategy is to find publications, posters, brochures, or videos that you like and would like to emulate. Then call the editor or producer and find out how their costs stack up — how many people worked on the piece, how much it cost to print and distribute, and so on. Or take a copy of several such pieces to your campus communications chief and find out how much similar products would cost in your market. Be advised that stated costs per copy can be deceptive sometimes. Some organizations include the cost of staff time in figuring a publication's cost, for example, while others do not. Some include the cost of distribution (which can vary a lot), while others consider only printing costs.

Another cost-effective strategy is to take a body of information and develop a "family" of pieces in line with your communications goals. For example, your department or college might be celebrating an anniversary. A good, in-depth story and a fistful of historic photos could be tailored for use in the campus magazine, a special promotional poster, a slide show for your anniversary banquet (that could then be used with alumni clubs around the state), and a page in the football program. Many campus staff newspapers print inserts for departments and divisions at low cost. The inserts not only reach all employees via the newspaper, but also are available at pennies apiece to the unit for its internal purposes.

Cutting publications costs

A penny saved is a penny to put toward your communications program, and there are many ways to save money in your publications programs. A good source of ideas for such savings is your campus communications or publications director.

Here are a few tips to get you started:

- Standardize the format and length of your publications, or go to a less expensive paper stock. Often, money is wasted on trimming or throwing away blank paper from press runs of odd-size publications. Acadia University in Nova Scotia saved money by reducing the weight of its newsletter paper stock, reducing type size — be careful it doesn't get too small for us older folks to read — and cutting pages, but not reducing content.

- Produce shorter publications. In the age of information overload, your audience might be more inclined to peruse a two- or four-page publication than read a 24-page publication. McMaster

University in Ontario has replaced a $26,000 community relations newsletter with a one-sheet report and a colorful "Coming Events" postcard, at a savings of $16,000.

- Produce publications less frequently. Many colleges and universities are scaling back the frequency of their alumni publications. The *California Monthly* magazine hasn't gone out monthly for many years; *Wisconsin Week* is produced twice a month. As resources get tighter and mailing costs rise, this is a common trend.

- Be flexible and have a time margin so the printer can fit your job into the most economical printing slot.

- Meet your deadlines: "rush" jobs will cost you more.

- Have all your copy in final form before you submit it to the printer, to avoid costly corrections.

- Consider using electronic file transfer, so the printer can translate your floppy disks directly into type composition.

- Limit color and simplify the design of publications. Every added color adds costs both in preparing the artwork and in printing. So do screens, bleeds, reverses, and specialty inks and papers.

- Reduce mailing costs. A visit to a bulk mail center or the U.S. postal service can save money. They can explain how to cut postal costs using the ZIP + 4 codes, by modifying the size and format of your mailings, by pre-sorting and bundling mail, and so on. Well-pruned mailing lists can also trim your costs.

- Consider creative distribution ideas — such as using campus mail, if it's free, or distributing materials at events.

- Standardize the look of campus letterheads and publications. Although this is a sore subject with some deans, directors, and department chairs, who prefer their own logos on their stationery, substantial money can be saved by standardizing institutional letterheads and publication formats, enabling the campus to print materials in bulk quantities and produce inexpensive templates for desktop publishing systems.

These are just a few of the many money-saving ideas out there; your colleagues can offer many others. The bottom line is this: there is not necessarily a direct relationship between the amount of money you invest in communications and their effect. If you are sharp at matching media and messages, then you will communicate more effectively.

chapter nine

A Rose By Any Other Name
Your message and the medium

Not too long ago, the University of California System undertook a project to conduct a statewide information campaign to reach the people of California with a message intended to engender support for higher education. A team representing the nine campuses of the UC System and the Office of the President worked with a former Bank of America vice president for public relations throughout fall 1994 to develop the campaign plan.

This was a skilled communication team, veterans of many successful communication projects and campaigns, yet it took many hours of meetings and discussions to lay the groundwork for the effort. The reason: the most critical element of the campaign was the message. The team knew the institution, the audience, and the tactics very well. But it was critical to present just the right message. In a brief statement, the message had to capture the essence of a complex and comprehensive institution so that the general public would relate to it.

When several messages had been developed, they were presented to a series of focus groups in northern and southern California. Some messages that the team liked ("UC: The Power of Excellence," and "Where would you be without UC?") were discarded based on audience feedback. Others ("UC: Improving the State of California," "UC: Our Products Perform," and "UC: It just might be California's most valuable resource") were refined further because of positive audience reaction. The latter was the one finally selected.

The team realized that, to succeed, the campaign would have to be a long-term project and the message would have to not only resonate with key audiences, but stand the test of time. In short, much of the work on the campaign went into developing the theme or message. Once that was decided, using the message — in every vehicle from alumni magazines and sports programs to UC hospital tray tents and posters — became relatively easy.

If you doubt the importance of a powerful message, just look at the advertising world around you. "Just do it," "We bring good things to light," "It's the real thing," "Quality is job 1," "Be all you can be," "A mind is a terrible thing to waste." You may be able to identify the products or organizations they represent just by the slogans with which they are associated.

This is not to suggest that your unit needs an advertising campaign or slogan, but just that you seriously think about the key points you want or need to make to your important constituencies and that you prepare to be consistent in your message. You can't promote your department as putting its highest priority on students one month, and then turn around the next month and say your main focus is research. Find a theme that works, that says what you are and what you care about, and stick to it.

As we have seen in earlier chapters, your message must be rooted in the reality of who you are and what you do: a rose by any other name is still a rose. In some ways, the process of message identification is critical to your leadership. The message that you craft and sustain may be the hallmark of your tenure as a leader. In essence, it is the case statement of your goals as leader of the organization. It conveys your sense of the legacy of your unit and your vision of its future. If you are clear in your message, those around you will be clear about your goals and will be better able to help achieve them.

There is an adage in the communications business that is wise to keep in mind: "Tell them what you're going to tell them, tell them, and then tell them what you told them." Repetition is vital.

This is principally true with your sustaining message. You can't deliver your message in one place, at one time, and expect it to stick. You should expect to return to it regularly, to constantly refine, repeat, and restate it. This is where you can benefit greatly from tools like the copy kit, which we will consider in this chapter.

But how should you develop this message and put it in writing or images? Usually, you will approach this task with a pretty good notion of what you want to convey.

In the UC campaign, for instance, the team knew from the outset that it wanted to convey why the University of California System is important to the citizens of California, even those folks who don't attend UC or, for that matter, know anyone who does. In short, the team wanted to convey that UC is important to everyone, not just UC students and employees.

You probably have some ideas about what you want to convey and how you can present your message convincingly. So, you begin the three-step process of composition:

- Distill your message.

- Garner and organize relevant supporting data.

- Compile that data into messages that appeal to the interests of your key audiences.

Distillation comes first

Distillation, the first step in the process, has many names. The editor of an academic journal may call it a synopsis or an abstract. A book publisher may call it a prospectus. Campus development officers might call it a case statement. By whatever name, this is the nub of your message that any audience can easily grasp.

Some writers distill easily and, in fact, cannot write a longer treatment until they have drafted a synopsis or abstract. Others arrive at the nub by a more circuitous path: they first must expand on the topic, outlining a logical train of thought with supporting arguments, before they can distill with confidence. If you are fortunate enough to have a communication team, you might present the team with this challenge and ask members to bring you some different options to consider. Or you might ask colleagues in the department to help craft this summary statement. Whatever method you follow, the distilled message becomes the core from which you can craft a variety of expanded messages.

Types of messages

There are two broad categories of messages that a campus leader will at some point be involved in distilling — the sustaining message and the occasional message.

The sustaining message

This message is one that shall be with you always. In a sense, it is the written reflection of the unit's mission statement made current and cogent. It describes an academic unit, its purpose, its programs, its relationship to the larger institution, and its service to society. It outlines the unit's activities and objectives, what it must do to sustain, improve, or change its programs and aims. It explains why the unit is valuable to its constituencies — educationally, culturally, and economically — and the ways in which the unit can remain significantly productive and effective through its own efforts and through public and private support. In short, the sustaining message is a stock paragraph, or several, that you can drop into a document as needed.

It will be the rare academic unit that can carry on an effective communications program without a consistent sustaining message. What might the sustaining message for a unit include? Robert L. Stuhr (1989), a financial consultant to colleges, suggests something like this outline:

Aims

Educational goals and programs

Important heritage and distinctions

Factors appealing to key constituencies

Campus environment

Accomplishments

Academic growth

Role in teaching, research, service

Meeting student needs

Faculty and administration

Alumni

Physical facilities

Financial viability

Extramural support

Status vis-à-vis similar units

Directions for the future

Existing programs that must continue

Changes in programs

New programs needed

Teaching trends

Research thrusts

Community service initiatives

As you apply this bare-bones outline to your own situation, you may realize that you have many of the pertinent pieces of your message already composed (in speeches, grant proposals, and the like). The job is already half-done. It's mainly a matter of compiling and composing. We shouldn't, however, underestimate the hard work of putting your thoughts on paper.

Here's the sustaining message that Amanda Perkins developed to describe her unit, its mission, and its programs:

In keeping with Midland University's quest for excellence in teaching, research, and service, the Department of Botany and Applied Ecology focuses on that branch of science that deals with plants — their life, structure, growth, classification, uses, relations with their environment — an ever-expanding academic field with profound theoretical and practical significance.

Our first task is to teach — undergraduate and graduate degree candidates and returning adult, special students — through a constantly evolving curriculum of courses. In order to teach, we must also constantly learn, for the faculty that is not itself at the growing edge of knowledge in its field is ill-equipped to develop the human intellect in others. Our third task is to serve — to extend to the wider community the fruits of our learning and the insights of our teaching that we may help lift the life of citizens to higher economic, social, and cultural levels.

The department traces its lineage to one of the first Midland chairs, that of natural history, which was one of the first departments to offer the Ph.D. degree. Through its basic science courses, the department serves as an instructional resource for the entire campus, as well as for an ever-growing roster of undergraduate majors in its applied-ecology sequence.

The department's research standing is at the highest level, attested to by the department's ranking among recipients of National Science Foundation grants. A vigorous outreach and continuing education program makes the department a partner with public schools, government agencies, industries, and individual citizens — in their thirst for new knowledge and in their concerns for a healthy environment. Department alumni worldwide are testimony to the department's quest for quality in over a century of educational service to the commonwealth.

The sustaining message also should lend itself to some further distillation. For the University of Wisconsin-Madison, for example, the sustaining message is, in essence, the university's mission statement. But when asked by the public to define the university in a nutshell, many refer to the Wisconsin Idea. This premise, first put forward more than 60 years ago, states that the borders of the University of Wisconsin are the borders of the state. This one phrase captures the commitment of service to the state that infuses the activities of the university's students, staff, and faculty.

Most of the messages you compose will be occasional messages, which tell about a particular program, project, or policy, or about your department or program at a particular point in time. Whether your message takes the form of a speech, an annual report, a news release, policy statement, World Wide Web page, or brochure, you can speed up the distillation process if you summarize your key facts on a sheet of paper, using subheads such as these:

The occasional message

What it is	Why it's offered
What it does	What it costs
Who does it	How you can do or get it
Who it is for	Why it's good
How it's organized	How it operates
When it happens	Where it's located

If you need help distilling a message, here are some ideas:

Six distillation models

- *Look at the lead story in today's newspaper* and you will see evidence of a reporter following that time-honored formula for reducing a report to its essence by answering the six classic questions: Who? What? Where? When? Why? How? Notice that these elements also appear in the list above. A journalist, working from your distilled message, could write a news story in short order.

- *Pretend you're out fund-raising and ask yourself this question:* "If I were to make a call this afternoon on an important potential donor, and he or she told me I could have just three minutes of his time, what message would I deliver about this program/project?"

- *Dip back into your experience developing course outlines or syllabi.* You had to distill a lot of information down into a sheet or two of paper, to which your students would pay attention and by which they would form their first impression of you.

- *Turn to the preface of this book* and see how the authors distilled the guts of this guide's message.

- *Pull some of the books from your bookshelf.* If there is any single best model for distilling a message, it's the back cover of a book. Book manufacturers have made a fine art of summarizing a book's contents in such a way as to stimulate a sale to a bookstore browser. Those words often work harder to *sell* than to *tell*, but they may inspire you.

- *Look at magazine ads* and see how advertiser can distill the essence of their products or services into a few images and a few words.

As we mentioned earlier, distillation is a way to focus your thoughts about what's important and to arrange those thoughts coherently. After that comes the challenge of elaborating on your distilled message with the specific supporting facts that will not only convey your thoughts to particular audiences but persuade them to your point of view.

Of course, a short memo or news item may require only a few more details than contained in the distilled message. But when you are undertaking a publicity campaign or a fund-raising effort, your task is to compose a multi-purpose narrative, *centered on your distilled message.* This becomes a resource from which you can draw repeatedly as you select and recraft its various parts to tailor messages to particular audiences and particular media. One tool that will provide all the background and basics you will need is the "communications copy kit."

Gathering data: The communications copy kit

The multi-purpose narrative is sometimes called a communications copy kit and its parts are called copy units. In essence, a copy kit puts in one place — in a readable outline — your distilled message, along with the supporting statistics, quotes, anecdotes, mission statements, and relevant history that would otherwise be tucked away in many different publications, file folders, and offices. It takes time to prepare a copy kit, but it can save many hours in the long run.

Since you know that your multi-purpose narrative is going to be modified and reconstituted in numerous ways, it makes sense to prepare your draft so that it's easy to reshape it as needed. Composing in outline form is the key here. Start with a framework of general statements that summarize the key points of your message (refer to your distilled message), add secondary supporting statements, and provide appropriate documentation for each secondary statement. Documentation will include:

- Facts that tend to prove it

- Opinions of authorities

- Opinions of constituencies

- Examples for elucidation

- Explanations for clarification

- Inferences that support your assertion

Some types of documentation — case histories, for example — can be attached as appendices so that details that are lengthy but pertinent don't get lost.

Don't worry about what your outline looks like. If you want to jot down a list of key, sequential topics and this form gives you flexibility, go for it. If a more formal outline helps ensure unity, coherence, and emphasis, use it. Just be sure you have some sort of "message map" in hand before you begin. Otherwise the piles of notes scattered around on your desk, bedspread, or computer screen will show up just as scattered in your message.

Converting data to messages:
The copy kit in action

To see the usefulness of outline-building, let's look at one of the challenges facing Perkins. Among her priorities for the year is to build up the reference library and update the student laboratories in the department of botany and applied ecology. She has developed a communications plan that targets audiences whose support she needs. And she has identified some affordable ways to reach these audiences through campus publications, public presentations, and other media, and by being ready to take advantages of serendipitous events. In short, Perkins knows she must hit on the theme of facility upgrades over and over again with different audiences in the months ahead.

Distilling. Perkins begins her copy kit with a terse distillation:

> Midland has an exciting and progressive new graduate program in Biological Conservation and Sustainable Development with great appeal to students. But its potential is already being constrained by outdated student laboratories and reference facilities. To upgrade these facilities will require at least $200,000. The department needs financial help.

General statement of need. Perkins then prepares a general statement about why the two areas of upgrade are important and how they will together enhance her department's offerings. In subsequent paragraphs, she describes the current status of the library — its strengths and shortcomings; what's needed to improve it; how it will benefit teachers, researchers, and the public; how much it will cost; how she plans to raise the money; and how others can help. Then she does the same for the laboratories.

Supporting data. For both the library and the labs, Perkins backs up her claims with data on student usage, describing facilities at comparable institutions and quoting faculty, authorities in the field, potential employers of students, and students themselves on facility standards. She also offers data from pertinent authorities on costs and impacts.

Preparing targeted messages from the copy kit. Perkins' copy kit at this point very likely reads like a detailed fact sheet, loaded with more information than anyone could possibly absorb at one sitting. *But no one audience will be receiving everything.* For some audiences, such as parents, she will prepare a message that uses primarily anecdotal information. The dean and college officials will be treated mainly to the "dollars and cents" and statistical data. Some messages will dwell more on the problems of the library, while others focus on the labs' deficiencies.

Perkins is very aware that, even though the benefits of her intended upgrades are overwhelmingly clear, there still are individuals or groups who may feel threatened by the change. She knows that frequent communication before, during, and after the project will soften those concerns. Her plan is to acknowledge and address those concerns head on and to enlist the aid of her potential critics in finding compromising solutions to problems that might arise along the way.

Alongside her copy kit Perkins will keep her department's sustaining message, accompanied by profiles of recent graduates and incoming students. When presenting the need to improve the library or laboratories, her message will always be in the context of the department's goals, accomplishments, and potential. Also, by having all of this information in hand, Perkins has a package that others can use to help spread the message.

Working from these several pages of data, Perkins and/or her assistants will put together the following messages that use appropriate media and that are slanted to her targeted audiences:

- A 300-word piece for the *Librarian's Page*, a newsletter of the Midland University library services. She will spell out the anticipated contents and uses of the updated reference collection and explain how the upgrade will complement other library resources, rather than compete with them.

- A formal proposal to the Midland University research committee for a $10,000 grant for one-time purchase of reference texts and a $50,000 grant for laboratory improvements. She will prepare proposals to five other funding sources, as well, acknowledging each foundation's or agency's particular traditions of support and the unique contribution each can make. The proposals will follow standard format, but will avoid jargon and obscure phrasing and will emphasize clarity and simplicity.

- An informal speech to be delivered to the Biology Journal Club, an organization of natural science graduate students. She will describe the department's plans and answer questions. She also will pointedly remind the students that they, and their younger brothers and sisters, are the main beneficiaries of the project and that they can help by talking up the project or even organizing a fund-raising activity.

- An article for the *Midlandite*, the alumni magazine, which traditionally profiles a different department in each issue. Perkins will ask the writer to focus on those activities and successes of her unit that have greatest popular application and appeal, and will stress the growing importance of education and research in applied ecology and environmental management. But she also will include a strong statement about the pending facility upgrades and their impact on Midland's continued strength in this field of biology.

- A short blurb on Perkins' electronic bulletin board update, which is also sent by email to faculty, alumni, and friends of the department. For this purpose, she will call attention to the longer article appearing in the current issue of *Midlandite*, but also add a special, short plug for the facilities funding.

- A speech at an alumni picnic. Perkins will focus on the department's contributions to Midland's mission and on the accomplishments of alums from her department. She will also describe the backgrounds and aspirations of several of the talented incoming students. (Perhaps a few of them will accompany her to the picnic and speak briefly.) She then will hit on the department's facility needs and invite the alums to come visit the department.

- An interview on the student radio station. Perkins will keep in mind that the largest group of listeners are undergraduates, so she will compose a message that emphasizes how much new facilities will improve classes and facilitate the students' work — writing term papers, for example. She will talk about opportunities for employment in conservation biology and sustainable development and for going on to graduate study.

- A presentation at the departmental faculty meeting. Perkins will update faculty on plans and the costs of upgrades, reminding them how their teaching and research will benefit from the projects. She may review with them the media and the audiences she has targeted and seek additional suggestions. She will distribute three "core" paragraphs about the planned upgrades that faculty can slip into their own speeches, articles, or presentations, as appropriate. Finally, she might distribute a boiled-down version of her copy kit for their reference.

- A story in the *Midland Bulletin*, the campus faculty/staff newspaper. Perkins will ask a campus reporter to prepare an item on the department's proposed library and laboratory improvements, looking for some angle like record enrollment in a particular discipline or an impressive "lead" gift for the library. She will provide the reporter with background on needs, costs, tentative timetable, and expected benefits, and make facilities available for a photo if desired. She will *not* ask the reporter to send a news release on the subject to the *Midland Daily News*, the city's morning paper, because she knows her topic is too parochial to get any coverage and she wants to maintain her credibility with the media.

If Perkins prepares her copy kit carefully and then uses it diligently to promote in every way possible her "occasional message" about the need for new facilities, she will be successful. It is most important to have ready this core of information that can be tailored to the point of impact. Of course, there is also a strategy for doing that.

Massaging your message to fit media and audience

It is clear that Perkins' strategy is to enlist the enthusiasm, goodwill, and support of each audience and, if possible, their fund-raising assistance. In each message, she has thought about the people she is addressing and has pulled from her copy kit units of information that are of greatest interest to them. Around that information she has subtly (and not so subtly) woven her own agenda. Journalists call these different perspectives on the same information the "slant" or "angle" of the story. She also has selected media that are especially effective with particular audiences. Then, in each situation, she has tailored the message to fit the particular medium.

Content and format

Since each magazine, newsletter, factsheet, or panel discussion is different, massaging the message to suit the immediate occasion is an important step. Massaging often involves shifting the focus and modifying the content and the length of the message.

At Iowa State University, Pat Parker, assistant director for international admissions, recognized that prospective students from abroad needed something different than the usual viewbook to help them decide whether or not to attend ISU. The institution, therefore, now sends out a special lightweight mailing piece — a folder that can be packed with the type of information overseas students want but that domestic students would find redundant. It describes the length of the academic year, what a credit hour is, exactly what the residence halls and off-campus housing are like, costs of health insurance, support services available, how to wire money, how to get from the Des Moines airport to the campus in Ames, an explanation of correct certification of academic records, scholarship availability, a table of estimated annual expenses, and application and admission procedures.

Example A

"It's a lot less sexy than our regular admissions pieces," Parker says (1994), "but it packs in a lot of information." It also gets results. ISU is among the top 20 colleges in international student enrollments.

Massaging a message also can entail modifying its style — assuming a more formal or less formal tone, adding or deleting jargon words, personal anecdotes, direct quotes, speculation, or analysis. Format changes, such as in paragraph and sentence length and the use of subheads, also are important considerations when tailoring a message to a particular medium.

Example B

When Clay Schoenfeld decided to seek a wider audience for the topics covered in his book on faculty retirement issues, he repackaged his subject in three different ways for three publications, each interested in the subject, but each with a slightly different readership and style of presentation. As you read the following excerpts, note the format as well as the content. The format of each article is meant to reflect the typography of the target magazine in the use and placement of titles, subtitles, subheads, and author's byline. It isn't absolutely necessary to tailor a manuscript in this fashion, but to do so says to the editor, "I've studied your publication and this piece is just for you."

For the magazine *Academe*, read by college and university faculty, Schoenfeld wrote an informal narrative piece that is a provocative call to discussion if not to action. Here is an excerpt:

Closing the Generation Gap
Should senior faculty sit back and enjoy benefits
that come at the expense of younger colleagues?

By Clay Schoenfeld

The University of Wisconsin Board of Regents struck a minor blow against discrimination the other day. Despite a loud protest by letter and phone from senior citizens, the Regents voted to end a policy of letting persons 62 and older audit campus courses for free.

Ex Officio Regent Burt Grover, state superintendent of public instruction, ever ready to stick his head in the lion's mouth, stated the argument that carried the day:

"Non-need-based entitlements are taking America down the tube. ... We ought not persist with policies that discriminate among the generations."

Grover is absolutely right. Too many relatively well-off senior citizens are enjoying a staggering array of perks reserved for the "golden oldie" generation, meanwhile reaping handsome salaries or generous pensions or even both. And that cohort includes some senior college and university faculty members, either still active or retired.

The ever-growing phalanx of the elderly partakes of those perks at the expense of our children, grandchildren, and great-grandchildren, burdened by a sluggish economy and mounting payroll taxes. Will senior faculty — active and retired — be, as the saying goes, part of the problem or part of the solution?

For the *Journal of Staff, Program, and Organization Development*, read by staff and faculty development specialists, Schoenfeld focused on different strategies for phasing in faculty retirements. For this audience he employed a more formal expository style and a cookbookish "how to" approach, of which this is a sample:

By Clay Schoenfeld
Emeritus Professor and Dean
University of Wisconsin-Madison

Phased Retirement as a Staff Professional Development Strategy
Whether the institution's goal is to encourage a reluctant person to retire, or to persuade an eager retiree to stay on, variations of a phased retirement policy can be an effective device for mitigating retirement shock on the part of the individual employee and on campus tables of organization.

Major demographic, political, social, and economic factors impinging on the college and university environment in the coming decade will have marked implications for individual and institutional development. The environmental factors playing upon higher education in the coming decade aren't going to go away; in fact they may increase in intensity. Professional, staff, and organization development people are in the front lines of a challenging time in colleges and universities.

For the *College and University Personnel Association Journal*, aimed at personnel administrators, Schoenfeld used an in-between declamatory tone, which is preferred by the magazine's editor:

Alleviating Retirement Shock on Individuals and Institutions

If I were still active in college and university personnel administration, I hope I'd be focusing on trying to evaluate the dimensions and impacts of the coming dozen years of retirement shock on college and university personnel policies and practices, and trying to come up with some imaginative strategies for alleviating any distortion in faculty/staff organization — and personal problems in the inevitable transition from work to rocking chair. ...

It all boils down to this: a wave of retirements is about to hit the country's campuses. It will take considerable leadership acumen on the part of personnel administrators if they are to see their institutions through a period of turmoil.

by Clay Schoenfeld, UW-Madison
Emeritus Professor and Dean

The articles excerpted above clearly had "product promotion" aspects, but also were an opportunity to share information that the author had worked hard to collect. The idea is to strike while the iron is hot. Don't let significant work go unnoticed. Share it while it's timely and get the greatest mileage out of it, reaching out to as many potential "clients" as possible.

The juggling of substance, style, and mechanics is not just a "journalistic trick." It's a valuable strategy for anyone who wants to reach a range of audiences. In fact, the recasting and reformatting of messages is something most faculty do fairly regularly in the process of teaching, getting published, or submitting grant requests. Metallurgy engineers, for example, may package their research results in one way for a professional journal, in a completely different way (in style, content, and format) for trade magazines in the metals manufacturing field, and in a third way for the classroom.

Readability

Crafting your message for medium and audience also requires that you pay attention to readability. Are your readers comfortable and familiar with the vocabulary and style of your message?

You may know about readability indices such as the Flesch Index, the Gunning Index, the Dale-Call Formula, and the Cloze Procedure. While each of these measures differs somewhat in principles and application, they generally calculate words per sentence, the proportion of "hard words" (that is, technical, uncommon, or jargon words, as well as those that are polysyllabic, like "antidisestablishmentarianism"), and the use of personal words and familiar phrases.

All of these indices provide a rating on the reading level and comprehension of your message. Continually applying one or more of these measures is a good way to guard against writing over the heads of your audience — or beneath them. However, you should not set out to make your writing rate favorably by, for example, using only short simple sentences of no more than 20 words or monosyllabics. Nothing would be more monotonous. Remember: you are shooting for an *average* sentence length of 20 words and an *average* of two syllables.

Also remember that an acceptable readability score does not mean that your material is readable, nor does an unacceptable score mean your writing is inappropriate for the intended audience. The indices will not pick up flaws in the sequence of ideas nor detect the absence of reader "signposts" — words and phrases such as "then," "but," and "because" — that make explicit the connections among ideas and keep the reader aware of the internal logic.

Nor will readability tests point out when you have broken the following "rules of the road" as defined by Paula LaRocque, writing coach for the *Dallas Morning News* (Yoe 1992):

> *Don't pile up a bunch of numbers in one sentence.* "He divided his study into 27 sets of four patients ranging in age from 44 to 62, each of whom was admitted under his care from 1989 to 1992 at three Chicago hospitals." Instead, break this into two sentences.

> *Don't have more than three prepositional phrases in any sentence.* "The blood hurries through hundreds of tiny arteries that run next to a small set of veins that drain warm blood from the heater and return it to circulation." Again, break it into two simpler sentences.

> *Don't fall into the passive voice.* "The term 'heater organ' was coined in 1980 by Block, who was a member of the Woods Hole Oceanographic Institute team that discovered it in swordfish; the phenomenon has been studied by them ever since, asking, biochemically, how it was accomplished by these ocean travelers."

> Instead you might say: "Block coined the term 'heater organ' in 1980 when he and his team from Woods Hole ... discovered the phenomenon in swordfish. Block and his team have studied the heater organ ever since, asking how, biochemically, swordfish stay warm and active in cold ocean waters." The idea is to keep noun and verb together and delete extraneous words.

> *Choose concrete over abstract terms.* Choose "on the job" rather than "When placed in an employment situation ... ." This especially applies when you are preparing memos dealing with pragmatic, non-academic issues, like the allocation of parking spaces or the scheduling of exams, or when you are preparing

comments for a parents' or alumni newsletter. Given
the choice, *all* readers prefer plain talk over obscure
academese. Save that for the research journals — or
be bold and remove it even from your journal articles!

Finally, a readability test won't necessarily help you adhere to
the principle that goes, "Talk like the folks you're talking to."
Your readability score can be A+, but if your semantics are
inappropriate for the intended audience, you flunk.

For example, when the advocates of "total quality management"
(TQM) — largely business and engineering school faculty —
introduced its precepts into higher education, they failed to
recognize that the language of TQM smacks of the corporate
board room and the shop floor in ways that set faculty teeth on
edge.

The American Association for Higher Education promotes the
term "Continuous Quality Improvement," which reduces the
discomfort, but many faculty members react negatively to putting
the label "customers" on their students.

In such cases, talking like the natives is the only way to introduce
new ideas with even a hope that they will be embraced and
accepted. This kind of sensitivity to the audience is not flagged
by readability tests.

Originality

You are not writing *Gone With the Wind*, but that doesn't mean
you should eschew originality in crafting your message. There
are not many new ideas, but there may be some new ways of
expressing old ideas.

When you look at the giants in the history of higher education,
you find that they often have a way of bringing a fresh or original
perspective to a fairly standard message. Former University of
California President and Carnegie Commission Chair Clark Kerr
is a case in point. In a recent speech at the University of

California, Berkeley, Kerr referred to the fact that it is possible to have both academic excellence and diversity (Weimer 1995).

At Berkeley, he said, we have the "Jeffersonian ideal — a meritocracy of talent combined with the equality of opportunity." It was a phrase repeated throughout the campus the following day. As he went on in his speech to call for the university to "preserve its position ... as first in excellence and first in opportunity," he had the captivated crowd totally behind his charge to it.

In that same speech, he described the position of higher education in the fierce competition for state resources in California: "Higher education is in a war of knives and it has no knife."

An original way of stating your premise or goal is likely to stick with your audience, and to bear repeating to others. Perhaps what makes presentations by Kerr and others so refreshing is that there is such a "sameness" to many of the writings and speeches of so many of us in higher education. That holds true for slogans, too.

Writing in *CASE Currents*, Bernice Ashby Thieblot (1994) reprised an earlier feature on "Name That Campaign," in which she illustrated the sameness of fund-raising campaign slogans. "A campaign still needs a memorable, thematic name — and it's still just as likely not to have one," she wrote. "If anything, today's larger, more amorphous efforts have names that are duller than before." Accompanying her article was a list of three columns of 70 words and phrases each; those 210 entries could be combined to yield represent the name of a fund-raising campaign. A greatly abbreviated list of her columns looks something like this:

COLUMN A	COLUMN B	COLUMN C
1. To Structure	A New	Paradigm
2. Milestones Toward	A Magnificent	Millennium
3. Innovating	A Global	Interface
4. Transforming	A Spirited	Ideal

COLUMN A	COLUMN B	COLUMN C
5. To Perpetuate	Traditional	Values
6. To Harness	A Vast	Technology
7. Envisioning	A Vision of	Vision
8. Toward	A Greater	Endowment
9. To Honor	A Tradition of	Learning
10. Advancing	Advanced	Advances
11. Quest for	A Commitment to	Quality
12. Time for	A Heritage of	Innovation
13. In Support for	The Enrichment of	Leadership
14. To Celebrate	A Century of	Service
15. Opportunity for	A Spirit of	Resolve

"Using this naming system is as easy as ordering from a Chinese menu," wrote Thieblot. "Simply scan the columns, select the terms that seem appealing and presto — your campaign has a name. ... Some combinations work better than others, of course. (Beware the unfortunate acronym — 'Advancing a Spirit of Service,' for example.) Even so ... there are 343,000 combinations here. You may find the right name for your campaign, one worthy of the coming millennium."

There's a lot to be said for originality — and humor, too!

Packing your message with punch

Though we don't have the precise text of Perkins' finished messages described above, she tested each for what Schoenfeld and Karen Diegmueller (1982) call the APPLAUSE factors:

Appeal. Ask yourself, who cares? Exactly what do they care about right now?

Plain Facts. What's the unadorned news or information?

Personalities. At least one living, breathing character in your message is worth a carload of statistics.

Local Angle. What's the direct connection between your message and the intended audience?

Action. Can you inject dramatic qualities into your message — people doing things, conflict, struggle, suspense, emotions?

Universality/Uniqueness. Is everybody doing it, or is this idea one of a kind?

Significance. Does your message make a difference? Does it have the crucial qualities of timeliness, proximity, prominence, relevance?

Energy Increment. Are you thinking and feeling deeply about the message yourself?

The 30-3-30 formula hits a moving target

Perkins also employed the 30-3-30 rule. Though it sounds like the label on a bag of fertilizer, it's simply a reminder that any message must simultaneously meet the needs of 30-second people, 3-minute people, and 30-minute people.

With any message you are constantly trying to hit a moving target. This is the day of the 10-second sound bite, the 25-minute lunch break, and the pocket digest. As a consequence, we are going to catch some of any audience for only half a minute; what we don't get across to them in that short time, we won't get across at all. So some element of any message must be designed for them: the lead of a newspaper story or the headline and artwork of a poster. The 3-minute readers/viewers can take a little more time, but not much, so something must pop out at them: the subheads of a brochure, for example. Then there is the person who will actually want to stick with us for half an hour, a person for whom we can reserve the full treatment. The consistent use of the 30-3-30 formula is the hallmark of an effective communicator.

Paying attention to structure

Perkins also made an effort to see that each message — whether delivered in print or in person — follows the three, basic structural components of good communication, to which Schoenfeld and Diegmueller (1982) applied the alliterative labels *framework*, *focus*, *force*. (For more on this topic, we also strongly recommend that concise and highly readable standby, *The Elements of Style*, by William Strunk, Jr. and E.B. White.)

Framework

The key here is to make the outline that you used in drafting your message pop out at your readers/listeners so that they never feel lost. Lead them along through your message. Here are some simple devices to make your main points abundantly clear:

- Enumerate them — "first," "second," "third" — as if you were highlighting a lecture on the blackboard.

- Use an abundance of connectives. No matter how clearly you think your framework shows through, lead your readers/listeners from one section to the next with terms like "Now let's ...," "As we've said," "You will remember that," and "In addition." In other words, always keep an audience oriented to the terrain of your message.

- Introduce each principal topic with a question. For example, "What are the factors that might encourage academic personnel *not* to retire at a conventional age?" "What factors might cause personnel to decline an offer to stay on at a college or university?" Each question would be followed by a discussion of the topic.

If your message is in the form of a research/development proposal, of course, your outline is a prescribed series of stylized subheads (abstract, statement of problem, and so on). But that doesn't mean that within each section you shouldn't try to make each point explicit.

Focus devices

Somewhere in every extended message, try to reduce the message to a picture your audience can visualize and with which they can identify — an event, a story, a real person, a metaphor or extended figure of speech, a personal anecdote, or other focus.

A real person

Midland University focused on a real person in both a news feature and a TV spot promoting the celebration of the fiftieth birthday of Midland's Department of Outreach and Continuing Education. Rather than hitting directly on the anniversary, the news feature made its point by profiling the department's first graduate, Paul H. Jones.

> When a young man came back to the family farm in Hudson County after World War II, he had a driving ambition to put his Medical Corps experience to work somehow, but no means were at hand.
>
> Then two things happened — the GI Bill for veterans and a "temporary" two-year Midland University Extension Center at nearby Elkton.
>
> So Paul H. Jones rode a surplus Jeep to night classes for three years to become Midland's first outreach program graduate. After getting a Midland B.S. in math, a Midland M.S. in physics, and a Stanford Ph.D. in medicine, Dr. Jones is now Gorham Marble Professor of Biomedical Engineering at the Massachusetts Institute of Technology. ...

A TV spot promoting the same anniversary focused on Professor Tom Taylor, enroute, on a cold morning, to serve the local community by leading a firefighters' workshop — a real person doing the kind of thing that outreach is all about.

The story

Another very effective device for focus is the story — a narrative that is written with a sense of drama and suspense. The following excerpt from the *University of Chicago Magazine* (1986) is hard to beat. It's institutional history, but written in a style that few can resist:

> The professor of Hebrew finished his lecture on Amos and wiped his sweating spectacles with a linen hand-kerchief. The white-waisted maidens closed their note-books and crowded out of Old Main. It was a Sunday morning in October. It was 1888. It was Poughkeepsie.

> The professor, still flushed with enthusiasm that always captured him when he taught the Prophets, was putting his notes away. ... Looking up suddenly, the stocky young professor of Hebrew, pumpkin-faced and long-haired, found himself face to face with his antithesis: a spare, square-shouldered individual with a distinctly businesslike carriage. The rich man held out his hand. "Dr. Harper," he said. "I happened to be up here for the day, and I wanted to talk to you."

> Dr. Harper smiled his sweet, unworldly smile. Living as he did in the dusty past, absorbed as he was in men and matters that might have been important twenty centuries before, it wasn't likely that he saw the sig-nificance of Rockefeller's coming to see him. The President of the Trust, the Moloch of Monopoly, never "happened" to be spending the day anywhere. But it wasn't likely that the round-faced professor of Hebrew would appreciate the fact.

> It wasn't likely, but it was so.

> Dr. Harper took his worldly visitor by the arm. ... Fourteen hours later they separated in New York, having come down from Poughkeepsie together. ... For the first time in his life, John D. Rockefeller had met a man his own size. And he knew it. He knew all about his earnest young theologian, all about his consuming selflessness, his prodigious powers as an educational organizer, his fantastic success at stirring up the coun-

try to the study of Hebrew. He had made up his mind this was the man to spend his money for him. That was why the richest man in the world happened to be spending the day at Vassar.

When the young Hebrew professor later left Yale to create some sort of educational institution "in," as the *Boston Post* put it, "Chicago of all places," nobody then, least of all the men who agreed to finance it, had any idea what kind of pig-in-a-poke it would be. Nobody, that is, but the man who was going to create it. And the University of Chicago that today is one of the world's great centers of learning is nothing but the lengthened shadow of William Rainey Harper. ... This is the story of the professor who met and mastered John D. Rockefeller and brought higher learning to mid America.

A personal anecdote

Your focus can be on a personal anecdote. In a *CUPA Journal* article, after quoting a psychiatrist to the effect that "the transition from being a worker to being a retiree is one of the most difficult and major changes most of us will ever face; people become stressed out as they try to adapt to a new situation," Schoenfeld wrote, "I can speak from poignant personal experience":

> Shortly after retiring as dean of Inter-College Programs at the University of Wisconsin-Madison, I called my successor just to see how he was doing.
>
> "May I speak to Dean Samson?" I said.
>
> "Whom may I say is calling?" a receptionist asked.
>
> "This is Clay Schoenfeld," I said with some authority.
>
> The reply: "Would you spell that, please?"
>
> Dean Samson had installed a new office crew to whom my name meant nothing.

An event

A focus can be a historic or other noteworthy occasion. Here a newspaper writer, Nathan Seppe of the *Wisconsin State Journal*

(1992) helps clarify and make more enticing a science story about an instrument aboard the Hubble Space Telescope:

> In July 1054, a new star appeared in the sky. People took note. It shone ten times brighter than Venus.
>
> That in itself would have drawn attention.
>
> But something else made a lasting impression on the Chinese and Japanese historians who recorded the supernova of 1054: The star remained visible in daylight for 23 days.
>
> The supernova of yesterday is a nebula today — a star that literally blew itself to bits. In this case it's the Crab Nebula in the constellation Taurus.
>
> The much-studied Nebula, a cloud of cosmic gases and dust that vaguely resembles a crab, is being studied anew. Scientists at UW-Madison are using a high-speed photometer aboard the Hubble Space Telescope to learn more about the Crab and the repetitive pulse of light that emits from the mysterious neutron star at its core. ...

An extended figure of speech can provide an apt focus. For example, Fritz Machlup (1991), writing about "A Recipe for a Good Graduate Department," starts out with — what else? — a recipe:

A figure of speech

> Take 12 juicy professors of different brands and ripeness and place them together with 50 preheated thoroughly selected students at different stages of preparation on the same floor of a building, around a fine collection of books and journals and well-equipped laboratories; stir them for five to six hours a day; allow them to boil over several times and keep them simmering near the boiling point. Most students will be well done after about four years.

The "recipe" and other focus devices may be all to the good in "literary" messages, you may say, but they have no place in more prosaic messages. Not so, says Judith Ruderman (1992). She offers this example of a proposal whose introductory statement broke away from the ho-hum to grab reviewers and win funds for a book:

> In the summer of 1979, an extraordinary conference took place in the Soviet Union. Considering its title, The First International Conference on the Unconscious, one could not help being surprised that the Soviet government would not only permit but officially sponsor such a meeting. Hundreds of guests were invited, including many prominent specialists from the West, to present papers on psychoanalysis, Freud, and the unconscious.

> These topics, as is well known, have been forbidden subjects for decades in Soviet journals and professional congresses. Psychoanalytic training does not exist in the Soviet Union, Freud's words are unavailable and his theory had been condemned as "bourgeois idealism." How, then, are we to explain this conference, the proceedings of which were considered important enough to merit a large three-volume publication under the imprint of the prestigious Soviet Academy of Sciences?

> In an effort to answer this question, I am applying for funding to further my investigation of psychiatry in the Soviet Union. ...

Force

No matter how clear your framework or how compelling your focus, somewhere in every message you've got to give the audience a brief, clear, concise, forceful capsule of your message. Editors of scholarly journals call it the "abstract" or, if it comes at the end, the "discussion" or "conclusion." Ministers call it the text of the day. We have referred to it above in its various forms as the "distilled message." Newspapers and news magazines call this the "lead" and they like it right up in front, as in this opinion piece by Kevin L. Kearns in *The Chronicle of Higher Education* (1991):

The Economic Orthodoxies Offered U.S. Students Won't Prepare Them for Work in World Markets

The American economy today is being radically transformed by the trade and foreign investment patterns established by the rise of Japan, the economic integration of Europe, and the de-industrialization of the United States.

Yet in spite of the massive changes underway, much of the academic community acts as though it's business as usual. Unfortunately, they're dead wrong. We need our best academic minds to help formulate a new national economic policy now.

Kearns tells us what it's all about right away. In other messages, particularly speeches, the "summary capsule" may be dropped in at a strategic point — today, it's often called a "sound bite." Politicians are especially adept at this, as in: "Ask not what your country can do for you," "Read my lips: No new taxes," and so on.

If your medium is a brochure or poster, you can add force to the essence of your message by giving it typographic prominence. Or you may use a powerful image to make your point. Photographer Dorothea Lange's haunting image of a woman's face as she sat by her hungry children became a powerful symbol of the Great Depression.

Whatever it may be called, the "force" factor leaves no doubt in audience minds about the message. It may come at the end of the first page or, more often, in the first paragraph or two. But don't spin it out so far into the story that your readers/listeners/viewers become impatient or irritated and lose interest.

Is it expository, demonstrative, or motivational?

When Perkins prepared her messages to various audiences, she not only used the above techniques but also used a mix of styles of delivery — expository, demonstrative, and motivational. Knowing these styles can help you craft your messages more appropriately.

The most common is the *expository*, a no-frills, straight-talk message of the type found in newspapers. Expository writing is also found in professional journals, but often appears less "user-friendly" there because of the academic jargon, the heavy use of passive voice, and the absence of real people or "actors" in the narrative. The expository style feels neutral in tone and does not convey emotion or strong opinion.

On occasion you may want to give an emotional cast to your message, to arouse feelings in your audience. Typical examples of such *demonstrative* messages are speeches of welcome, fund-raising brochures, and thematic editorials. Through your choice of words (that is, superlatives, descriptive terms, and nouns and adjectives that imply a judgment or opinion) and your delivery, you draw the audience's attention to the manner of presentation as well as the message itself.

In *motivational* messages you try to elicit a specific reaction by providing the audience with a motive, with something that prompts a person to act in a particular way. Your goal may be to arouse awareness of a subject, to give information the audience needs to acquire understanding, or to persuade in order to influence feelings, beliefs, or actions.

The late Kenneth E. Eble (1990), University of Utah professor of English, obviously knew what he was doing in combining expository, demonstrative, and motivational messages in the following excerpt from an address to department chairs on "Communicating Effectively":

Expository — just the facts. Despite a general faculty fondness for being let alone, a chairperson cannot avoid the necessity of communicating and the desirability of communicating well. The presence of students and the bureaucratic necessities of processing, if not educating, them, require a good deal of communicating. And the oddity of people being together but not talking sooner or later affects a department. Some member or members of a faculty will want to break the silence. If all that is forthcoming is routine, functional communication, the notion can be established that the chair has become a mere functionary.

Demonstrative — showing feeling. If chairing a department is often looked upon as a sacrificial act, and the performing of it a drudgery, it is because too little is made of its opportunities and joys. Writing and talking and communing with students and faculty are recognized pleasures of academic life. For a chairperson they are twice blessed. They are not pleasures stolen from preparing classes and papers, but central requirements of the chairperson's job. And for chairpersons, as for the faculty and students they serve, joys are greater for being shared joys, individual achievements greater for their part in the shared achievements of others.

Motivational — spurring to action. Recognizing the importance of communication should be a central aim of inducting new chairpersons into their jobs. Among the expectations to be carried out by a chairperson: A chairperson must try to leaven the deadliness of much academic prose. There is much that is pleasurable, comic, and thought-provoking in any place where large numbers of students and faculty are brought together daily. Some of this should be communicated by a skillful department chair who is willing to challenge the distinctions between poetry and prose, song and speech, dance and marching to an academic two-step. In any department of size, there should by all means

be an internal publication or publications — a newsletter that has some literary as well as news-imparting
merit.

Developing and tailoring the message: A case study

To summarize the steps in preparing and delivering a message, especially one that will be recast in several ways for several purposes, let's look at another of Perkins' efforts — this one, to disseminate information about the department's new master's degree in Biological Conservation and Sustainable Development.

To begin, she reviews her sustaining message and uses it to distill her "occasional" message in the form of a factsheet. This step not only provides a road map for composing the brochure but also serves as a document for distribution until a more finished product is available. Since the audience is mainly prospective graduate students and their advisors, she takes the added step of more or less aiming the message at these groups.

**A New Midland University Graduate Program
in Biological Conservation and Sustainable Development
The Department of Botany and Applied Ecology**

What it is: A study and research regimen leading to a master of science (M.S.) degree.

What it does: Introduces students to a professional career in environmental management.

Who is it for: Qualified recent B.S. graduates and returning adults with academic backgrounds in biological fields or professional experiences in resource conservation/development.

Why it is offered: Government agencies at all levels, planning commissions, and industries have a growing need for trained personnel with a knowledge of environmental issues, skills in environmental impact assessment, and a commitment to economic development in concert with biological conservation.

How it's organized: Depending on the student's credentials, a minimum of 18 graduate course credits plus thesis or field project in lieu of thesis, all under the direction of a major professor.

Who does it: A team of department faculty members under the leadership of A. Wilmot Campion, with Eugene Odum, Georgia, in consultation with an interdisciplinary advisory committee.

When it starts: Fall quarter, 1996. A student may enter in any subsequent quarter.

Where it's located: The B&AE Department office is at 110 Mendel Hall. Most classes will be in that building. Field experiences will take students to a wide range of settings in the Midland area and throughout the state.

What it costs: To the regular Midland University resident and non-resident graduate tuition, the program adds a fee of $30 per quarter to cover necessary special instructional materials and logistical expenses.

About student support: A limited number of scholarships, fellowships, teaching assistantships, and internships are available to particularly qualified applicants.

How to learn more: Stop in at the Department Office, write Midland 3250, call (609) 637-8200, fax (609) 637-1333, or email bae@midland.edu for a complete program description and application/criteria information.

The underlying rationale: "By and large, our present problem is one of attitudes and implements. We are remodeling the Alhambra with a steam-shovel, and we are proud of our yardage. We shall hardly relinquish the shovel, which after all has many good points, but we are in need of gentler and more objective criteria for its successful use." — Aldo Leopold.

The department home: The B&AE Department offers a balanced environment among teaching (undergraduate and graduate), research (basic and applied), and service, outreach and continuing education. One of the original Midland disciplines, the department today is a campuswide instructional resource, a research laboratory of international repute, and a reservoir of public services widely extended. Alumni worldwide attest to the department's focus on the individual student.

With this information in hand, Perkins now turns to developing the general information brochure, using material from her factsheet and from additional data in her copy kit. This is aimed principally at prospective graduate students. It includes the following components:

- A catchy front cover for the 30-second reader

- Main points highlighted for the 3-minute reader

- Documentation/description for the 30-minute reader

- The sustaining message on the back cover

- The ready adaptation to a poster format

- The relatively non-scholarly, persuasive tone

- The factsheet outline forming the skeleton

- An introduction with an appeal to the audience

- A utilitarian conclusion

- The ready expansion into a more detailed document whose tone and format would be tailored to the audience in question

Below is the text of the brochure that Perkins developed. She got help in editing, design, and layout from staff in the Midland publications office, but it is her own factsheet that lends it clarity, completeness, and cogency.

(COVER)

Illustration accompanied by this text:

By and large, our present problem is one of attitudes and implements. We are remodeling the Alhambra with a steam shovel, which after all has many good points, but we are in need of gentler and more objective criteria for its successful use. — Aldo Leopold

(Succeeding Pages)

For graduate students seeking careers in a "gentler, more objective" environmental management

MIDLAND UNIVERSITY
Announces a new Master of Science (M.S.) Degree in Biological Conservation and Sustainable Development

Offering a professional focus to multidisciplinary environmental studies and a promising career ladder

(Succeeding Pages)

Wanted: Qualified graduate students for careers in environmental management.

For two years in succession — 1993 and 1994 — *U.S. News and World Report* lists specialties in environmental management among its "Best Jobs for the Future — Hot Tracks in 20 Professions."

Now you can prepare yourself for just such a career through a new graduate opportunity.

Midland University announces a Master of Science (M.S.) degree in Biological Conservation and Sustainable Development through Midland's distinguished Department of Botany and Applied Ecology (B&AE). The program, beginning in the fall semester of 1996, is meant for recent B.S. graduates and returning adults with academic backgrounds in biological fields or professional experiences in resource conservation/development.

You join a program rooted in ecological research, economic principles, esthetic perceptions, and field experiences.

The program seeks to serve present student and public needs and help form more sensitive policies in our relationships with the environment. The program is directed by Professor A. Wilmot Campion, who obtained a Ph.D. under the famous ecologist Eugene Odum at the University of Georgia. Campion also worked with the Chesapeake Bay Commission.

You can custom-build your own academic program of study.

Midland has a rich array of graduate course offerings. Around a core of required activities, in consultation with your major professor, you can select those courses that best suit your academic background, your career goals, and your prior field experiences. You are expected to complete at least 18 graduate course-credits plus a thesis, or a field project in lieu of a thesis.

New core courses provide a professional focus within a multidisciplinary experience.

Required:
> Biological Aspects of Environmental Impact Assessment
> Biological Conservation and Sustainable Development Seminar

Recommended:
> Principles of Applied Ecology
> Urban and Regional Planning (in Department of Earth Sciences)

Suggested:
> Environmental Management (in School of Forestry and Environmental Studies)
> Environment: the American Experience (in Department of History)
> Environmental Risk Assessment (in School of Business Administration)

As a BC&SD major, you are eligible to compete for varied forms of financial support:

- The Populus Award

- Midland University Graduate School fellowships

- College of Letters and Science scholarships

- B&AE Department teaching assistantships

- Internships with the regional office of the federal Environmental Protection Agency, the State Department of Environmental Management, the Pontiac County Planning Commission, the City of Midland Park and Pleasure Drive Bureau, and the Midland Association of Real Estate Developers.

(BACK COVER)

The Department of Botany and Applied Ecology Mission Statement

(Refer to Perkins' sustaining message on page 195.)

Between the factsheet and the brochure — and her original copy kit — Perkins has plenty of material from which to create a poster that will grab a student's attention. She also has all the key statements and data needed for a story in her alumni newsletter, a speech at a local environmental clean-up company, or a news release to local media announcing her program. Here is Perkins' news release:

Midland University Office of Public Information

Contact: Sally Jamieson 637-3333
10 Dec 95 1400

FOR IMMEDIATE RELEASE

MU Launches New Ecology Program

To meet a growing need in both public and private sectors for environmental management specialists, Midland University will introduce a new master's degree program in "Biological Conservation and Sustainable Development," Susan B. Aristes, vice president of academic affairs, announced today.

Instruction will begin with the start of the fall quarter of 1996.

Based in the Department of Botany and Applied Ecology, the 18-credits-plus-thesis-or-project program will draw on academic resources campuswide, Aristes said.

"We're looking for highly qualified recent graduates or returning adults with strong academic or experiential credentials and a commitment to economic development in concert with ecological conservation," Letters and Science Dean E. Howard Harrier said.

Dean Harrier added: "There's a demand for such people in government agencies at all levels, planning commissions, and industries."

A limited number of fellowships, scholarships, assistantships, and internships will be available to particularly qualified applicants, according to Amanda Perkins, B&AE chair.

Heading the program will be the department's newest faculty member, Prof. A. Wilmot Campion, a University of Georgia Ph.D. in ecology with Chesapeake Bay Commission experience.

"We seek to serve present student and public needs as well as help form future sanative policies in humankind-environment relationships," Campion said today.

A multidisciplinary advisory group will monitor the program.

"We're delighted to see this program emerge at Midland," William E. Dollard, head of the state Department of Environmental Management, said today.

The Midland Association of Real Estate Developers also expressed support.

A brochure describing in detail the program and application criteria is available at the B&AE office, 110 Mendel Hall, (609) 637-8200.

The new graduate program joins other related Midland programs in seven departments.

"My office will ensure that each has a distinct focus," Aristes said. "I see collaboration, not competition."

B&AE is one of Midland's original units and now enjoys an international reputation in ecological teaching, research, and public service.

Two things that Perkins might add to a release: a little bit of history on how the program came to be and a couple of quotes in support of the program from the dean or president and from the CEO of an environmental business. Her student intern can call these sources and get a couple of pithy statements from them regarding the program and how it will fill an important need in the community.

She will then send the release, along with her brochure, to the editor of *Bioscience*, who is going to do a piece on environmental degree programs around the country for a summer issue.

Clearly, Perkins knows how to distill a message and get plenty of mileage from her copy kit!

As we have illustrated, there is nothing particularly difficult or magical about coming to grips with your message. It is the essence of what you say when your neighbor asks about your department or college.

But the message is also an expression of your vision for your unit or your institution and, as such, it must convey your energy and enthusiasm. Again, consistency and the ability to state your premise in a short abbreviated form also are important pluses.

In February 1995, while playing golf at the Pebble Beach Pro-Am Tournament, former President George Bush was asked by a television announcer what he was doing these days. His answer: "Barbara and I are working to spread a 'thousand points of light' in our community." Succinct. Catchy. Caring. Consistent. Elements of a strong, successful message.

For further consideration ...

Gearing up for the hard work of writing

Do you have trouble gearing up for a communication assignment? Writing is hard work!

You may draw some friendly tips from the extensive research that Robert Boice, a professor of psychology at the State University of New York at Stony Brook, has done on the travails of new faculty (*The Journal of Higher Education*, January/February 1995). He is a prolific writer on subjects relevant to academic leaders and his points apply to the writing process.

Reliable success at communication, Boice says, "begins with finding *motivation*." As if you didn't know that.

But what you may not know is that, from his observations of what he calls "quick starters," motivation seems to come best not from waiting for the proverbial spirit to move you, but "in the wake of regular involvement, not in advance of it." Boice suggests that writers immerse themselves in communication "while cheerfully imagining that once working, they will enjoy the discoveries and interactions."

The second developmental category, according to Boice, is *imagination*, which comes not from consulting the stars, but from "notes and ideas ... listed-and-gisted into outlines," followed by "conceptual outlines, where each point is written out informally to see what can be said, to look for clarity and direction."

The third stage: *fluency* — the ability to pace yourself and avoid stress, to face the disappointment of imperfect performance, the right expectations to deal with lack of ready appreciation by a chosen audience, the habits of self-study that promote improvement.

Control is the fourth developmental stage. By control, Boice really means self-control: freedom from big swings in mood, regular attention to little things that block progress — "constant self-study and identification of inefficient habits and beliefs."

A sense of *audience* is crucial, says Boice: "Audience ... is more than asking and listening; it ideally grows with a movement away from self-focus, ever outward. First we discover what we can say, then what is worth saying to others. In other words, a sense of audience means to understand and to be understood."

Finally, *resilience*. Effective communicators: (a) are less reactive to distractions, (b) think out their work in preliminaries, (c) display less impatience and perfectionism, (d) minimize the mindlessness that accompanies the stress and overloads that haunt academic leaders, and (e) practice ways of reducing their fatigue. But the "mainstays of resilience," says Boice, are "timing and audience" — "wasted efforts undermine resilience; the efficiencies of pacing and exteriorization cultivate it."

And now, as with every bit of communication, we need a conclusion. Boice supplies one from his research: "We know that work at patience and pacing belongs amid the complexities" of communication, and that "understanding audience expectations is just [as] important as trying new innovations" in techniques or technology.

chapter ten

Breaking Through
Mating media and audiences

If a tree falls in the forest and no one is there to hear it fall, does it make a sound? That old philosophical question has some resonance to this discussion of matching media and audiences.

The most carefully written speech will not have the desired impact if the audience is inappropriate or inattentive. An urgent electronic message about an emergency departmental meeting will be effective only if your colleagues are in regular "electronic" touch with you. Just like the tree falling without a witness, if your message is delivered and no one is listening, it *won't* make a sound!

In the preceding chapter we saw how a simple message can be tailored to suit various media and various audiences. This chapter is intended to help you make sure that the medium you pick is the most efficient and effective for the audience you want to reach.

Matching message and medium requires that you be aware of a medium's style and content and shape your message accordingly. In chapter five, we discussed how to evaluate a medium to get a sense of its audience and what they want or expect to hear, see, or read. Ideally, when drawing up your communication plan, you evaluated media and decided which would be appropriate for your message.

But in real life, enthusiastic souls inevitably race ahead, preparing a message before figuring out how to deliver it or picking a medium before considering the audience. So if you have not already done so, this is the time to turn back to chapter five for a list of media options and tips on how to pick a suitable carrier for your message.

There is no reason why the scholar-historian who writes for respected professional journals cannot also write history textbooks and provide television commentary on the historical aspects of current politics. In fact, most outstanding faculty and administrators owe some of their success to their ability to communicate well — whether in the classroom, to a TV camera, or in a scholarly paper. To communicate expertise in a variety of media requires an awareness of media-audience links and a willingness to reach beyond the professional formats that are comfortable, familiar, and "safe."

Fortunately, more and more faculty are taking the plunge. Mason Smith (1993) reported that 83% of faculty at the liberal arts colleges he surveyed had communicated to the public through some form of popular media in the preceding five years. Of those, 65% had communicated through quotes in a newspaper or magazine, 54% through one or more popular articles, and 41% through radio or television appearances. Why did they do it? The leading answer: "To communicate with the public and to enhance my college's visibility."

The smart campus leader realizes that it is vital to expand communication beyond the group of colleagues down the hall — and that *when communicating with a broad range of constituencies, you have to use the medium of communication to which each attends.*

Thinking in "circles of influence"

In some ways, this might prove the most important chapter in our book because of the growing glut of information confronting our key audiences. The ability to aim and shoot your message in ways that will break through the clutter of information will determine your success.

The "circles of influence" approach is one way to think about the media you need to use to reach your key audiences. Draw an archery target on a piece of paper, put yourself in the bull's eye, and then define your audiences on the rims of the concentric circles surrounding your bull's eye, placing those closest to you in the innermost ring and working outward to those audiences furthest from you. By and large, these concentric circles also mirror spatial relationships, with those in the closest circles physically closest to you or your program, and those at the outermost rings furthest away.

Department Chair Amanda Perkins, for example, might define her target of circles of influence as follows:

In the circle surrounding her are her most immediate audiences — departmental colleagues, students in her courses, the dean (her boss), her support staff, her family, and her close friends at Midland and in the community. These are the people with whom she interacts on almost a daily basis and thus communicates with most intensively.

In the next concentric circle are the other students in her department, other departmental chairs and faculty colleagues at Midland, campus administrators with whom she most often inter-acts, her most involved alumni, important donors, her contacts in industry, and her professional colleagues at other institutions. These are people with whom she operates frequently, but not daily.

The third circle contains those a little further removed — the rest of her alumni; parents and families of her department's faculty, staff, and students; faculty, staff, and students at the institution who have some direct contact with her department; prospective students; the university's board of trustees; and close community contacts (e.g., fellow Rotary Club members).

The fourth circle might include other colleges and universities, community or government leaders, the general alumni body, and Midland faculty, students, and staff who have no direct contact with her department.

Her outermost ring will hold the general public, policy-makers, and alumni and contacts who are national or even global and with whom she has little direct contact.

(If she carried this exercise to the ultimate extreme, Perkins could draw these circles until she reached the outermost rim, which is the group that will never have any contact with or influence over her department.)

When you, like Perkins, complete this "circles of influence" chart, you will have a conceptual view of the audiences with which you are communicating. This makes it easier to begin to identify the media that are most appropriate to reach them.

But we need to recognize first that we spend the bulk of our communications "capital" on communicating with those in the innermost circles. We communicate with them most frequently, most directly, and in the greatest variety of ways. Hence, they know us best. As we get further out, our audiences get less frequent, less targeted, less direct, and less varied communication from us.

It is important to note that your message needs to be communicated first — and most influentially — to this innermost circle, because they are at the center of their own "circles of influence." It's important, too, to note that the audiences on our circles interact with each other and with those in proximate circles.

Before we discuss the communication vehicles that these "circles of influence" suggest, there are a few other things to keep in mind about matching media and audiences.

Media of influence

Despite the sophisticated communications in our world — or maybe because of them — the most influential means of communication remains the oldest form of communication — person to person. If a colleague knows and trusts Perkins and she tells him something specific about looming budget cuts, he will believe it, no matter what he might read or hear to the contrary. If the college president tells the alumni board what is really happening in the admissions program, the board members will take her word over what they read in the student newspaper. Personal knowledge and experience continue to head the list of information sources that people trust and use most to form their opinions.

This is one reason why your innermost circles of influence are so important. Since they are presumably hearing about your programs, plans, and problems "straight from the horse's mouth," they are very credible sources of information to those around them.

The influence of personal contact was evidenced in a recent media relations study, conducted by Lehigh University (1994, Office of National Media Relations), in which 192 universities were queried about the effectiveness of their national media strategies. When respondents were asked to grade various methods of contact based on their success in placing news stories, they gave "personal contacts" an A, followed by phone calls (B) and down the list to tipsheets and press releases, which garnered Bs and Cs.

The next most influential form of communication is secondhand or proximate knowledge. For example, the wife of one of Perkins' colleagues may not have heard directly from Perkins on the latest budget cuts, but will be a credible source because her husband has passed along the information to her.

Beyond that, direct communication on a subject in the form of a personal letter or note is more persuasive than a newsletter that goes to hundreds of people. And an authoritative report, or white paper, on a subject generally carries more weight than a press release.

One of the least credible sources of information is the news media — and yet it is one of the most influential because it reaches so many people. In surveys, people continue to put the news media far down the list of credible sources of information, but anyone who has had to deal with a negative story in the press knows that it is very influential and very powerful. We will deal more specifically with the news media in the next chapter.

This discussion of media of influence is, simply, applied common sense. If you think about how you form opinions and what information sources you personally consider most credible or most influential, you will no doubt come to a similar conclusion. Looking at media this way again reinforces the importance of the internal audience and reinforces two of our most important points:

- Your message must reflect the reality of the situation. (If it doesn't, those in your innermost circle of influence will do you in.)

- Good external relations are built on excellent internal communications. (If not, those in your innermost circle of influence may be sending messages that are in direct conflict with yours.)

Circles of influence and media targeting

Considering our prime audiences using this circles of influence model can give us some insight into ways in which we might best communicate with them. In general, the circles closest to us will hear from us in the greatest variety of ways, while those on the outermost rim may learn of us only through the mass media.

Matching the media with the audiences in the intermediate circles is the biggest challenge. As with any good communications strategy, it is best to gather a little "ground truth" before deciding on how best to reach a particular audience.

That can be achieved in several ways. Market testing is one approach: you might experiment with a vehicle — whether a speech, a letter, a radio spot, or a new publication — and then test it with some small segment of the desired audience. Another approach is to steal good ideas from your colleagues around campus or at other colleges and universities. If they have been very successful with a particular audience, such as prospective students or prominent alumni, their strategies also might work for you.

Going back to our circles of influence, we might attach some new "media" values to the rings we have drawn. Perkins, for example, might look at her circles of influence and identify the following communication options.

For the circle immediately surrounding her, she would record the following communication devices: personal communication (talking one-on-one), meetings, personal notes and letters, memos, electronic mail and phone calls, budget documents, facsimiles, Post-It™ brand notes, visits, and progress reports.

For the next broadest circle, she might use many of these same devices, though less frequently, and others, such as newsletters, bulletin board postings, information racks, speeches, pamphlets, reprints, clipsheets, promotional materials, and the like.

In thinking about the next circle out — general campus audience, community leaders, colleagues at other institutions, etc. — Perkins will begin to depend on less "personal" communications and more on the campus and/or student newspaper, the local media, press releases, annual reports, other direct mail pieces, speeches and presentations, panel discussions and conferences, programming for local TV and radio, articles in professional journals or special interest magazines, special events, and perhaps an electronic bulletin board.

As Perkins reaches out to regional and national audiences, she will use even less personal means of communication, such as story ideas for national and regional newspapers and electronic media, letters to the editor, op-ed pieces, advertising, presentations and displays at national conferences and events, a World Wide Web site, exhibits at events such as the state fair, and promotional materials that can be sent to a large audience — for example, brochures about the department for all the state's high school guidance counselors.

New communications technology can bring the audiences in the outer rim right to your front door. Students or alumni from Japan, for example, can come into your Web site in Alabama for the cost of a telephone call and get a plethora of information from you directly. You can do this without the expenses of publishing and mailing materials, and without having to depend on a Japanese newspaper to pick up a story about your department or institution. The only hitch is that this technology is relatively new; although it's attracting growing numbers of users, those numbers may not yet be significant enough among certain audiences. (See chapter thirteen.)

In using these circles of influence to match media and audiences, you can avoid both gaps and communications overkill.

Let's say that the department of botany and applied ecology is doing a special Earth Day open house in April and is cooperating with the city parks department in the effort. To publicize the event, Perkins is making a speech to the Midland Rotary Club. Using her circles of influence chart, she and her staff have decided to target the audiences in her first three circles of influence. After her speech, she writes a letter and circulates her speech to those in her innermost circle. She makes sure that all audiences in these three circles get the open house flier, brochure, and poster. At the same time, she works through the campus and local press to get the word out on the event, uses her community contacts to publicize the event in the local schools, and urges her colleagues and students to communicate in ways similar to those used in their innermost circles of influence.

In this way, she can best match her audience and communication strategies. She also can avoid expensive communications over-kill, like producing a full-color poster, an ad in a regional newspaper, or a mass mailing to far-flung audiences — all of which are unlikely to significantly boost her audience.

This example illustrates, too, the importance of using multiple strategies in reaching a given audience. If a local high school student sees a poster for the open house in his classroom, hears his teacher announce it, sees a local newspaper article on it, hears a PSA (public service announcement) on the radio, and talks to his mom who heard Perkins' Rotary Club speech, he will form a greater impression of the event than if reached through only one means. And he just might attend! And for future reference, Perkins and her colleagues will want to survey those who attend the Earth Day Open House to assess which of their communication strategies were most effective.

In Lehigh's media relations survey, respondents were asked how they decide which media are most important to their institution. Nearly half said they target the media on a strictly geographical basis — local, regional, and national (reflecting a circles of influence approach). Said one news director surveyed, "Local and national media are important because that's where administration and constituents expect to see us."

Trends in communication and media choices

In advertising her Earth Day Open House, Perkins used a number of media — letters, speeches, posters, and newspaper stories — to reach clearly defined audiences. Several of these medium-audience matches were among the means that colleges and universities have traditionally used to reach key groups, with great success. We will discuss them in detail below.

But there are some trends in the communications game that you need to consider before you adopt any approach. One is that people are becoming more visually oriented and, at the same time, reading less. In terms of the general public audience — that outermost circle of influence — it is worth noting that twenty percent of the adults in the United States are functionally illiterate. This group is not likely to be a target audience for academe for most purposes, but that statistic should remind us that if our aim is to influence public opinion on an issue, one out of five adults will be lost "off the top" if we craft our message using the printed word only.

Another trend, as we have mentioned, is the growth of electronic communications through email, computer information services, electronic bulletin boards, and the Internet. This has created new opportunities for getting your message out — rapidly and at a relatively low cost — but it has also created a division in your audience. There are the "haves" (those who use such services) and the "have nots" (those who lack the equipment, expertise, and/or interest to use those services).

A third trend on this list is the burgeoning amount of information hitting every member of our society. An added complication is that the advent of voice mail, cellular phones, fax machines, and electronic mail have given many messages a character of urgency that they may not warrant. The time it takes to cope with messages from all sources is time that members of our targeted audience cannot spend on our message — if it doesn't simply get lost in the crowd. As the mail, fax, phone, and electronic messages accumulate, it is becoming more common for folks to just scan material rather than read and digest it. This has implications for how we select media to communicate with busy audiences.

As we discussed in chapter five, the greater your control over a medium, the easier it is to deliver your message at the time and in the manner that you want. The mass media represent forms of communication over which you have the least amount of control; we will devote the next chapter to methods for dealing with this special "audience."

For our purposes in this chapter, we will focus on communication devices that are most often used by academic professionals to reach special audiences. Tracking our discussion of circles of influence, we have organized these devices into three categories: "personal," "printed," and "electronic." Most often, your targeted audience will be reached through a variety of these means.

Person-to-person communications: Meetings, letters, speaches

Most academic adminstrators spend a lot of time in meetings, on the telephone, and writing letters. Within the past few years, more and more time also is going into electronic mail.

These are four key ways to keep in touch with those closest to you. Each merits some discussion here.

The meeting

Audiences: Departmental faculty, staff, students; deans and administrators; alumni; donors; community leaders

Meetings are a primary, expected, and generally successful means by which campus leaders communicate with faculty, bosses, subordinates, and students. Meetings can be a very effective means of communication — and they can also be a waste of time. With schedules in academe as full as they are, meetings with mutiple participants also are increasingly difficult to schedule. Therefore, it's worth spending a little time on when *not* to have a meeting.

No academic leader should fall into the habit of using a meeting to pass on information that can better be transmitted via memos, email, or telephone. Too often, colleagues schedule regular meetings just to keep in touch when a short phone call, note, fax, or email message may work as well, or better. And too often, meetings are held simply because they have been scheduled. We shouldn't hesitate to cancel a standing meeting if the agenda is not substantive enough to warrant it and, if there are only a few agenda items, find another way to consult or reach consensus. A conference call, which is often much more convenient for participants, may suffice. Consider your meetings critically, noting the cost of the time spent in travel and attendance by all the participants and weigh that cost against what is accomplished at the meetings.

One-on-one meetings

Meetings are effective ways to regularly communicate with your superiors and your staff. Meetings should generally be consultative, held to discuss options in implementing policy, to form policy, to plan, and — most important — to receive and give advice.

Such one-on-one meetings with your closest associates are perhaps the most effective form of communication. As you get into a regular meeting habit, you also come to know the most effective way to meet with each individual — from the very structured and decision-oriented to the more creative, idea-generating form.

Departmental meetings

Meetings are also a very effective and efficient way to communicate and consult with a number of people at one time. They are a must when it comes to all planning and policy-related decisions.

Timing

A lot rides on your timing of meetings. Regularity is important in order for your colleagues to arrange their schedules accordingly. So your call should always be for the same day of the week or month at the same time, at least during any one term. In case of an emergency meeting, give as much advance notice as possible and encourage those who can't make it to send a deputy.

Preparation

To get the most from the meeting, you should have a detailed agenda, with action items for discussion and decision at the top, to save time. It helps to list action items first and to designate who will take the lead on each item. Distribute it to all participants several days in advance, in print or by email. A structured meeting always produces more results than an unstructured meeting.

If you are in the habit of having a standing meeting, you might have regular agenda items for personnel, budget, equipment needs, policy issues, upcoming events, and the like that you revisit each time to report on progress and to structure your presentation. Computers make it relatively easy to update your agenda.

Strategy

The meeting you chair doesn't have to be a dull inconvenience for your colleagues. For one thing, if it's a meeting that does not require full faculty participation, you should not invite people who don't need to be there or who will not profit from it. An alternative is to invite people only for the time scheduled for their particular contribution or interests.

Be sure that all elements are coordinated and that people, information, and services (audiovisuals and so on) are on hand as needed. It is important always to go into the meeting knowing what you want to achieve from it.

To make your meeting an interesting collegial event and an effective communication tool, give your colleagues some ownership in the agenda. Circulate a call for agenda items ahead of time, be sure to include items that have been suggested at the previous meeting, and give credit to those who came up with the suggestions.

Direction

If you are leading the departmental meeting, it is important to do so in a way that invites participation, but keeps the meeting on track. One way to make meetings more efficient is to assign a time frame for each discussion/decision item and stick to it. If, as moderator, you hit a topic that ignites long discussion, you can always carry discussion over to another time or have a subcommittee of those most interested in the topic come up with some resolution and report back to the full committee. We know one university administrator who conducted his staff meetings with all members standing up, on the theory — which usually proved correct — that meetings would be shorter that way.

A bonus

Don't neglect the opportunity that a faculty or departmental meeting affords to build unit morale. One strategy is to always begin your meetings with reports of "good news" — grants won, faculty and student accomplishments, and so on. Another is to show appreciation.

Follow-up

It's a good idea to jot down action items that come from meetings, to ensure follow-up. A summary (minutes) of the meeting is very important. If you don't provide one, the participants will draw their own conclusions, which may or may not be perceptive. The summary should take the form of a succinct memo. If there's a deadline for submitting data or reporting on accomplished action, state and underline the date in the memo's Subject and repeat it at the end of the memo.

The letter or note

Audiences: Departmental faculty, staff, students; alumni; donors; parents; colleagues; prospective students.

This is your most official form of communication and, in some respects, your most powerful. It creates a permanent record of your communication. Letters mark the official actions of colleges and universities: acceptance to the college or department, appointment, review, evaluation, congratulations, sympathy, reprimand, and so forth. Everyone reading this book no doubt writes dozens of letters a month, but may benefit nonetheless from a brief discussion of how best to use them.

A positive force

Linda Weimer knows a very successful academic administrator who keeps a raft of notecards in the top drawer of his desk. He makes it a point to write at least two or three thank-you cards or congratulatory notes each day. It is a practice that has paid off handsomely for his department through the years.

A simple note of thanks or congratulations to a parent whose son or daughter has made the dean's list, to an alum who has received some special recognition, to a colleague who has written a book, to a dean whose school has been highly ranked, to a staff member who has done an especially good job on a project, to a student who turned in an especially good paper: these communications send a strong signal about you as an administrator — that you are paying attention, that you care about your unit, and that you believe in recognizing good work. This simple thing can have profound effects on the morale of your unit and the way you are viewed by that close circle with whom you have personal communication.

A negative force

Inevitably an academic administrator finds from time to time that he or she also must send bad news in the form of a letter. It is desirable in that case to follow up or accompany that communication with another form of personal contact — a meeting or phone call. If a faculty member has had a grant proposal rejected by the dean and you must communicate why, it is best to do so face to face or through a phone call as well as in writing. If a student's problems require that you write him or her a letter, it is also wise to have a conversation with that student as well. There are also times when legal issues are involved and it is best to seek some advice about what can and cannot be said before putting anything in writing.

Beyond
the immediate circle

Most of us are accustomed to writing letters to our supervisors, our employees, our colleagues, and our students, but the letter also can be a very powerful and personal tool to reach a broader audience.

Many campus leaders, for example, write an annual letter to the faculty, to share their thoughts about the institution they lead, or they mark important moments in the institution's life with a letter. When James Duderstadt (1995) announced his resignation as the president of the University of Michigan, this is the letter he sent to his colleagues:

September 28, 1995

An Open Letter to the University Community

Dear Members of the Michigan Family:

For many years I have given speechs on the changes occurring in the world, in higher education, and in our University. In this letter I continue that theme of change, but in a more personal vein.

After serving for almost a decade as provost, acting president, and president, Anne and I have decided that this will be our last year as leaders of the University. It is my intention to retire from the presidency and return to the faculty of the University next summer.

We want to thank all of you both for your support and for the privilege of serving the University in these leadership roles. It has been a wonderful and exhilarating experience, primarily because of the extraordinary people who learn in, work for, sacrifice for, and love Michigan. It has also been a satisfying period in our lives because of the great progress made by the University during these years.

While there is no perfect time to step aside from a leadership role, Anne and I have decided that this year may be the best both for us and for the University. Through the efforts of countless members of the University, most of the goals we set in the late 1980s have now been achieved. Today, in 1995, by any measure, the University is better, stronger, more diverse, and more exciting than at any time in its history, due to your efforts.

National rankings of the quality of the University's academic programs are the highest since these evaluations began several decades ago.

Through the remarkable efforts of our faculty, the University now ranks as the nation's leader in research activity.

Despite a decline in state support over the past two decades, the University has emerged financially as the strongest public university in America. Our endowment has increased four-fold to over $1.3 billion. And, with almost two years left in the Campaign for Michigan, we are already at 90% of our goal.

A walk around the University reveals the remarkable transformation in our environment as we approach the completion of our massive effort to rebuild, renovate, and update all of the buildings on our campuses. The University Medical Center has undergone a profound transformation placing it in a clear leadership position in health care, research, and teaching.

And perhaps most important of all, through efforts such as the Michigan Mandate and the Michigan Agenda for Women, we now have the highest representation of people of color and women among our students, faculty, and staff in our history.

It is clear that as we approach the 21st Century, the University of Michigan has become not only the leading public university in America, but that it is challenged by only a handful of distinguished private universities in the quality, breadth, capacity, and impact of its many programs and activities. Throughout higher education, people now look to us as truly "the leaders and best."

It is natural to take great pride in what members of the Michigan family — faculty, students, staff, alumni, and friends — have accomplished. Working together, we have indeed built a truly extraordinary university. But we have built a university for the twentieth century, and that century is rapidly coming to an end. It is now time to lead the University in new directions, to transform ourselves to better serve a rapidly changing world. And I believe that such new directions may benefit best from new leadership, fresh visions, and untapped energy.

To this end, I have informed the Board of Regents of my intention to return to the faculty at the end of this academic year. This will provide the Regents with ample time to complete the search for my successor. This transition period will also allow me to provide the stable leadership necessary to keep the University on course until a new president has been selected.

Although we have had many opportunities for leadership elsewhere, Anne and I remain deeply committed to Michigan. Indeed, after 27 years on the faculty, then as dean, provost, and finally as president, we are maize and blue down to the level of our DNA. We look forward to serving the University in new ways in the years ahead. And we look forward to many more years of working with the marvelous people who make up the Michigan family. Thanks for the opportunity to serve!

Sincerely,
James J. Duderstadt

By sending out this letter, the president was able to convey a consistent message about his decision, the reasons behind it, the areas in which he felt he had made the most important contributions to the university, and his aspirations for the future of the University of Michigan. It is very unlikely that much, if any, of this message would have gotten through if he had simply sent a letter to his Board of Regents and relied on the *Ann Arbor News* to report his decision to the public and the community.

Letters can be especially effective in times of crisis — in the wake of major budget cuts, a natural disaster, a broadly publicized campus crime, and the like. The president of the University of Southern California wrote to all parents and alumni — thousands of people — in the wake of the 1992 Los Angeles riots. Though costly, the strategy no doubt paid off with families who decided, partly based on the president's communication, not to yank their children out of USC. But as important, it sent a strong signal that the university was looking out for their students and gave close associates firsthand information about the incident. Similarly, officials at Homestead Community College in Florida wrote letters to students and families in the aftermath of Hurricane Andrew.

In years past, some colleges and universities have sorely neglected a very important group — parents. The only regular communiqué has been the tuition bill.

Today, however, most campus officials realize that 18- to 21-year-olds tend to leave out a lot when they talk to their parents about life on campus. This is partly because the students don't think particular issues are important enough to pass along, partly because the students have not paid sufficient attention to those issues. On the other hand, students *do* tell their parents about the things that bother them about college.

Parents can be powerful allies — or, if shrugged off, relentless adversaries. As Allan Tucker and Robert A. Bryan (1991) remind us:

There is a large, amazingly effective grapevine out
there among the general public that operates to either
the advantage or disadvantage of a college or university
concerning how it treats students. Parents of students
currently enrolled talk to parents of students yet to be
enrolled, and as we all know, bad news travels faster
and farther than good news.

The wise campus leader will, first of all, pay real attention to
student issues (not enough laboratory sections, inadequate library hours, poor quality food, and so on) and respond to them.
You should also make it clear to your office staff that students
are "clients" or "family members" and will always be treated
with patience and friendliness.

Second, if you receive complaints from parents, respond promptly
and personally. While most complaints may be at least partially
inaccurate, the concern behind them is genuine. And because
parental concern is not a trivial emotion, you can't turn the
complaints over to a secretary to handle or set them aside to for
a more propitious time. You have to respond without much delay
or testiness. This is not just the proper thing to do; to procrastinate
is to invite the parent to write to higher authority.

Handling complaints promptly and thoughtfully, of course, is not
the only way a campus leader can help build a positive image of
the institution in the minds of parents. Fortunately, students are
far more often satisfied than sad or frustrated. You should make
an effort to notify parents about their sucessful offspring. While
virtually every student will tell his or her parents about getting
good grades, the parents will be elated to have that news echoed
in a congratulatory letter from you. A scholarship won, a thesis
prize secured, and so on — these happy occasions all warrant a
personal letter from you.

These practices hold true for other constituencies as well. Handling complaints promptly and thoughtfully and recognizing
important achievements by colleagues, students, and alumni

helps an academic leader build a positive image of the institution in the minds of important people.

Visits/special events

Audiences: Departmental families; prospective students; prospective employers; alumni; donors; parents; colleagues; other campus administrators; the general public.

There is no substitute for a personal visit to your department or division for someone to learn about you and, it is hoped, form a positive impression. It has been shown, for example, that one of the single most important factors for high school students in determining which college to attend is the campus visit.

In tailoring your message for a host of audiences, don't overlook this possibility. Your faculty and your students are invariably your best ambassadors. And to invite others to come into your unit and experience the energy and excitement that you and your colleagues feel about what you are doing can be a powerful means of education and motivation.

Most departments and divisions are very experienced when it comes to visits from prospective students and colleagues from other institutions, so we will concentrate here on audiences that might not as readily come to mind in terms of visits or special events.

One such group is so close to home that it may not be obvious: the families of your faculty and staff and close colleagues in other units. They are people whom you may see at social gatherings or official functions and who may know a lot about you, but a visit to your department or division to hear a series of faculty lectures or meet some of your outstanding students would enhance their experience and make them much better ambassadors for you. In planning for their annual open houses, many campuses make an extra effort to target their own faculty and staff, urging them to bring their families to campus for the day.

Another such group: the parents of your students. If your campus hosts an annual parents event of some kind, maybe you can get involved and piggyback on that event a tour or reception at your unit. If the parents can meet and talk to your faculty, it should help dispel the myth that students are taught primarily by graduate students or that they get very little personal faculty attention.

Visits by prospective employers also are important. The prospective employers of your graduates can be a demanding group. Quite simply, they generally want people who can contribute the most to their operations. And they expect colleges and universities to produce those people. In turn, the record of every academic unit in placing its graduates consistently and successfully in the marketplace is a key element in that "outcomes assessment" by which institutions of postsecondary education are increasingly being measured today.

While no amount of employer relations can substitute for turning out accomplished graduates, any 360-degree communications program will include regular contact with prime employers of those graduates, if only to keep them cognizant of your academic unit. In that regard, there is no substitute for personal contacts — on their turf or yours — with employers, in groups large or small, and individually.

Some academic people call this contact "the grin and grip grind." True, it's a matter of interpersonal relations, but it also involves some varieties of communication.

Special events provide a similar opportunity for positive impressions that can be beneficial to your department or division.

Special events

Any department can and should take full advantage of campus events that are planned — open houses, special anniversary celebrations, etc. — or that are part of the inevitable cycle of campus life, such as orientations, move-in day, new-student welcome activities, commencement, and class reunions.

These occasions may give parents, alumni, and members of the public their only opportunities to meet and talk with campus personnel, view the facilities and grounds, and get a sense of campus life. For you, these are opportunities to better understand the parents and their expectations, to learn from alumni who know campus history, or to get a feel for public interest and attitudes regarding your institution and unit. You also might find that these events yield some skilled volunteers for special campus or unit needs.

In addition to getting involved in events that are already planned, think about special events that you can plan for your department or division that will serve your goals. Bringing in a famous speaker or scheduling a symposium on a topic of current public interest, for example, can attract widespread campus interest and spark some valuable media coverage. In general, events take a lot of time and energy, especially for support staff, so it is better to plan wisely and to do one or two high-impact events well rather than try to do too many with little positive result.

Speeches

Audiences: Alumni; donors; parents; community groups; colleagues; other campus administrators; the general public.

If you are a faculty member or campus administrator, you are inevitably going to give speeches — probably a lot of them.

The speech is an essential medium for communicating in person to a broad audience — and it can be incredibly powerful and influential.

At the same time, there is no prospect more terrifying to most of us than standing before a group of people and giving a speech. *Parade* magazine years ago ran a brief story noting that sociological research had shown that the only thing the average person fears more than public speaking is snakes.

It might help to remember Franklin D. Roosevelt's six-word formula for speeches: "Be sincere, be brief, be seated."

James Carville, chief manager of Bill Clinton's 1992 presidential campaign, in a post-election press conference, let us in on a trade secret. "You think my job is to stuff a candidate's head full of sound bites, like pounding sand into a bottle. Not so. My big job is to develop a focus." It was Carville, you may recall, who posted that big sign in Clinton campaign headquarters: "IT'S THE ECONOMY, STUPID!" (Walsh 1992).

Just so, an academic leader as speechmaker must avoid rambling and focus on the cardinal objective — to hammer home a key point or two, what some people call "the vision thing."

As Richard W. Conklin (1989) put it:

> The vision goes beyond the functional case statement. It paints with a broad brush, creating a compelling picture. The vision positions the institution as a place with a special purpose. It is never a depiction of the institution as it is; it is always what the institution wants to be. The vision is never accomplished; the institution is becoming. ... If you articulate the vision, you've done enough.

By "paints with a broad brush," Conklin is speaking qualitatively, not quantitatively. Vision painting is to be brief and to the point.

This "vision thing," of course, is only a component of any speech. The *substance*, which is equally important, takes its signal from the particular audience and/or occasion. Nothing is more ineffective than the speech that doesn't acknowledge the interests and needs of listeners.

For example, when Perkins addresses a high school assembly, as she is frequently invited to do, she combines her disciplinary credentials with a broad current public interest in ecology to talk about the "The ABCs of Ecology." Her speech conveys substance — what ecology is — and, by her choices of words and example, her speech conveys vision — her personal sense of ecology's importance in the world.

It starts out something like this:

> As you students may know, the word "ecology" has been lying in the dictionary for some 100 years. But as you also know, the term is now flitting about in your vocabulary, like a bat emerging suddenly from a cave into bright sunlight.
>
> Now you may well ask, what exactly does the word *mean*? What does it *do*? What can *I* do with it? Is it one of those complex things that only a scientist can really understand and use? Or is it something within the grasp of a high school student like me?
>
> Well, there are all sorts of approaches to ecology, because ecology is a very rich word; that is, you and I can put it to many uses.

Perkins then elaborates on several of those approaches, in terms that students understand and with examples that relate to their experiences and interests. Because she knows that many of the students are likely to associate ecology just with scientists, she explains how anybody can be ecologists, which she then broadly defines as "people who see that everything is connected to everything else and for whom this understanding is an important driving force in their lives." In other words, she shows that her message about ecology is meant for every member of her audience.

Perkins fleshes out her topic and finishes with a more refined vision message that applies specifically to studies in applied ecology, that is, her hope that more students will take an interest in ecology as a career, possibly study at Midland in her unit, and go on to serve society in this increasingly important area. Then she fields questions. Ten minutes of "speechifying" is plenty for high schoolers.

Perkins did a good job of practicing what two consummate scholars/lecturers, Jacques Barzun and Henry F. Graff (1992), preach:

> The first and most important facts to ascertain before preparing any sort of talk are "How long am I expected to speak?" and "Who and how many are expected to attend?" The first answer determines the amount and kind of material to present; the second, the vocabulary, tone, and degree of complexity that are appropriate. ... A good rate of delivery is 125 words a minute. It allows for variations of speed as well as pauses for rest or emphasis.

Speech mechanics

In terms of complexity, if you are addressing a League of Women Voters meeting, you can count on a degree of sophistication. If it's a mixed public audience seeking diversion, the requirements will be quite different. Whatever the group, audiences quickly sense whether you're taking the trouble to speak in their vernacular.

Barzun and Graff suggest these devices, regardless of audience character, to hold their attention:

- Repetition of key points

- Proper and steady enunciation

- No distracting body movements

- No "ers," "ums," "ya knows," and so on

- Independent clauses first, then the dependent

- Topic sentences first, then the balance of the paragraph

- Plenty of direct address

- Plenty of asides — "as you know," "now let's return to," and so on

- Key and/or colorful terms emphasized

- Tell 'em what you're going to tell 'em, tell 'em, and tell 'em what you told 'em

Write or recite?

Writing out a speech is OK, provided you write as if speaking or if you are reading before a learned society or at a formal event. *But never read an informal speech or popular talk.* Speak from notes or memory — it's a recital of your ideas, not a proclamation.

On the other hand, in front of an audience, some people have serious difficulty remaining calm enough to present their thoughts in a logical fashion, no matter how they rehearse. If notes or a written speech guarantee a smooth start, use them, but *recite* whatever sections you can. Once you begin feeling comfortable with the situation, you may find it easy to abandon your props for the remainder of the speech.

If reading, look up from the page frequently and put plenty of feeling into your voice. Use pauses to emphasize a point and to heighten dramatic effect and give naturalness to your speech.

There are several things you can do in preparing a speech that will make it much easier to read — whether it's a speech you deliver or one for a superior to read:

- Print the text in large type (14- or 18-point) with double-spaced lines.

- Number each page clearly at the top.

- If a long word breaks at the end of a line, do *not* hyphenate. Rather, jump to the next line and type the *complete* word.

- Never end a page in mid-sentence, and preferably not in mid-paragraph.

- To avoid mispronunciation of a name (or other tricky word), inquire about the correct pronunciation in advance. Then put the word in brackets and spell it phonetically with accent marks, or write the accented syllable in capital letters.

- Use many short paragrphs so you can easily find your place after looking up at the audience. You may also want to use sectional subheads *for your convenience*, but not to be read.

- Mark paragraphs or lines that can be dropped if time runs short.

- If you are using index cards, include only what you need. For some people, a list of key words or phrases is enough; others need more detail. Make your notes easy to read at a quick glance.

- If you are using papers, do not staple the pages. Most formal speeches are delivered at a table or podium. With a loose sheaf, you may easily and quietly lift and move pages aside as you finish reading them.

- If you are supplementing your speech with audiovisuals, check in advance on availibility of such things as blackboard space, easel, electrical outlets for slide projectors, blinds, or curtains.

Whether reading from notes or speaking from memory, you should always *rehearse.* You need to rehearse in order to appear comfortable with your material and to get an idea of how long the speech will take. Through rehearsal you find the gaps in your logic, refine your transitions from topic to topic, and perhaps discover that the anecdote you chose really doesn't make the point you had in mind. The more effort you put into preparation, the more effortless your speech will appear. Mark Twain said it best: "It takes three weeks to prepare a good informal talk."

What about a sprinkling of levity? Barzun and Graff offer this sage counsel (1992):

Humor, anyone?

> Nothing is harder than telling a joke well; half the audience has heard it before, and if it has no bearing on the subject of the lecture, the hearers, after their

dutiful laughter, are as cold as when the lecturer first opened his mouth. Begin seriously ... then, having taken thought about the place within the subject where the collective mind probably stands. ... Gather the minds to that place. ... Then carry on, with a dash of humor or wit if truly relevant and fresh. An audience commonly wants to be pleased and is therefore not hard to please; it wants to think well of the lecturer, and he is honor-bound not to defeat that generous impulse.

Talk the language of your audience

Over time you may develop the guts of a speech that you can adapt to a fairly wide range of community constituencies. The operative word is *adapt*.

For example, if Perkins were to adapt her "ABCs of Ecology" speech for a talk to members of the Pontiac County Farm Bureau, her terms would be redolent of agriculture and she'd picture a farmer as a hands-on ecologist of sorts. In adapting the material to a meeting of urban planners, she'd likely ditch all those "things" in her high school assembly talk for terms more technical.

Talking the language of the audience is — pardon the expression — the art or science of "community," of forming a bond with your listeners. Another aspect of that art or science is focusing on the audience: try to "localize" a speech as much as possible. To do so, you may get some help from your campus news service. You can also put your office staff to work rounding up the kinds of data or documentation that is pertinent to your particular audience. If one of your clerical people has especially good "digging" skills, let that person work on rounding up budget figures, stories of recent accomplishments by local students, and other appropriate information. If you give your helpers clear guidance as to what you need, they can save you hours of time — and make you look good.

Finally, if you know you will be giving a number of speeches to fairly defined groups of people, develop the habit of saving in a folder the anecdotes, enrollment figures, and other items that come across your desk with any promise as speech material.

Direct communications:
Using media you control

When you can't rely on person-to-person communications, the next most reliable way to deliver your message is through direct communications — that is, communications you prepare for a mass audience over which you have complete control. These can be newsletters, annual reports, pamphlets, videotapes, radio public service announcements, recruitment packages, proposals — even posters, fliers and press releases.

In short, "direct communications" implies that you have control over the content, format, and delivery of the message. There are a host of such communications coming from academic departments and divisions. We have selected just a few of the more ubiquitous varieties to highlight in this chapter.

The newsletter

Audiences: Departmental faculty, staff, and students; campus administrators; other campus colleagues; alumni; donors; parents.

In any academic unit of any size, writes Eble (1990), the leader "should enlarge communication beyond that necessary to unit functioning. A unit in which communication is frequent, varied, and open, and which has the force, lightness, and direction that a good academic leader can provide is less likely to foster wranglings, misunderstandings, and sulking."

A periodic newsletter best serves that purpose for faculty and, particularly, for unit academic staff, professional/technical personnel, classified employees — whatever your campus may call them — who otherwise may feel out of the loop. Staff often are on a unit's front line; they interact frequently with students and the public, creating those all-important first impressions of your unit. Academic leaders often wrongly assume that non-faculty employees are less interested in the unit's mission and accomplishments. The same leaders can be quite ignorant of the influence that their staff people have on campus among their peers and how they initiate and carry out many fruitful activities in the "lower ranks" on behalf of their units. In some cases, staff people, not faculty, are the most *visible* flag-wavers for the unit and need to be well-informed of unit activities.

Think of a newsletter as achieving six objectives among your staff members:

- Creating awareness of the unit's goals

- Providing information on significant developments that affect the unit and employees' lives

- Allowing employees to be more effective goodwill ambassadors

- Encouraging favorable attitudes and enhancing employee performance

- Satisfying employees' desire for news about what's going on in the unit and with their peers

- Recognizing staff's contributions to the unit and the institution

The key term is *news*letter. The writer essentially assumes the role of a rural weekly newspaper editor. Along with dispensing necessary official announcements, policy statements, and cheerleading editorials, you can feature the personal human-interest stories and items about team players doing things that are interesting and/or significant and that will generate eager, regular readership. This doesn't mean the newsletter has to be cutesy or overly clever. But a newsletter with a friendly touch can pay real dividends, not only in staff morale but in ensuring that key administrative messages reach everyone.

For example, when Midland's faculty development officer, Helen White-Morgan, launched a program to better train Ph.D. students in academic career skills, she made sure a suitable story appeared in the campus *Bulletin*, so that departmental secretaries, who have frequent contact with grad students, could help pass along information about the program.

If you are in a research-focused or interdisciplinary unit, a newsletter is a low-cost, high-value means of distributing news of your unit's research activities to other departments, agencies outside the campus, businesses, funding agencies, and the news media. The last group will probably scan your newsletter regularly — if the format is tight and the content is timely — for story ideas ("news leads"). The former groups may be spurred to contact you or your faculty to arrange collaborative efforts or at least exchange ideas.

A departmental newsletter can take the form of a one- or two-page fast-copied, monthly flier; a division may put out an eight-page quarterly; a campus may distribute a weekly tabloid bulletin or newspaper to all members. But remember: in reaching out to your constituents, spirit is as important as form and frequency of publication.

A few tips on putting out your newsletter (Evans 1993, Taylor 1993):

- Develop a mission statement to give your newsletter a focus.

- Use your mission statement to help you distinguish between good and bad news ideas — or appropriate and inappropriate material.

- Establish a policy for the handling of controversial topics.

- Study other periodicals; an idea that worked for somebody else might just work for you.

- Get ideas from your readers. Conduct formal surveys, bind in a card inviting suggestions, encourage phone calls, or establish a "Readers Write" column.

- Cultivate volunteer correspondents to represent key categories of your readers.

- Invite guest editorials or essays.

- Read all of your institution's news releases, catalogs, and other publications. Just because something went out in another medium doesn't mean you can't adapt it to your newsletter.

- Check your back issues and do follow-up stories on "whatever happened to ..."

- Turn dreary "mandated" topics into palatable articles, by conveying heavy cargo through charts and graphs, for example.

- Always keep the readers' needs foremost in your mind.

- Work hard to get strong material.

- Write well.

- Take the time to think up catchy headlines.

- Vary the format occasionally — with a screened box, for instance.

- Evaluate feedback from your audience and adjust your approach accordingly.

The annual report

Audiences: Campus administrators; donors; grant agencies; alumni; colleagues at other institutions; policy-makers; community leaders.

No matter where you sit in a campus hierarchy — as program director, department chair, dean, chancellor, or trustee — somebody is above you, wondering how you are doing. And perhaps the most ubiquitous means of communicating to that "somebody" is an annual report.

It's a valuable habit to squirrel away a copy of every bit of correspondence or record that could conceivably be included in some form in an impending annual report. These materials, collected in a drawer or file folder, become the raw contents of your report.

So what should you be saving and how should you present it? Far from being just a chilly arithmetic balance sheet, an effective annual report presents a clear account of where your academic unit is going, how it is getting there, what it did specifically during the year to stay on track, and what it needs for continued progress in the future.

A brief preface

If filing an annual report is a requirement, it's appropriate to start out with a preface something like: "In keeping with the requirement that. ..." But the preface should also, as Eble writes (1990), "leaven the deadliness of much academic prose" by "addressing the issues currently animating faculty and student conversations" and lifting the level of the report to a visionary plane.

For example, in an "Annual Report of the Dean of the Faculty of Arts and Sciences," Harvard's Henry Rosovsky acknowledged that he and his faculty "operate without a written constitution and with very little common law" and "there is no strong consensus concerning duties and behaviors." As a remedy, Rosovsky proposed a bold step:

> I advocate the creation of a Faculty of Arts and Sciences Commission that would attempt to specify — in broad terms — the principle parameters of citizenship: teaching loads, other obligations to students, proportion of graduate versus undergraduate teaching, limits on outside activities, and similar matters. ... As a faculty, we must reach a new and explicit understanding concerning what we should expect of ourselves and our colleagues.

Executive summary

Sticking to the 30/3/30 formula, which we described in the preceding chapter, you should include a one-page summary of highlights for the busy superior given to scanning documents. Also, give him or her a lively series of chapter headings, each a strong declarative sentence rather than a label. For example, not "Faculty Accomplishments" but "Faculty Set New Pace in Scholarly Productivity," or something like that, so if the headings are all that your superior reads, you will at least have conveyed the essence of your message.

Contents

What you have to say and what impression you wish to make will dictate the contents of the report. You can often supplement and enhance the basic structure with such features as a chronological record of unit advances through the years, the story of a particular program in some detail, profiles of one or two representative individuals — faculty, staff, students — a flow chart of unit operations, pie charts of income and expenses, an account of an average day or week, a dramatized version of how and where the unit's graduates are working, presentations of new findings and services, a wish list of needed resources, and so on.

Strive to elevate the report in tone and substance above the routine and mechanical. Convey a sense of the philosophical moorings of your position, the challenges of shared, dynamic leadership. Make the report warm and human and understandable. And cement all sections together into one logical, interesting whole.

Format

The lower you are in the administrative hierarchy, the more conservative your report's format or "look" probably should be. A department chair, for example, can use whatever format he or she would use for normal corrrespondence with the dean, lest there come the charge of expensive window-dressing. A chancellor or president, on the other hand, may choose to illuminate an annual report with photographs and artwork, so that it can do double duty as a general public relations document for wider audiences. It's sometimes difficult, however, to be frank and explicit enough to meet the needs of a system CEO or a board of trustees in a report that is also going to prospective donors, students, or key government officials. It's much better in such a case to develop multiple editions, wrapping special messages around a core of set material.

Annual reports not only keep the administration abreast of an academic unit's mission, accomplishments, and needs, they have at least four other advantages:

- They become ready background reference for you in drafting other documents, such as research-and-development proposals.

- They serve as standards and spurs for internal audiences.

- Their presence in the files will cause future campus historians to praise your name.

- They can be useful as planning and policy-making tools.

Leonard Wenc (Santovec 1992) illustrates the last advantage. When he came to Carleton College (MN) over 25 years ago as director of student financial services, one of his first assignments was to deliver a report to the board of trustees. "That report was successful in showing where we were and where we were going," he says, "so I disciplined myself to do this on an annual basis."

After the close of each fiscal year, Wenc gathers pertinent data, adds it to a database, and generates a report using five- and ten-year benchmarks, then adds some proposals. The president tosses out about half of those ideas, but he uses the others, according to Wenc. "If I was batting that well in a baseball career," he chuckles, "I'd never have to work again."

So Wenc advocates using the annual report not only for presenting data but also for reflection and shaping policy: "I'm always amazed at the number of my colleagues that don't do an annual report and then complain about not being brought into the strategic planning of an institution. But that's because no one knows what they're doing."

Visual media: The poster

Audiences: Students; department faculty and staff; other campus faculty, staff, and students.

The surest way to grab attention is graphically. If you need reminding, just wander your campus and check out the posters on bulletin boards, sandwich boards, billboards, walls, trees, telephone poles, whatever.

The art of *writing* posters is best summarized with a KISS: "Keep It Sound and Simple." Tell WHOM you're addressing, WHAT you're announcing, WHERE it's happening, WHY it's important, and HOW people can take action. Say it in succinct terms. Then, stop.

The art of *designing* posters is not so simple. If you strive for academic respectability and credibility, your unit's letterhead carries a compelling message. On the other hand, if you want to attract special attention, it might pay to seek the help of a student artist.

Poster size is a question of setting. Most interior bulletin boards encourage or even impose a limit of 8 ½" x 11" or 9" x 12" sheets. On exterior surfaces, almost anything may go. Let discretion be your guide.

Distribution will be no problem if your campus has a service, often operated by students. If not, you're on your own. First, list the places where the students you want to catch are most likely to spend time. Then, get a box of thumbtacks (for interior bulletin boards), a stapler (for exterior boards), and a campus map. Find a student to do the legwork, letting him or her chart the most efficient route. If you are planning to poster only a limited number of *departmental boards* and you have sufficient lead time, you can mail the posters to the department secretaries with your request for cooperation.

On many larger campuses, your poster will either be removed or covered over by other posters in such short order that generally you need not worry about dated material still hanging about. And if the dates on your poster are written large in the first place, there is little chance of an outdated poster confusing anyone. But if your campus requires that those who put them up take them down, then be sure to schedule your student to go back with his or her map and reclaim them when they have served their purpose.

Posters will always be with us, but high-tech is catching up as an equally effective way to reach students and staff.

For example, when the University of Vermont was hit by the measles a few years ago, officials posted vaccination information on a computer network, then put a message about it on terminals in the library and in campus laboratories. To reach those who were not using computers, the university placed the vaccination message on the campus closed-circuit TV system and sent a voice mail message to every campus telephone.

The information was available to the campus community two hours after university officials met to discuss the problem and two hours before the story could be reported on a local TV news program or in the press. Now, that's fast — and effective! (Hardin 1993)

The periodical

Audiences: Alumni; parents; donors; students; prospective students; prospective employers.

Alumni and donors (they are often one and the same) are among the most important audiences of any college or university. As a group they show virtually unlimited loyalty; any effective communications program will cherish them accordingly.

There is virtually no limit to what your good alumni can do for your unit and the campus provided:

- You keep them fully informed about the objectives, policies, progress, and problems of your unit.

- Your unit serves society well and can make them proud.

- You give them an opportunity to perform challenging tasks for your unit.

Every institution cultivates its alumni through an association. Some associations are part of the institution, some are independent, and some are quasi independent. Each arrangement has its advantages and disadvantages, in terms of the association's publications. Internal alumni associations may be easier for the institution to control, but their publications may be less independent and seem less credible to their readers.

The more decentralized an institution, the more alumni loyalties tend to lie with the divisions and departments within that institution. So, unit heads should develop their own periodicals, to communicate directly with their graduates.

But before you create a publication, examine your *campus* alumni magazine and its circulation. Is it automatically sent to all alumni or only to those who subscribe? Is there any way to find out how many from your unit receive it? If it's going to all of your alums, can you arrange with the editor to develop a page or a column or even a special issue devoted to your college or unit? Would that meet your needs? Or is there more you want to say to former students?

If the answer is "Yes, much more," then it's time to determine the costs and expected benefits of your own periodical and exactly which grads you want to reach. Kinship with alumni varies by discipline, by size of academic unit, and by emphasis on baccalaureate versus advanced degrees. For example, large professional schools or some departments in the humanities may keep track only of their former graduate students. A good deal depends on the gestalt of your unit *and* the availability of support for compiling and maintaining mailing lists. If the benefits are sound and the audience is clear, then you should move on to the planning stage.

Several characteristics mark an effective periodical aimed at alumni, although the relative importance varies according to the periodical:

- Reports on what's happening on the campus today (with a histocial perspective)

- Human interest reports about alumni

- Interpretations of current events in the light of developments in higher education

- Focus throughout on the significance of the alma mater's mission and the role of alumni in its accomplishments

Most division or department alumni periodicals tend to be too parochial; they fail to address the issues affecting higher education as a whole and fail to relate the impact of those issues on the unit.

What should your periodical look like? Flash is less important than substance — well-written, thoughtful articles. Your publication can be a four-page sheet, a simple eight-page newsprint tabloid, or a larger glossy piece. Some units publish annually, while others go biannually, quarterly, or bimonthly. (Remember: increased frequency will help keep mailing addresses more current; the U.S. Postal Service will return undeliverable mail *and* give you the new address for only a limited time after an addressee has moved.)

Whatever the form of your periodical, someone has to prepare it — that is, write articles and other features, organize the gathering of class information (if that is to be included), and arrange the logistics of printing and mailing. This can take a considerable amount of time and skill and should not be simply delegated to the nearest warm body.

Midland University has an Alumni Creed that goes like this:

"We believe that the graduate is a member of a society bound by a spiritual tie of faith in the ideals of higher education." Corny as that may sound, Midland alumni seem to believe it.

The alumni of most institutions feel the same way. Department chairs and deans who don't mine this rich ore of support by putting out an alumni periodical are missing a sure bet. Why would an academic leader not communicate systematically in some way with the people into whom the institution placed such an investment of time and resources, in order to help engender support for oncoming generations of those same types of students?

The proposal

Audiences: Granting agencies; trustees; administrators; and donors.

The proposal is a time-honored form of direct communication and no population is better versed in its use than faculty. There is no compelling reason to go into much detail on this form of communication because, by the time you become an administrator, one thing is sure: you can write proposals.

It is worth mentioning here, however, that proposals are finding currency with new audiences. Traditionally used for winning grants, proposals are also becoming a common tool in private fund-raising. Whether called a "case statement" or a "statement of need," communications prepared for donors are, in essence, proposals. You are most likely to succeed if you organize well, write well, and take into account the donor's point of view.

Just as grant proposals are tailored to a particular agency, so should documents prepared for donors be tailored to their special interests and needs.

One of the best outlines for preparing proposals comes from Judith Ruderman of Duke(1992). Many of these tips also apply

when it come to approaching for support your most generous alum
or your most tight-fisted dean or president:

1. Give your proposal a title or headline that is
   diagnostic but not catchy or trendy.

2. Begin with a capsule statement, abstract, or
   executive summary — whatever you prefer
   to call it — in which you distill the jist of the
   proposal or its main points. It's a good idea
   to draft this statement before you write the
   proposal so that it can serve as a guide for
   the text — even if you revise the summary
   later. If you can't write that summary now, it
   could mean you are one of those people who
   likes to write the summary last — or it could
   mean your idea is not defined enough yet to
   qualify for funding.

3. The body of the proposal begins with a statement of the problem or need, demonstrating
   its importance and the significance of your
   project in solving the problem or meeting the
   need. You stress how your solution is innovative and suitable for the task. If a bibliog-
   raphy is in order, append it to the proposal.

4. The narrative continues with the objectives
   of the project. Be very clear about what you
   hope to accomplish.

5. Next come your procedures or methodology
   for meeting the stated objectives. It's impressive if you can include a proposed timeline.

6. An evaluation plan for your project follows;
   that is, a plan for determining if the objectives have been met.

7. Next you will present the needed resources
   — your personnel and facilities for undertaking the project. This includes you. With

whatever evidence you can muster, with all due modesty explain your particular qualifications, employing testimonials if you have them. But don't include a full vitae here; append a tailored version of your résumé to the proposal.

8. The final section the proposal is the budget, itemizing major categories of expenses. (Some people say a little padding never hurts; others underestimate, intending to come back for more. We advise a realistic budget without frills the first time.) So that your figures are clear and accurate, get some help from the campus office of research administration. And keep the total amount requested realistic in terms of the source in funding projects similar to yours.

Modified to fit your specific audience, these eight points should help you better communicate your needs and improve your chances of securing the resources to meet them.

The fact sheet or brochure

Audiences: All.

And now we come to that most basic medium of communication, practically regardless of audience — the fact sheet or general brochure.

No matter what other media you can or can't match to what audiences, develop a comprehensive, complete, yet brief statement of academic unit history, mission, operations, and goals. The ideal format is a 4" x 9" folder that will fit readily into a standard #10 business envelope as well as into a purse or breast pocket; can be attached handily to another document; and is easily updated as needed.

In some ways, a brochure or fact sheet is akin to the one-page "quick use guides" that accompany the many-paged users' manuals for such equipment as VCRs and telephone answering machines. It's the bare basics in one compact sheet.

The uses to which you can put such a utilitarian publication are multiple. Robert S. Topor, a former university publication information director, has prepared a readable guide to the way academic leaders ought to plan, prepare, and evaluate fact sheets and brochures — *Marketing Communications* (1993). Its approach is based on information collected from targeted audiences.

For detailed examples, we refer you to chapter nine, in which Perkins lays out the essentials of her new master's degree program in both a fact sheet and brochure.

Indirect communications: Using media outside your control

To reach a broader audience with your message, you will rely on indirect communications — getting coverage or stories placed in the campuswide newsletter, newspaper, or alumni magazine — over which you have minimal influence. (See chapter seven.) At the same time, to reach the general public with your message, you will almost certainly need to rely in large part on the news media over which you have *no* control. The next chapter is devoted to working with news media.

chapter eleven

A Special Audience — The News Media

Dealing with the gatekeepers

Earlier in this book, we described newspapers, television, radio, and news magazines as independent agents — media outside our control. We also referred to mass media reporters and editors as gatekeepers because their judgments determine how much of what we offer as news material is accepted and passed along to the readers, listeners, and viewers.

In this sense, *the media gatekeepers are an audience in their own right:* the information that you deliver must first appeal to *them* and meet *their* criteria before it can reach a wider audience. In other words, you must prove yourself a credible source of information and provide material that is truly newsworthy. This concept applies whether you are trying to woo them or to cope with their unwanted attentions. To deal with this special audience, you must first understand the media — which we will try to help you do in this chapter.

What is news and what makes a campus newsworthy?

The classic definition of news is that it's an *interesting, unusual, and/or significant event occurring within the past 24 hours*. It has also been defined as *information that is factual, not generally known, and that will be interesting to many people*. We might also add that *controversy almost automatically means news*. If your institution has enacted controversial policies, is conducting controversial research, or has an expert who can discuss some aspect of the forces at work in a public controversy, you can almost be guaranteed media attention.

Every event has a frequency or time-span in which the event unfolds and takes on meaning. The closer the frequency of the event to the daily, twice-daily, or hour-by-hour time frame of the news medium, the more likely that the event will be seen as news.

Significant vs. eventful news

That requirement — that news be a definable event occurring in a definable time frame — means that much of what happens on campus, be it a long-term minority student recruitment effort, a five-year study of community health practices, or a lifetime study of cell biology, does not strictly qualify as news. On the other hand, what goes on at your institution, even if very slowly, often has an overriding *significance* that ultimately demands acknowledgment from the media.

The late Bob Doyle, veteran reporter of the former *Milwaukee Journal*, who later became vice president for public affairs of the University of Wisconsin System, once explained why news media editors want news about your institution:

> They want it because higher education news has two inherent "I"s.
>
> One "I" is for Interesting. It attracts attention because it's close to the interests of many people — present and

potential parents, present and potential students, alumni, staff, faculty, employees, taxpayers. News about higher education helps create an audience for advertisers and — in the case of newspapers — for editorial writers.

The other "I" is for Important. Higher education news enables newspapers and broadcasting stations to fulfill their obligations to keep the public informed about significant events and trends. It stimulates discussion and generates reader/listener response. It helps the taxpayers and voters to decide who are the Good Guys and who are the Bad Guys.

Importance of "event" pegs

Reporters often respond more positively to your phone call or press release when you provide an "excuse" that permits them to put news of an ongoing higher-education activity into their *event-dictated format.*

Three quick examples:

- When the head of the five-year health study reports his preliminary two-year results in a public health journal, your unit can prepare a news release that media can run on the day the journal is distributed. Summarize the contents of the report and briefly review the goals of the project.

- The day before your annual report on minority recruitment is officially released, send a copy to the media with a press release and background information and arrange for them to interview the key players.

- On the day that the cell biologist makes a presentation to a major scientific meeting, ask a campus science reporter to distribute a story that explains the scientist's findings and summarizes the work leading up to it.

In other words, capitalize on *dated events* to tell your significant and ongoing stories. (Often science or medicine reporters respond better than other reporters to ongoing activities; they know that basic research is only sporadically event-related.)

Understanding the culture of the news media

Besides the newsworthiness of your activities, many other factors affect the delicate tension between your institution and the news media. The sooner you recognize and understand these factors, the sooner you will achieve a reasonable working relationship.

News media are businesses and subject to business bias

You have to recognize that you are dealing with a business whose primary mission is to make a profit by selling a service. That service consists largely of news, entertainment, and self-help tips. Only by attracting and holding audiences can a news medium stay solvent and flourish — and only by helping the news people accomplish their task can you expect to occupy their pages and airwaves.

Through a process of what is called social control in the newsroom, newspaper publishers and radio/TV station owners can bring subtle pressures to bear on reporters and editors in support of the faith that what's good for business is good for us. At times that can make campus boosters out of reporters; at other times, just the opposite.

Media are active in community conflict resolution

News media play a role in conflict resolution, tension control, and community cohesion. In a small city, that tends to mean that the media downplay controversy. In a large city, the media tend to serve as liaison among conflicting subsystems, airing more fully any conflict-related information.

News media bear a legal and ethical responsibility to serve the public interest

Their public interest obligation is one of the reasons why they should be interested in you and your institution. By tradition or statute, they are common carriers of uncensored information, theoretically covering all sides of an issue. Thus, don't expect a mass medium to "sell" your institution's viewpoint (unless that happens to be in the medium's interest) or to consistently purvey your view alone. That doesn't mean that news media can't be influenced; of course they can. But controlled? No! And we wouldn't want it any other way in an open society.

There is no denying that "freedom of the press" can take disappointing turns when the reporter covers a perspective that radically differs from your own. Perkins was reminded of this tendency when the press release announcing her new graduate degree program was picked up by the *Carthage Globe-Times* in the home of rival State University. Here's the story that ran:

State U. Pres Views New Midland Program with Alarm

In the wake of the announcement yesterday that Midland University is inaugurating a new master of science program in biological conservation and sustainable development, State University President J. Kenneth Thomas today expressed concern that "we're spreading our educational resources too thin."

"There should be some sort of commission review or otherwise we'll see competitive programs like this cropping up all over the place," he told the Downtown Carthage Rotary Club at its Monday luncheon.

State University holds claim to being the public center for environmental teaching, research, and service, he said, while as an independent institution Midland has "no business in the act."

> Midland President William Bradford Jones was unavailable for comment. According to a Midland press release, the new program will provide students with a specialized curriculum in ....

Perkins was and embarrassed stunned by Thomas' reaction. While she had consulted with faculty peers at State before developing her program, her president apparently had not talked to Thomas to get his cooperation on the program. On reflection, Perkins chose to look on the bright side. As she told her colleagues, "Without Thomas' reaction we might not have made it into the *Globe-Times* at all, much less on the front page. Besides, they spelled our names right and gave a pretty good summary of our program." She also might have added that Thomas ended up looking defensive and a bit mean-spirited in his attempt to claim a monopoly on the discipline, something that did not enhance *his* image. The moral: don't lose sleep over media you can't control.

Open records, open doors

In their role as objective representatives of the "public," the media are strong advocates of open records and open meetings laws, which provide all citizens (including reporters) with access to certain information about activities of tax-supported institutions. The scope of such laws varies from state to state and they generally have less impact on private educational institutions. Since media tend to push the interpretation of the law as far as it will go, it behooves you to know to what kinds of meetings and records the law applies — and to be sure your faculty also understands them.

In a public institution, you can expect that reporters probably will have rights to view financial documents; names, titles, and salaries of employees; contracts and grants; and internal memos. Personnel actions, performance evaluations, and litigation proceedings are generally not open. Again, if you don't know your institution's policy, it pays to get a copy and read it.

Experience has shown that, even if they gain access to the records they seek, many reporters don't have the time or energy to scrutinize them in detail. Often your honest summary of their contents is accepted at face value by reporters *if* you have established credibility with them and show a willingness to provide the original materials if requested.

News media are bound by deadlines and limited by space

Reporters live and die by deadlines. It follows, then, that you should be aware of those deadlines.

Deadlines vary, but generally, morning papers are based on information collected and written up before 5 p.m. the previous day. So the first deadline for a morning paper generally occurs between 4 p.m. and 6 p.m. Final deadlines are later in the evening. Printing occurs during the night, with slots often left open on the first page to tuck in any urgent evening developments.

The evening paper's deadline occurs around noon. After spending part of the morning preparing their stories for the current day, the reporters then spend the afternoon tracking down stories for the following day. The best time to contact these reporters with your ideas is after 1 p.m.

Weekly newspapers commonly publish on Thursdays or Tuesdays and must receive your material three working days ahead of publication.

A morning TV newscast is based on material collected the previous day. Unlike print editors, newscasters can add or drop any new material up until the time of the broadcast. However, the electronic media face the same limitation as print — the fact that most Americans leave work by 5 p.m. and go home, making them unavailable as sources of information.

Nevertheless, morning papers generally have a small staff on swing shift, monitoring news that comes in through the night.

A submission that isn't current or that is delivered minutes before a deadline has little chance of getting any timely media coverage.

Each news medium is really a *collection* of submedia

Newspapers and magazines have a variety of sections or pages, each focusing on particular subject matter (from science to classifieds to sports) and using various styles of composition. In like fashion, radio and TV have discrete time-blocks — for national news, local news, weather, and sports. Recognizing the particular character of submedia — their philosophical bent, topical emphasis, technical specialty, and so on — will help you target your message more effectively. For instance, if Perkins hopes for a spot in *Better Homes and Gardens*, she would likely target its "Environment" section. If she seeks time on local WERA-TV, she would probably find the most willing reception from the editor of the noontime "Farm and Home" hour.

Media people are educated — but they're not academics

Reporters and editors are individuals, each with his or her particular professional background and personal bent. You may find one more open to your message than another.

Beyond dealing with individual differences, however, you may bump up against a traditional suspicion that academics and media gatekeepers have of one another. Some call it a "copy paper curtain." This schism is nowhere near as sharp as it once was, especially with more and more former mass media reporters taking jobs in campus news offices and almost all reporters now having a college education. But the tension definitely still exists — probably fed by the sometimes considerable income differences between reporters and academics.

Media people often are skeptical about the relevance to the real world of what goes on within ivied halls. Among academics there is a parallel skepticism about the capacity of news people to understand complex issues and report them clearly. (Actually, good journalists hate to make errors and want their stories to be accurate.)

Problems also arise when news editors are poorly prepared or even averse to dealing with one of the most important activities at many institutions — research. For example, when the gate-keeper of your local paper has science phobia and the paper also lacks a science reporter, your best hope is to try to cultivate the interest of another reporter. If you have the time and inclination, you can bring the news editor around to visit your labs and chat with your most articulate researchers. In this way you can gradu-ally remove the mystery from research.

One way to part the copy paper curtain is to become familiar with the reporters and editors who cover higher education. Ask them to stop by when they are on campus. Put names with faces. Treat them respectfully but don't try to be pals. Honor their commit-ment to objectivity.

Find out what news interests them most and least, how they prefer to hear about news — telephone, fax, electronic mail, and so on. Then give them a summary of what's newsworthy at the moment. They may put more credence in the news judgment of your campus science editor, in which case he or she may be your best conduit for news.

Developing a personal rapport with reporters paid off at Midland College. Before the vice president for university relations came on board, relations between President Jones and the media were strained. Though he answered media inquiries honestly, he was shy and uncomfortable with reporters, so he tried to avoid them. The media interpreted this as arrogance. Consequently, he was consistently cast in a negative light by media writers whenever Midland was the focus of controversy. The harsher the media treatment, the more Jones tried to avoid reporters.

It didn't take the new VP long to size up the situation. She quickly recognized not only that the president had great integrity, intel-ligence, and personal charm, but that he was at his best in *informal* situations. Over a few months she persuaded Jones that he could break the tension with the media if he would periodically meet them in his own surroundings in a relaxed gathering — not a press conference, but a brown-bag lunch in his office. The first brown-bag brought a thaw in relations that continued to improve with subsequent sessions.

News media are tied to the "beat" system

News people are systematic in their approach to gathering information. They also try to avoid stumbling over one another in pursuit of the same story. Hence, the beat system. Each reporter has an assigned beat — courts, city hall, business, education, and so on. When an event fits neatly into a beat area, there's no problem. But when an event is relevant to two or more beats, it can get lost in the newsroom shuffle — or wind up with comprehensive coverage.

Don't hit every editor or reporter at a newspaper or radio station with the same announcement. Direct your information to the person who has the most control in deciding whether it gets used; usually that's also the person most likely to use it. Also, keep track of changes in beats on your daily local and regional media and update your contact list often.

To arrange interviews, Robert S. Topor, a specialist in higher education public relations and author of *Media and Marketing: A Powerful New Alliance for Higher Education* (1993), lists the following as the most likely opportunities for radio or TV coverage:

Type of Program	Gatekeeper
Interview or talk show	Show producer
Newscast	Assignment editor
Review of event or performance	Beat reporter
Public service announcement	Community affairs unit
Community calendar	Calendar compiler
Editorial reply	Public service director

13-plus commandments for good media relations

To ensure the best possible relations with the news media, and to increase your chances of being heard by the media when you have something to say, the late Robert Doyle suggested these still valid "commandments":

1. Use the open door policy — with a vengeance. Let the reporters know they're welcome in your office, whether they can find any news or not. I know one case where, when you walk into the president's office, one of the first things you see is a sign on an empty desk reading "Press Desk." It has a phone, a word processor, and a supply of paper.

2. Talk and write in plain English. Strive consistently to say what you have to say clearly and simply in short sentences. Declare war on "gobbledygook," "bafflegab," and "academese." Every discipline seems to develop a special vocabulary, and that's fine, but shelve it when you're talking to the public. On the other hand, don't talk down — either to reporters or to your other audiences.

3. Know your business. The academic administrator who wins the respect of the news media is one who obviously knows all about his or her unit — its history, mission, operations, plans, people. He or she doesn't have to give vague answers. He or she is a dependable, fluent source of information.

4. If possible, make the top person in the unit the spokesperson. Let the reporter talk to the boss, the person who makes the policy decisions and is in the best position to know all their nuances.

5. Adopt a straight answer policy. If you can't answer, say so and explain why. Don't hedge or evade. If the news is bad, face up to it. If somebody has goofed, admit it. You'll be better off in the long run through the trust you generate via frank and honest dealings.

6. Get acquainted with reporters, editors, and photographers. In spite of the adage, familiarity often breeds respect and goodwill. Pay an occasional call to the media's offices so you can learn something of their environment and *weltanschauung*. (Getting to know editors and reporters as individuals works to their benefit and yours.)

7. Try to develop a nose for news. Read varied news stories and listen or watch varied newscasts. That's the best way to learn what editors think is news. Watch especially what they disseminate about your unit and institution so you'll spot the news interest in a similar event or situation the next time. (Learn to think visually for television and to think locally for the hometown media.)

8. Give reporters tips on news other than that of your unit. Maybe you know of an interesting and untold story that has nothing to do with higher education — some kind of human interest or business success story, for instance. The best thing you can do for a reporter is to give him or her a good story.

I recommend against giving anything else — such as a gift at holiday time which could embarrass both of you if it were returned. If it were kept, the reporter might lean over backward to make sure you hadn't influenced his or her news judgment to the extent that he or she might not give as good a break as you deserve. (The exception to Doyle's rule is a note of thanks if a reporter has done a particularly good job of covering an issue or event.)

9. Be fair in releasing news. If you issue a news release, give it to all outlets simultaneously. But if a reporter shows enough enterprise to dig up a story on your unit on his or her own, it's his or her story. Don't feed it to a competitor. (Since different media have different deadlines — morning, evening, midday — fairness also requires that you attempt to alternate your release times so that all the major papers and networks get a crack at being first on one story or another.)

10. Take the initiative in releasing news. If you're doing something that you're reasonably sure is newsworthy (or if you or your staff have expertise that ties well into current events or into a medium's particular focus), speak up, either directly or through your campus news service, depending on local ground rules. (Most campus news services discourage your independent contact with the media, but are very happy to act on your behalf — if only you will let them in on the news!) You don't have to write a news release — a note or memo may do just as well. Or a phone call. If they want more, they will let you know.

11. Base your actions on what you think is right, not how you think they'll look in the media.

12. Don't ask to OK a reporter's story. That's a good way to lose friends fast among news media people. It's like telling the reporter, "I don't think you are competent to report accurately what I've just told you." Many good

reporters will check back with their sources on a complicated story if they have time. (If it is a complex topic or issue and you have the time, you can help prevent errors by providing the reporter with a background sheet enumerating the key points and providing relevant figures or statistics. Also, "checking back" is standard policy with most campus news services when they prepare news releases on behalf of your unit.)

13. Try to understand the reporter's deadlines. Every reporter has had the experience of calling a campus office for information in connection with a fast-breaking news story. The reporter may have 10 minutes to get the information written and to an editor. The official says he or she is busy and suggests that the reporter call back Monday for the information. Media relations have just hit a new low with a frustrated reporter. (To avoid this situation in your unit, discuss with your office staff, academic staff, and faculty the importance of responding promptly to media inquiries. They themselves need not necessarily do the responding, but they must make sure that *some* knowledgeable person does, immediately.)

Doyle summarized his advice this way:

> One. Keep your door open.
> Two. Do your job well.
> Three. Use plain English.

Here are some other commandments to keep in mind:

- Remember whose side you're on. Stable relations with media depend to a certain extent on you playing your "role" and letting them play theirs. In cases where controversy is involved, reporters like to investigate on their own; they get confused and suspicious when you act like an investigative reporter. While they expect honesty from you and expect you to comply with open records laws, they also expect that you will represent your institution's interests. They do not expect you to provide negative information that they don't know exists or to answer incriminating questions that they haven't asked.

- Never call a reporter to ask if he or she received your news release. This tops all reporters' lists of "irritating things." If they don't respond to your news, they were not interested or are too busy to respond now.

- Do not call a reporter when he or she is close to a deadline. Find out those deadlines for the reporters you deal with most often and leave them in peace at those times.

- Don't underestimate a reporter's or editor's knowledge or intellect. They talk to a lot of people and digest and synthesize a lot of information. There's a good reason why the PBS show *Washington Week in Review* uses media reporters as its panel of expert observers of the political scene: they know what's going on and are sharp analysts of public opinion and social trends.

Getting your message into the news media

Work with your news or public information office

Use your public information office as your liaison; the staff are experts at working with the media. As Sally Pobojawski, science reporter at the University of Michigan, explained in a letter to journalists (1992):

At the University of Michigan ... information officers receive an average of 35 requests for assistance from members of the media every week. We can provide first-hand information about a scientist's research, publications history, availability, personality and interview style. We can cut through the bureaucracy, we can persuade publicity-shy scientists that talking to a journalist won't trash their reputations, and we can soothe wounded egos when a scientist gets "misquoted."

In addition to responding to media requests, we make an active effort to bring news to the attention of national, state and local media. The days when public information officers could simply churn out press releases and wait for reporters to call are over. Tomorrow's research announcement can make today's story obsolete.

So, sometimes we call. And mail press releases, if the story can wait. And send faxes if it can't. Our goal is not to pressure journalists but to provide timely, accurate and useful information.

The best thing you can do to increase your coverage by media is to help your media relations or news service work for you. Here's how:

- Feed your news service stories with lots of appeal that are based on credible sources.

- Provide your news service with a list of trade publications and other media in your discipline that you know have news sections and an inherent interest in your activities.

- Encourage your faculty and staff to "think news" and become more aware of the news potential of their activities.

- Encourage your faculty and staff to be available when your media relations professionals call on them to provide assistance or talk with reporters.

Give stories a hook — and a human angle

If you do your own news reporting, then, whenever possible, tie your story to a current event. Whether you are calling a reporter or preparing a press release, do your research so that you can craft a lead or an angle that gets the editor's attention.

The natural corollary to a good news hook is to highlight the human element. We often fail to tell the human story behind our accomplishments. Put real people in your stories and describe their struggles to overcome obstacles and the random chance that sometimes leads to success.

Also, take the initiative on issues of real concern in education. If you have faculty who research and lecture on bilingualism, access to education, tuition and public funding of schools, and similar topics, make them visible and available to the media. The public expects people employed in the educational system, including those in colleges and universities, to be experts in education rather than in medieval languages or trinomial equations. Try to capitalize on this interest in educational trends.

Be patient

Remember: when a story is played by one medium, it has a good chance of catching the attention of other media. Don't make the mistake of thinking that local media coverage doesn't count. A good story develops a life of its own, appearing in places you never expected to reach. Besides the wire services, which monitor your local media and thus are very important sources for many *other* media, there are the enterprising reporters and editors who keep track of what is being covered elsewhere. For example, specialized reporters of print and electronic media regularly skim major technical and trade publications, such as *Chemical and Engineering News* or *Medical World News*. Thus, information that originally attracted the attention of specialty publications may be featured in the business or medicine section of the regular news media.

Use the appropriate delivery systems

There are a number of ways to contact the media — telephone, fax, email, news release, and so on. Ask the reporters you deal with most often which delivery systems they prefer.

The telephone and email

Telephone is the primary means for reporters to collect promising news items and track down corroborating information. Hearing a summary of an item and having a chance to ask a few probing questions let a reporter immediately decide whether the item merits attention or not. Many prefer the telephone over paper communication. Recently, however, some have gone almost entirely to email communications.

It is important that you not contact reporters with mundane items, just hoping for a little publicity. You will end up irritating them and losing your credibility. Wait until you have something really worthwhile. Then, call them during the slack part of their day.

Finally, be persistent in promoting a story — but also know when to quit.

The news release

The news release or press release should be a tightly crafted, objective description of an event, activity, or policy action. It is delivered to the media by mail or, if urgent, by fax. Some reporters now accept material by email. In cases where the campus is one of the area's biggest newsmakers, there may be a direct electronic link to distribute releases to the media.

Though most media will not use your release verbatim, it helps reporters frame your message accurately and provides background information and quotes from spokespersons. It makes a reporter's job easier, which in turn benefits you.

In setting up a news release, the information of greatest importance is at the top — in the first one or two paragraphs. This is called the *lead* and it includes all the who, what, why, when, and where facts. Supporting information is arranged in subsequent paragraphs in descending order of importance, the inverted pyramid structure. Thus, if an editor cuts a two-page story after the first page, the reader still receives the essential information.

Releases commonly use short sentences and the active voice. Paragraphs are also short — generally one or two sentences long. Any technical word is replaced with a more common term or the word is defined. Basically, a press release aims at the reading level of someone with a high school education.

Though some writers use catchy or dramatic wording in their lead to hook the reader's attention, newswriting should not be flowery or express personal opinion through excessive use of adjectives and adverbs. Stick to the facts.

Finally, the information in a news story is commonly attributed to someone — to the scientist doing research, to the dean of admissions reporting on enrollment trends, or to the president making an announcement. Frequently, the attribution occurs in the form of a direct quote.

Press releases follow a set format. They are most often printed on 8 ½" x 11" letterhead, have wide margins to allow for editors' notations, are double-spaced and one-sided, are no longer than two or three pages, and have a brief capsule headline. Each new paragraph is emphasized by a deep indent of six to eight spaces. Commonly, only one space is inserted between sentences.

At the top of the page are the contact names and phone numbers of the in-house reporter and/or the faculty source. (It is critical that somebody *actually be at those phone numbers* to respond to media queries following the release of the story.) Also near the top of the page is the release date. Sometimes you attach an "embargo date," which means that the story is not to be printed or aired before the specified day and hour. Embargoes generally are used on research stories, which first must be announced at a scientific meeting or by the funding agency. Use embargoes sparingly.

To indicate that there are additional pages following the first sheet, type "more" at the bottom of each page. Each additional page beyond the first page (which has no number) is marked at the top in a distinctive journalistic style; for example, "Academic rankings — add 1," "Academic rankings — add 2," and so on. Many institutions, however, have dispensed with the traditional format and now simply put just the page number at the top center of each subsequent page. The end of the story is indicated by the number 30 (-30-) or by two or three hash marks (###).

A topic that is technical or that has important aspects that cannot easily be included in a basic release may be accompanied by a *background sheet* that provides additional details or explanation.

On the next few pages is a news release in standard format. We print it in detail here to show its organization and style.

Note that the most newsworthy information is put into the first few paragraphs. This release accompanied a press conference, as is noted in the story. The press attending also were given a written statement by the chancellor and a copy of the actual "Pledge," which was signed in a "media moment" by the chancellor and the four school superintendents. This particular story received front-page coverage in the *Los Angeles Times* as well as the local media, then was picked up by *The Chronicle of Higher Education.*

A few weeks later, when faculty and students had scheduled a demonstration to protest the UC Regent action on affirmative action, the UC Berkeley chancellor sought to get out ahead of the news with a follow-up story on The Berkeley Pledge and what had happened since the early September press conference. That news release, in part, follows the first release.

Letterhead

FOR IMMEDIATE RELEASE

9/7/95—File #14246Contact: Jesus Mena
 (510) 642-3734

UC Berkeley commits $1 million in new partnership pledge to California's K-12 students

Oakland — At an East Oakland high school, Chancellor Chang-Lin Tien today pledged to California's youth that the University of California at Berkeley will do everything possible to give them the opportunity to receive a first-rate college education, no matter what their race, ethnicity, or gender.

Flanked by superintendents of four Bay Area school districts, Tien immediately committed $1 million to launch The Berkeley Pledge, a statewide effort to revitalize the partnership between UC Berkeley and the California school system.

In a speech to students at the school, Tien said he wanted to reassure students that, following the UC Regents' action in July, UC Berkeley remains committed to its celebrated diversity.

The Regents' decision eliminated race, ethnicity and gender from consideration in student admissions by 1997, but it also called on UC campuses to "take relevant actions to develop and support programs" that increase "the eligibility rate of groups which are 'underrepresented' in the university's pool of applicants," Tien said.

"As a public university, our campus has a historic responsibility to serve all of California," said Tien. "Our commitment has made Berkeley an international model for excellence through diversity. We do not intend to retreat from our commitment.

"We want all students to know they have an opportunity to receive the finest education at Berkeley — no matter whether their skin is white or brown, no matter whether they attend schools in the inner city or the suburbs," said Tien. "We pledge to keep opportunity alive."

-more-

Endorsing UC Berkeley's Pledge were Waldemar Rojas, superintendent of San Francisco Unified School District; Jack McLaughlin, Berkeley Pledge — add one superintendent of Berkeley Unified School District; Herbert M. Cole Jr., superintendent of West Contra Costa County Unified School District; and Terry Mazany, representing Carolyn Getridge, superintendent of Oakland Unified School District.

The four Bay Area superintendents are the first of the K-12 administrators throughout the state who will be asked to sign the pledge by UC Berkeley in the coming months.

The press conference was held at Fremont High School's Media Academy, a student journalism program with a stellar reputation. The school was selected as the site because its population includes substantial numbers of disadvantaged students who reflect the obstacles faced by inner city youth.

Beginning in 1997, UC will be the first major university system in the country that will no longer consider race and ethnicity in student admissions.

Tien has acknowledged that maintaining diversity will be a major challenge. The Berkeley Pledge, he said, is an example of the creative approaches needed to ensure the university meets the needs of California's diverse population.

The Berkeley Pledge has three basic components:

- First, the UC Berkeley campus will work to ensure that all students who show potential, yet face major obstacles, are linked to outreach programs that can help them build their academic records. The K-12 school superintendents agree to help identify these students. Furthermore, school administrators will enhance their collaboration with UC on issues of teacher training and curricula development.

- Second, the campus will work to ensure that students who are admitted can afford to attend UC Berkeley. The campus has already pledged to raise $60 million in student scholarships over the next five years and is committed to developing financial aid packages to make UC Berkeley affordable.

-more-

- Third, students recruited to the campus will receive the academic support they need toeinsure they succeed.

Berkeley Pledge — add two

This includes faculty and graduate student mentoring and intensive discussion sessions to address specific needs of these recruited students. Advanced campus programs will help motivate exceptionally talented students to attend graduate school.

The Berkeley Pledge enhances the coordination of existing programs, expands the scope of others, and creates new ones as resources permit.

Outreach services already provided by the campus are extensive. In 1994-95, these programs reached thousands of students in more than 300 California schools.

Tien has appointed a faculty task force to review current programs and recommend improved coordination as well the possible creation of new ones. Martin Sanchez-Jankowski, professor of sociology, will chair the Outreach Task Force.

The UC Berkeley campus also has created The Berkeley Recruitment Corps, which will step up efforts to recruit the state's very best students. The effort will be headed by Vice Chancellor for Undergraduate Affairs Genaro Padilla and Rick Russell, Jr., president of the California Alumni Association and a UC Regent.

Among the most innovative and vital components of The Berkeley Pledge is the proposed Berkeley Academy, an intensive summer program that will draw young people from throughout the state. It will offer advanced courses, providing academic skills that will be essential for college entry. The Berkeley Academy will also work in collaboration with high school teachers, offering opportunities to participate in summer institutes at UC Berkeley and increasing teacher interaction with campus faculty.

Tien emphasized that today's announcement is just the start of his outreach campaign. He, along with other top campus leaders, plans to visit students and schools throughout the state as the campus strengthens its partnership with the California school system.

###

FOR IMMEDIATE RELEASE

10/10/95—File #16262   Contact: Jesus Mena
                                        (510) 642-3734

California Superintendent of Public
Instruction and UC Berkeley join
hands on the Berkeley Pledge

Berkeley — California Superintendent of Public Instruction De-laine Eastin has agreed to serve on the policy board of The Berkeley Pledge, a statewide outreach program launched last month by UC Berkeley Chancellor Chang-Lin Tien.

"I will work hard to strengthen the ties between higher education and K-12," said Eastin. "The Berkeley Pledge is a wonderful idea. It's a win-win situation. I hope it can become a model for the whole state."

The endorsement by the state's top public school educator reflects the breadth of support The Berkeley Pledge has garnered since it was first announced by Tien on Sept. 7.

Tien announced The Berkeley Pledge in an effort to preserve the campus' celebrated diversity despite historic changes in University of California Board of Regents' policy on student admissions. Beginning in 1997, UC will be the first major university system in the country that will no longer consider race, ethnicity or gender in the process of student admissions.

Tien committed $1 million of discretionary funding to The Berkeley Pledge and said he would recruit additional funding from private sources and foundations.

Since the time of the announcement, William K. Coblentz, a prominent San Francisco lawyer, has donated $25,000 to The Berkeley Pledge. Tien personally has contributed $10,000 of the pay raise given him by the UC Regents to the fund as well.

Furthermore, United Way has added The Berkeley Pledge as one of the options for donors to its annual drive through employers in the San Francisco area.

The UC Berkeley partnership with the schools is exemplified by the work being done with the San Francisco Unified School District.

UC Berkeley faculty, including Tien, have worked with the district to revamp the Galileo High School curriculum. ...

###

The strategy behind the second release was to get some positive news out and to set the proposed faculty/student demonstration in some context — emphasizing that the campus was taking steps to maintain its diverse student population despite the Regent policy. The effort paid off. The ABC News reporter sent to cover the Oct. 12 demonstration spent the previous day doing a story on The Berkeley Pledge, visiting San Francisco's Galileo High School, and interviewing campus officials, including Tien.

The press kit, or packet, is a news release accompanied by supporting materials. It provides media with an organized collection of pertinent information to help them report on a particular event or activity. The press kit is indispensable for meetings, forums, press conferences, exhibits, and institutional celebrations. You can distribute the kit at the event or mail it in advance. The kit generally includes a press release, an agenda of events with correct names and titles of participants, a copy of the key speaker's statement or speech, a fact sheet on the subject, biographical information on participants, reproductions of any graphs or charts, and a fact sheet on the sponsoring institution. It may also include recent relevant news articles, photos, or a glossary of terms.

The press kit

The purpose of the media advisory, which is akin to an invitation, is to notify the media about upcoming events and/or activities, explaining the who, what, why, when, and where of the occasion. The advisory is brief and to the point, generally a page or less. The Widmeyer Group, communications consultants, says this about advisories (1992):

Media advisory

> Send advisories to your state/local media list, which should include journalists who regularly cover education issues or related issues. Make sure you send an

advisory to your state and/or local wire services for inclusion in their "daybook" listing of events. Even if you know that a reporter or news organization will likely not attend your event because of time limitations or other reasons, send an advisory anyway; they may want to contact a wire service or freelancer to cover the event for them, or schedule an interview for a later date.

Send advisories at least three to five days in advance, but not more than a week, unless holidays interfere with the timing. An advisory sent too far in advance can get lost in the shuffle.

If your event is public, send your advisory, or a modified form, to the media's community calendars as well.

A sample media advisory follows:

Media Advisory   For more information:
March 10, 1995   Amanda Perkins
Release: Immediately   (512) 820-7095

Open House at Midland Department

The Department of Botany and Applied Ecology at Midland University will host prospective students, their parents, and teachers at a special open house on Saturday, March 15, 1995, from 10:00 a.m. to 4:00 p.m. at Wayland Hall on campus.

Laboratories will be open to demonstrate the department's facilities and to show off current research projects of honors undergraduates. In addition, a special exhibit, "Art in Biology," will feature a unique collaboration between art and science programs at Midland.

Chair Amanda Perkins will make a brief address and introduce faculty at 12:00 noon during the buffet luncheon in Room 12, Wayland Hall. Wayland Hall is located at 110 Forest St. Parking will be available in the lot at the corner of Forest and Lake Streets.

-30-

Note: Facilities and refreshments will be available for the media in Room 8. The new electron microscope in the cellular biology laboratory, the undergraduate projects, and the art exhibit will offer several interesting photo opportunities. The art exhibit includes a series of colorful ceramic sculptures entitled "Houses of the Sun," depicting stylized plant cell interiors.

A tip is what it sounds like — a suggestion to a reporter about a topic that should make a good news story. Tips are often made over the phone, particularly if you know the reporter.

The tipsheet

You also can send them out in the form of a *tipsheet,* which ranges from a memo focusing on one topic to a couple of pages of "mini-releases," issued monthly or quarterly, describing several or a dozen activities on campus or in your unit. Each topic usually gets one to three paragraphs, which may begin with a catchy title and lead. A phone number is provided for any follow-up.

Reporters want good stories. They will do your work for you if you'll give them your ideas.

For example, every college town newspaper likes to cover graduation with a profile or two of interesting graduates. All you need to do is tell reporters who those graduates are and how to reach them.

Here is an excerpt from a tipsheet of student profiles put out by the public information office of Southern Illinois University at Edwardsville prior to a recent graduation:

Undergraduate degree candidates:

Joyce Ann and Judith Marie Baudendistel, twins from Fults. They are both candidates for bachelor of science degrees in business administration with specialties in management information systems. For four years the twins went to the same university, majored in the same discipline, worked in the same office as student workers. They are already employed, working for the same company. They can be reached in Fults at (618) 458-6550.

Of course, you should select for your tipsheets stories that will interest the community. What plays in the *Podunk Press* will not necessarily work in the *Boston Globe*.

Tipsheets are an especially good way for science units to interest the media in the work of their researchers. Here is an excerpt from a quarterly tipsheet prepared by the Public Information Office, University of California, Santa Cruz. In this example, the tips could actually stand on their own as short news releases:

Recycled-paper mills produce fewer toxic substances than mills using virgin wood

Producing recycled paper is dramatically cleaner for the environment than making paper products from virgin wood fiber, according to a study by Daniel Press, environmental policy analyst at UCSC. Press found that, relative to mills using virgin wood, recycled-paper mills generate a fraction of the toxic substances such as chlorine, chloroform, ammonia, acids, and solvents that are commonly released in paper manufacturing.

Although the number of mills producing recycled paper remains relatively small industrywide, the environmental impact of paper manufacturing could be greatly improved through the use of recovered wastepaper, Press concluded. He based his study on data reported to the Environmental Protection Agency by pulp and paper manufacturers from 1987 to 1992.

"The pulp and paper industry has been one of the dirtiest industries in the country," says Press, who spoke Sept. 1 at a meeting of the American Political Science Association in New York. "This study confirms the problems faced by the industry, but it also shows the enormous improvement that is possible with new technology and manufacturing processes."

(The last paragraph compares toxins produced per ton of finished product by the two kinds of mills.)

Contact: Daniel Press (408) 459-3263 or dpress@cats.ucsc.edu.

Exploit your academic expertise. Every campus or unit has individuals with specialized knowledge in everything from aardvarks to zymurgy. But the media can't call on your experts to comment on an unfolding story unless they know the experts exist.

Experts list
(print or electronic)

Many institutions annually prepare a list of experts by topic areas (with a phone number for each) and distribute the list to media, especially to local and regional outlets.

Note: Before you include anyone's name on your list, be sure that the expert is actually willing to talk if called upon by media. If your expert's accomplishments have been covered by media in the past, mention it in your listing, as evidence that the expert knows how to work with reporters.

With computers, it's not difficult to customize lists of experts for targeted news beats, such as politics or medicine. Many institutions now have their experts data bases on the World Wide Web as well.

You may also want to investigate ProfNet (Professors Network), a cooperative of college and university public information officers linked via the Internet to give journalists and authors quick and convenient access to expert sources among their faculties. It also can be used by campus leaders to survey what's going on at other institutions.

ProfNet enables journalists to send an electronic-mail query for information on any topic of interest to several hundred campus public information officers and to a wide range of academic, government, and corporate entities oriented to scholarship and research. Started at the State University of New York at Stony Brook, the service has become so successful that it has spun off into a private corporation that operates through an annual fee to participating institutions. Here is a portion of a typical daily ProfNet transmission to members:

Date: Mon, 19 Aug 1996 10:19:22 -0400

From: @alpha.vyne.com

To: ProfNet@alpha.vyne.com

Subject: PN 1737: Poverty and Welfare/ Phonics/ Black Bears

Reply-to: outbox@vyne.com

PROFNET SEARCH 1737

August 19, 1996

[Sent Monday at 10:20 a.m. EDT]

SUMMARY

DEADLINE TODAY:

1. Poverty and Welfare – MSNBC
2. Crime and Incarceration – MSNBC
3. Early Sewing/Weaving Machines – Asian Wall Street Journal

BEHAVIOR/RELATIONSHIPS:

4. Internet Addiction – Huntsville Times

BUSINESS:

5. Performance Review Tools – San Jose Mercury News
6. Southwest Airlines – Providence (RI) Bulletin
7. Country Stores – [Lightly Cloaked]

EDUCATION:

8. Choosing Educational Software – Bucks County Courier Times
9. Phonics versus Whole Language – Electronic Learning

ENVIRONMENT:

10. Control of Black Bear Populations – Bay City Times (MI)

HEALTH/MEDICINE:

11. Medical Trivia – Ladies' Home Journal

LAW/CRIME/JUSTICE:

12. Self-Esteem and Prostitution – Author (Nimbus Publishing)

RESEARCH/FACT-CHECKING:

13. Dietary Supplements – Microsoft's Encarta Website
14. Light – Independent Film & Video Monthly

SCIENCE/TECHNOLOGY:

15. Technology and Construction Site Management – Modern Steel

MEMBER ITEMS:

16. Marketing Position Description – West Virginia University
17. Anniversaries and Capital Campaigns – Marian College

QUERIES

DEADLINE TODAY

1. POVERTY AND WELFARE - MSNBC. Alice Rhee seeks leads on experts by 3 p.m. EDT today who can discuss poverty in the U.S. — and especially the link between poverty and the welfare system. What is the likely prospect as the federal government turns responsibility for welfare over to the states? This is in connection with new statistics on poverty being released today by the Bureau of the Census. Please call Alice at (201)-583-5208 and be prepared to fax leads (brief bio and perspective on topic) on suggested sources to (201)-583-5511. (Note: Since we've provided the fax number, you don't need to ask for it. Thanks.)

BEHAVIOR/RELATIONSHIPS

4. INTERNET ADDICTION – HUNTSVILLE TIMES. This is James McWilliams, technology writer for The Huntsville (Ala.) Times. I'm doing an article on "Internet addiction," and I need to know if there actually is such a thing. Is using the Internet three hours a day any more an addiction than watching television the same amount of time? (Many Americans watch much more TV than that.) Which is generally healthier: the Internet or television? What separates an addiction from a pastime or recreation? Please respond by sending email to jamesmc@traveller.com, or by calling (205) 720-6913, my pager. Thanks.

BUSINESS

5. PERFORMANCE REVIEW TOOLS – SAN JOSE MERCURY NEWS. I'm writing a story about a new type of performance review tool called 360-degree feedback. I'm interested in speaking with professors of management who might be familiar with this. I'm most interested to find out if this type of review works and what are the

pros and cons of using it.> Sherri Eng email: SEng@sjmercury.com HEALTH/MEDICINE

11. MEDICAL TRIVIA – LADIES' HOME JOURNAL. Elizabeth Meyers seeks leads on medical experts and others who can provide some quick answers for several medical trivia questions she is currently researching. Experts will be quoted.

Why are some people ticklish and others not?
Why does hitting your funnybone feel so odd?
Why do your teeth sometimes hurt when you eat hot or cold foods?
What happens when you crack your knuckles?
Why do some people bruise more easily than others?
Why do you have odd dreams when you eat certain foods before bed?
Do overweight people and muscular people burn calories in the same way?
Why is it so difficult for women to lose weight in the hips and thighs?

email: emeyers@nyc.mdp.com Phone: 212-455-1062

RESEARCH/FACT-CHECKING

13. DIETARY SUPPLEMENTS – MICROSOFT'S ENCARTA WEBSITE. Experts needed to supply information about the safety and benefits of vitamins, minerals, herbs, and amino acids when taken as supplements. Also needed are experts who can speak about the history of supplements (i.e., when companies first began isolating and packaging micronutrients as pills and other formulations), and recent trends in supplement use. The story will be written as a magazine-like update to Microsoft's multimedia encyclopedia on CD-ROM. No direct quotes will be used. Phone (201) 656-6992 or email 102651.2616@compuserve.com. > Ingrid Wickelgren

[END]

Please Note: A reply to this message will not reach us at ProfNet.

To contact us by email, please respond through a new message directed to one of the addresses below. Many thanks.

————

TO CONTACT PROFNET AND OUR VIRTUAL COLLEAGUES

BY FAX: 516-689-1425
BY PHONE: 516-941-3736 or 800-PROFNET
BY EMAIL:

Member Items: profnet@vyne.com (Kevin Aschenbrenner)
Hiring Line Items: ForHL@aol.com (Dan Forbush)
New Member Signup: newaddress@aol.com (Rita O'Brien)
News Links: hall@vyne.com (Alan Hall, Quadnet)
Technical Support: kuffer@vyne.com (Jason Kuffer, Vyne)
To Change Address: newaddress@aol.com (Rita O'Brien)
Other/General: 76550.750@compuserve.com (Dan Forbush)

TO REACH OUR WEB SITE:

http://www.vyne.com/profnet/ (Name is "member"; password is "newt" — system is case-sensitive)

SciNews-MedNews is another electronic forum, available through CompuServe for campuses that want to post research news — and for journalists who are searching for research news ideas. *NASW Online*, another service on CompuServe, features a message board and a library of article abstracts for members of the National Association of Science Writers.

In May 1996 the American Association for the Advancement of Science inaugurated *EurekAlert!* Reporters who register with this service can receive announcements on new research before the information is formally released to the media or published in journals. Campuses that want to disseminate information through EurekAlert must register and pay a fee. If successful, the service — at http://www.eurekalert.org/ — is likely to inspire similar services in other discipline areas.

One way to ensure simultaneous release of news is to call a press conference. (Depending on the immediacy, this can be announced by phone or mail.) Yet even a press conference won't ensure equal treatment among the media, because the time of the conference will automatically favor one or another. For example, a 10 a.m. conference will work better for a noon news broadcast

The press conference

and a late afternoon newspaper, while a 2 p.m. conference will be to the advantage of an evening newscast and a morning newspaper. The solution: stagger press conference timings. If you hold one in the early morning, hold the next in the afternoon.

You'll want to be conservative in your use of press conferences, however. Since they signal that you've got an interesting, important announcement, be sure you have one. If you "cry wolf" too often, you may some day have a good reason to call a press conference but nobody will come.

What's interesting and important in the eyes of the news media will depend to an extent on the size of the city in which you're located and the number of other substantial news sources in that city. For example, Iowa State University dominates the news scene in Ames, while the University of California, Los Angeles is only one of many newsworthy organizations in the area. The introduction of a new dean of agriculture will bring reporters to Ames from as far away as Des Moines; a new dean at UCLA may draw only the student newspaper.

If time allows, print up copies of the speaker's text and hand it out at the press conference, along with other pertinent materials such as charts, statistics, or institutional policy statements, and a list of the names and titles of any other participants. Try to hold the conference in a space of adequate size and with adequate electrical outlets and lighting for electronic media. Be sure to make provisions for parking and press access to telephones.

Freelancers and magazines

Magazines try to provide both entertainment and in-depth coverage on select topics of interest. They get their story ideas through many of the same routes as news media — press releases, tipsheets, personal contacts, and so on. For a college or university, the best chances for attention occur in regional magazines or in specialty magazines in science, the arts, business, and consumer news.

Relatively few magazines today accept stories from "unknown" writers. Years ago, magazines were less demanding about the credentials and experience of those who submitted pieces. No more. Today's magazines generally depend upon a staff of in-house writers, experienced *freelance writers,* or a combination of both. *Ghostwriting* is also common: a magazine writer works closely with a scientist or other personality, capturing the story in the first person but making sure it is well-written and meets the publication's style.

Editors are constantly seeking story ideas to assign to writers; writers search just as determinedly for stories to offer editors. Thus, access to both editors and established freelance writers (sometimes called contributing editors) can be pivotal when trying to get your story into a magazine.

Freelancers tend to specialize in subject matter or a genre of writing. This specialization gives them increasing familiarity with the major players in a field and they tend to come back to these people — their *contacts* — for stories. Freelancers also develop a group of client magazines to which they regularly pitch story ideas or from which they receive assignments.

If you have a personal working relationship with a magazine editor or freelancer, cultivate it. If you don't have anything going on in-house that interests them, tell them about an exciting project at a sister campus or the work of a colleague across the country. The important thing is to stay on their list as a source of ideas, as someone with his or her finger on the pulse of higher education.

If you do not have personal contacts, it is best to leave cultivation of this medium to your public information office, which can pursue your topic suggestions through its own contacts. Or, ask your PIO to help you develop a relationship with a couple of freelance writers.

Though we generally think of the "news" side of the mass media as our primary target, we should not overlook the rich opportunities on the editorial side of the newsroom. Many newspapers, magazines, and television and radio news programs regularly

Op-ed pages
and letters to the editor

carry opinion pieces from the public. Called "Op-Ed pieces" (Opinion/Editorial or Opposite/Editorial), these opinion pieces are good vehicles for explaining complicated policy issues and responding to public concerns and misconceptions. They often cover topics not communicated through regular news coverage.

The backgrounds of Op-Ed writers run the full spectrum from professional freelance writers and political figures to the owners of small businesses and members of volunteer organizations. The only real qualifications are to write reasonably well and make a valid and interesting point, with information and arguments to back it up. It helps, of course, to have an affiliation that would seem to qualify you as a spokesperson for the message you present. For example, someone writing on problems in the trucking industry is more likely to get the attention of the editor if the writer is a member of the Interstate Commerce Commission, the Teamsters Union, a citizen group that has studied causes of big rig accidents, or the author of a recent book on the subject.

On issues in higher education and a myriad other specialty topics, your administrative officers and faculty are a rich source of knowledge — and you should urge them to contribute their opinions.

To get an Op-Ed piece into the paper or electronic media, contact the editorial editor and pitch your piece. Explain what you want to say, why you feel the piece should be published or broadcast, and why it is relevant — especially to that medium's readers or viewers. Most papers have an Op-Ed approval process that can take ten days or longer. Many larger daily papers will require exclusivity, meaning you can't send the piece to any other outlets.

If a pitch is accepted, the author prepares a piece whose title, length, and style match similar Op-Ed pieces in that medium. Be focused: make your points clear and sharp, back them up with data, and include a local angle if possible. Include a brief biography, giving your name, title, organization, and any special current activity related to the topic.

You can, of course, get your views into newspapers faster, but in less depth, by writing a letter to the editor. Depending on the newspaper and the tone it sets — or permits — for "letters" discourse, you may feel that you are either carrying on an intelligent dialogue with readers or descending into a mud hole.

Whatever the local flavor, *you* maintain a firm but non-vindictive tone in making your arguments. And *always* make a response via the letters page if the paper publishes a letter that distorts or misrepresents your institution. If you don't, that untruth will stand unchallenged and, to the uninformed, it will become truth. So that you yourself don't have to write all such replies, have a cadre of fellow colleagues who will pitch in on request. Certain letters should logically be written by the parties most knowledgeable about the topic in question.

Publicity agents

Because of the time, energy, and attention required to get a meaty story or profile about an academic unit into national media — magazine, TV, radio — some institutions hire a public relations firm to help them identify stories that will "sell." The firm's agents go out and push those stories until they sell. This is fairly expensive, for example, but it can pay off well for a business or medical school, or in a particular crisis situation.

The advantage of using PR firms is that they make it their business to know key people in the major media outlets, to know the kinds of stories those people want right now and how they want the stories delivered. Because the agents work for numerous clients and thus peddle numerous stories, public relations firms can always deliver *something* acceptable to editors — which means the media pay attention to them. Sooner or later, *your* stories will be chosen.

If you decide to go this route, do your homework and shop around. Talk to colleagues in units of *similar size and character* and find out who they've used and how it's worked out for them. Talk to your public affairs or information officer for his or her input.

Remember that hiring a firm doesn't necessarily mean less work for you. You undoubtedly will have to prepare considerable material for the firm to review and also prepare your "stars" on how to respond when the "call" finally comes.

Reporting and releasing research news

When announcing research findings, there are three audiences a faculty member must please — his or her professional peers, the funding agency, and the media. To keep everyone happy and maintain academic credibility, we suggest the following protocol:

1. Make your first public announcement of a major research finding through a paper in a refereed journal or in an invited presentation to an appropriate learned society, thereby both sharing your scholarship initially with fellow scholars and acquiring the cachet of peer review.

2. Arrange with your campus news service in advance to prepare a news release, which you check for accuracy and which the news service then makes available simultaneously to all local, regional, and national outlets, using the embargo dating method mentioned above.

3. If the funding agency and the learned society are interested, arrange with their public information personnel for a collaborative release or several releases.

4. If you've generated friendly relations with a particular reporter, and you know that he or she will respect the embargo date, tip him or her off that a release is forthcoming and offer to provide additional background information. Thus the reporter can be prepared when the release comes out.

5. Once the report of your finding is in the
public domain, make yourself available to
the news media and, if need be, initiate
clarifying reports for popular consumption.

How this protocol plays out in actual practice was well-illustrated
by the way the organizations involved handled the release of a
big story — the apparent confirmation of the "big bang" theory
of how the universe was created, based on research funded by
the National Aeronautics and Space Administration (NASA).

George Smoot of the Lawrence Berkeley Laboratory and the
University of California, Berkeley, the team leader, touched off
the announcement by presenting a paper at a meeting of the
American Physical Society in Washington, DC. Public relations
personnel from NASA staged a follow-up press conference at
which Berkeley, NASA, and the American Physical Society
simultaneously distributed press releases. The next day, team
members appeared on all major TV network newscasts, which
were then followed by features in Sunday newspapers and weekly
newsmagazines.

By adhering to such a responsible strategy of media relations,
scholars help the public learn what their tax dollars are buying
and at the same time avoid any charges by peers of self-aggran-
dizement.

With the above items as your general model, here are some
additional tips.

If you are a researcher being interviewed by a reporter:

- Find out what brought him or her to you, why he
or she is doing the interview, and what he or she
knows about the subject. The answers will give
you a starting point for discussion and will also
signal to you whether the reporter has precon-
ceptions or biases about the research that could
present a problem.

- If your subject area is complicated, cannot be explained without the use of technical terms, or involves a lot of numbers or statistics, you would be wise to provide the reporter with a written summary of the key points, in plain English, along with a glossary or clarifying illustrations. A reprint of a popularized article that you felt did justice to your research can also be helpful background to the reporter.

- If you are not really ready to give an interview — the results aren't final, the journal article has not been accepted yet, or you just don't have the details fresh in your mind — don't do it. Reassure the reporter that you do want to talk, but ask him or her to call back later in the day, the week, or the year as appropriate. Keep in mind, however, that if you told your campus news officer that you were ready and then you waffled, your odds of subsequently getting the attention of either your news service or the media will plummet.

- Be prepared to see your research transformed into a simple story that lacks your jargon and skips the details dear to your heart. The price for reaching average citizens is that most research must be described in simpler terms than faculty are accustomed to. This does not mean, however, that it is less accurate in making the key points.

- Though one of Doyle's 13 commandments was not to ask to check a reporter's story, the ground rules are a little different with science stories. Because there is greater potential for errors in reporting research news, you may ask the reporter to read quotes or figures back to you before the story is published or aired. Some will, many won't, and some will call to double-check the details with you as they are writing the story.

If you are working with in-house campus reporters, they almost always submit a draft to you for review or will read the draft to you over the phone. Note: This is not an invitation to rewrite the story. Rather, it is your opportunity to correct errors of fact or omission, *period*. If you go beyond that, don't expect to see that reporter — or his or her colleagues — at your doorstep again. When given copy for review, deal with it immediately and return it promptly; in-house reporters are on deadlines, too.

If you are preparing or coordinating a unit's research news coverage:

- Never issue a release to the mass media that your parents or the fellow across the back fence wouldn't understand. Your job is to translate the complex ideas and jargon into a simpler message. While remaining accurate, use familiar words, analogies, and other figures of speech to convey the findings.

- Don't issue a release or encourage a reporter to pursue a story if the results are too preliminary to have been verified. Never exaggerate the importance of results or raise false hopes. Always be wary of the researcher who seems overly eager to get quick publicity.

- Don't make a claim that a finding is "unique" or the "first of its kind" unless you can substantiate it. Today, few researchers are solitary pioneers. Commonly, teams at a half-dozen colleges or universities work on parallel tracks, building directly and indirectly upon one another's findings.

  Though you have no obligation to do so, you may make your research announcement more appealing and credible by mentioning important contributing research accomplishments at other institutions. Reporters, who like to describe trends and put research findings in context, will appreciate your effort.

- The advice we offered earlier about using the "human touch" applies especially to research stories. Liven your story with a humorous or wry remark from the researcher; his or her description of the anxiety and anticipation surrounding the last, critical experiment; more information on graduate students who may have been on the research team; a comment on the particular difficulties of dealing with the animals, people, materials in question — anything that makes the research come alive to the reader or viewer.

Responding to media inquiries (friendly and otherwise)

While we emphasize the importance of adopting a straight answer policy, we also acknowledge that there are occasions when reporters will approach you with obvious bias or preconception about your activities. In such cases, it may be naive to be totally unguarded and open. When you sense that you are being sized up as a target for a lopsided exposé, take reasonable precautions.

In general, when the media calls or when you agree to appear on radio or TV for an interview on a controversial issue, follow these helpful tips, abstracted from "The Media Assistance Plan," Office of Vice President for University Relations, Michigan State University, 1993:

- Get the reporter's name and his or her publication/station.

- Be fair, friendly, and factual.

- Don't hesitate to demur if asked to comment on matters outside your areas of expertise.

- Don't say anything you aren't willing to have attributed to you by name.

- When offering a personal opinion, make sure the reporter understands you're speaking for yourself and not your colleagues or institution.

- Never assume you'll see the reporter's story before it is published or broadcast.

- When an interview is for broadcast, remember the people in television and radio news usually can report only the barest essentials of a story, so select two or three key points and focus on those.

- Be creative in how you present ideas. Use analogies and other figures of speech to reach your audience.

- Many reporters won't accept "off the record" statements. (Others will, but with no intention of honoring the agreement if you have provided them with a juicy nugget.) Unless you and the reporter have a long-term working relationship, the safest stance is to assume that *anything you say within their earshot may be quoted.*

- Keep your institution's news service apprised of contacts from media, especially on policy or personnel matters, and ask them for assistance any time you need it. (The news service works hard to maintain credibility with the press; it's important that they know what *you* are telling reporters. They also need to know if reporters are following up on tips from the news service. Let your news service know when their efforts pay off.)

Some points we would add to the above:

- Be cautious in answering hypothetical questions that begin with "if," such as "If you had designed this building differently, would that accident have occurred?" Don't take on the role of the omniscient; it usually leads to trouble.

- Don't be drawn into a thoughtless, emotional response by accusatory, leading, or inaccurate questions. Sometimes a reporter's question is simply ignorant, sometimes a ploy to prompt you into revealing more than you wish. If *you* set the agenda by presenting your message in clear, simple language with sufficient quotable quotes, a reporter won't need to provoke you in order to get the story.

- Don't confirm a name or a fact in a controversial story. Some reporters will call and say: "Joe Jones told us that Sally Smith is suing your department and we're just calling you to confirm that information and get your comment" — when Jones has said no such thing and the reporter is just on a fishing expedition. Be wary of such calls and either give no comment or tell the reporter you will get back to him or her.

- Though it may be uncomfortable, don't feel compelled to fill the silences or empty spaces in a conversation. If you have no more to say, *stop talking* or switch to a topic that *you* want to discuss.

- If you have time, prepare and distribute a press packet that provides a brief summary of the issue in question, along with any pertinent statistics and a tight quote or two, names of the key players, a copy of any statements they have issued, and brief background on your institution. Interviewers are glad to have the additional material.

Finally, we might also recommend *Media Guide for Academics*, by Joann Ellison Rodgers and William C. Adams (1994).

Keep your expectations realistic

Don't be upset if the media fail you periodically — if they don't respond to accomplishments that truly merit notice, if they give you only three paragraphs rather than twelve, if they don't run a promised story for three months, or if they give more attention to a handful of protesters than to the major event your institution has sponsored. As one observer has put it, "Go for the long-term benefit. Think of media relations as a sustained effort that will allow you to get your viewpoint across most of the time."

Remember: only very occasionally will your unit appear in front-page or top-of-the-hour stories and those are, unfortunately, most likely to involve controversy or tragedy. More often it will be represented in a Saturday science feature somewhere in the middle of the newspaper, part of a commentator's column, an announcement of awards received, a radio interview with a graduating senior, or a few seconds of footage of your unit's recent dinosaur dig. It's the *cumulative* effect of modest but positive and creative stories and coverage that counts.

For further consideration ...

"Misquoted?"

Many campus administrators live in mortal fear of being badly misquoted by news media or having their institution misrepresented in a news story.

What to do if it happens?

The answer seems to depend on who you ask.

Campus directors of public relations tend to recommend that you keep your cool (*CASE Currents*, July/August 1995):

> "Try to engineer a resolution that would allow a continued professional relationship with the reporter."
> — *Alexis Henderson, University of Maryland System*

"Call the reporter and describe the problem as an inaccuracy, leaving the reporter's news judgment out of it."

— Ruth Wardwell, Chapman University (CA)

"Present a reasoned argument, not an emotional tirade."

— Peter M. Gigliotti, Shippensburg University (PA)

"Complaining is worthy of your time only if the content and context of the information is substantive."

— Lou Cartier, University of Nebraska at Omaha

"Remember, we're all human."

— Joe Hargis, Carleton College (MN).

"Be patient."

— Vern Lamplot, University of Arizona

"Never give a quote over the phone; use a fax machine."

— Mary Burnett, Rhodes College

Reporters, on the other hand, are more defensive:

"I never have the problem because I use a tape recorder and take incredibly careful notes."

— Ann Blackman, Time

"I go back to the interview on audio, and we usually find some agreement on why we disagree or who is mistaken."

— Claudio Sanchez, National Public Radio

"Frequently it turns out not to be a misquote but only that they don't like what a story says."

— Garland L. Thompson, Black Issues in Higher Education

"When something comes out that a person obviously said and it make him or her look bad, the person suddenly misremembers."

— Anita Sama, USA Today

When reporters call

John D. McIlquham, president of *The NonProfit Times*, has some suggestions on terminology that academic leaders should studiously avoid when approached by the press (May 1993):

- "Assess" as in "We must wait until all data are in before we can assess our next course of action." Any reporter knows "assess" is a synonym for "stalling."

- "Best overall interests." A clumsy, tired phrase used to explain your action in reaction to an opposing position or to justify your own position when you win — signifying nothing, really.

- "Box," as in an organizational chart. Denotes rigidity, isolation.

- "Claims" as in "We have certain claims against him and he has certain claims against us." News media persons will translate as "We owe him money and he owes us money," whether that's accurate or not.

- "Process." Another vague synonym for stall, as in "The report will be released when the process is completed." (As McIlquham points out, "process" is the term used by astronomers to describe the evolution of the universe's boundaries.)

- "Real world." An overworked phrase used to suggest that one's position is grounded in reality, while an opposing view is hopelessly lost in space.

- "Study." A respectable term in academe that unfortunately has acquired the connotation of an excuse for inaction and delay.

- "Sufficient information." What persons poor in lexicon say they need when they lack ammunition. Reporters recognize that "I lack sufficient information" is often just a dodge.

- "Opinion," as in "Here's my opinion, for what it's worth." A reporter may not grasp the distinction between personal opinion and institutional dogma.

"Camerability"

When going before the TV camera, here are some recommendations from Robert S. Culkeen of Westfield State College (MA) and Elizabeth A. Natale of Trinity College (CT):

- *Dress for Success.* Wear something with a collar for a lavaliere mike. Go easy on makeup. Avoid high-contrast clothes, especially bright pinstripe shirts or, for women, red shirts, shiny jewelry, tinted glasses.

- *Do Your Homework.* Anticipate tough questions. Prepare the messages you want to get across in short "sound bites."

- *Practice.* Rehearse with a camcorder.

- *Keep Your Ears Open* — for distracting noises that would contaminate the interview. If they intrude, repeat your point.

- *Watch What You Say.* Assume the interview begins when the reporter arrives.

- *Put Your Body in Neutral.* Don't rock, swivel, frown, gesticulate wildly.

- *Look 'Em in the Eye.* Play to the camera.

- *Size Things Up.* Tailor the length of your comments to the questions.

- *Don't Look Back.* Avoid "As I said before." Repeat your original point.

- *Turn "No Comment" Into a Comment.* Say, "That's an interesting point, but what's even more important is ...."
- *Stop Talking.* Say what you want to say and then quit; don't ramble.
- *Maintain Control.* Lead the interview in a subtle yet sure manner.
- *Stay Put.* At the end of the interview, don't move until told you can.
- *Just Say "No."* If you're embarrassed by a poor performance, express your reservations before the taped interview airs.
- *Have Fun.* Your ease will come through.

chapter twelve

From Crises To Campaigns
Communications tips for challenging situations

The résumé of a chief advancement officer recently crossed our desk that strikingly embraced the diverse challenges that face campus leaders (Weimer 1995). Under "Professional Experience" appeared the following entry:

> Developed communications campaign strategy and materials for the university's $500 million capital campaign, the largest by any public university at the time it was launched. It is now eight months ahead of schedule with more than $400 million pledged.

That was an achievement in handling the good news, a campaign. Further on, there appeared a partial list of crises that had faced that professional's institution in the past four years:

- Indictments by the county Grand Jury of 12 senior employees, including two vice presidents, the executive assistant to the president, the athletic director, and faculty department heads for altering state documents to purchase alcohol

- Investigation of university leadership by the Texas Rangers and the FBI, and allegations against the chair of the Board of Regents for using his position for personal gain and profit

- Allegations of scientific misconduct and alchemy against a distinguished professor of chemistry

- A racist attack by the student newspaper against a black legislator, and a racist theme party for fraternity pledges

- Allegations of mismanagement and misconduct in food service operations

- Two major NCAA sanctions and penalties, and theft of the university's new collie puppy mascot

- Charges of sexual harassment and date rape against members of the marching band

And this is only a partial list!

Most campus leaders don't face this magnitude or diversity of crises. Nevertheless, almost every campus leader will face some crisis — large or small.

Also, with the continuing budget squeeze, every campus leader must, to some extent, become a fund-raiser and conduct fund-raising campaigns. Other sorts of "campaigns" require a communication strategy as well, such as establishing a new academic major, raising student fees, and passing a city referendum to allow for a new campus building program.

The crisis typically comes out of the blue, allowing little time to plan a response. The organizational change or capital campaign, on the other hand, allows for extensive planning and strategizing, which may begin long before the event. The common thread is that both kinds of events require extraordinary communication efforts, internally and externally. This chapter is intended to provide you with some insights and communication tips for dealing with such challenges.

Communications in a crisis

Even the best-managed operations will at some time face unforeseen circumstances: accident, natural disaster, disease, crime, scandal, or trouble between town and gown. They also will face "foreseen" circumstances — budget cuts, reorganizations, strikes, or new mandates to their departments. Depending on their impact, these "circumstances" could portend a crisis. It is how a leader copes with such situations that truly tests administrative mettle.

In some sense, a crisis could be defined as an event, or series of events, that involves your institution, division, or department and that will likely attract attention — probably negative — from the media and from others outside your immediate circle. You might add to this definition that it is a situation most likely to affect perceptions of your unit and of your leadership. A crisis threatens the well-being and security of individuals within the institution and threatens the institution's good image.

These features are summed up by Laurence Barton, author of *Crisis in Organizations* (1993), in his definition of a crisis: "A crisis is a major, unpredictable event that has potentially negative results. The event and its aftermath may significantly damage an organization and its employees, products, services, financial condition, and reputation."

Recognizing a crisis situation

Murders, suicides, fires, earthquakes, burglaries — they happen every day, on campuses as readily as anywhere else. It is not hard to recognize such a crisis situation when it confronts you. But what of situations that "sneak" up on you?

Fred Volkmann, vice chancellor for public affairs at Washington University (MO), recently offered this partial list of topics in higher education that are on the media's radar screen at the moment (1995): tuition policies, teaching quality, faculty workload, faculty and administrative salaries, animal research, student drug and alcohol abuse, research fraud, and donor influence on campus policies.

No academic administrator is immune from having a seemingly innocuous circumstance or problem turn into a "crisis" situation. Amanda Perkins, for example, has a star faculty member who was recruited at a blue-chip salary that is higher than the state governor's salary. Several of her departmental faculty work at home on Tuesdays and Thursdays and are seen by their neighbors doing yard work in summer. Her department has several foreign graduate students who speak English as a second language and who teach undergraduate course sections in ecology. And a number of research projects in her unit involve animal research.

Each situation can be found on Volkmann's list; each has the potential to become the focus of a local news story and mushroom into a crisis situation. In such cases, simple perception can be a problem. If a full professor is mowing his lawn on Thursday morning, is he goofing off and not earning his pay? If a Chinese graduate student has a heavy accent, are her students unable to learn from her? If animals are being studied in the laboratory, are they being abused? Those in the know would answer, "Of course not," but others may jump to the wrong conclusions.

Beyond that, Perkins and her peers have "unforeseen crisis potential": assistants who may pilfer from cash accounts, faculty who may grow a bit too familiar with students or colleagues, or associates who may move a few decimals in reporting their research results. In short, it's people who make up our colleges and universities, and people are capable of doing things that are illegal, or at least ethically and socially questionable.

To guard against such situations, be alert to the potential for perceived or actual wrongdoing in your division or department. Scanning the local newspapers and the *Chronicle for Higher Education* will give you some insight into what is "potential crisis" material to the media. We suggest that you develop background files on today's explosive issues in academia so that you have information handy when you need it.

Many crises simply aren't avoidable, but campus leaders can take steps to prevent those that are. Your best protection against crises is to have firm policies on all potentially troublesome situations, to convey those policies loud and clear to the parties concerned, and to monitor and enforce those policies daily. Tight fiscal controls, a well-understood code of departmental ethics, good security measures, and a policy of being up-front and open about potential areas of concern with bosses, employees, students, alumni, and the press can minimize unexpected crisis situations.

For example, Perkins faced her four "potentially troublesome situations" head on:

- She included the salary of her star faculty recruit in the press release announcing his arrival and explaining why he was such a great catch for Midland, thereby leaving the press nowhere to go with the story.

- She made teaching and communication training mandatory for all new graduate students in her department and had them pass a language test before putting them in the classroom with under-graduates.

- She talked at a faculty meeting about public perceptions of faculty workload and the need for her colleagues to talk to friends and neighbors about the work they do and the schedules they keep.

- She brought in the campus photographer to take a picture of lab assistants playing with the rab-bits being used for research, for an Easter feature in the campus newspaper that subsequently was picked up in a sympathetic story and carried across the state by the wire services.

In short, in recognizing a potential crisis looming, a good offense is sometimes the best defense.

The chancellor's residence at the University of Wisconsin-Madison was being refurbished and repaired in anticipation of the selection of the new university leader. When Donna Shalala accepted the job as chancellor and was preparing to begin her term, she recognized the potential for negative publicity over the building project. She suggested that the University News Service get the story out and fast. One afternoon, months prior to Shalala's arrival on campus, a press tour and briefing were held at the residence, complete with "before" and "after" pictures of the house and a breakdown of all expenses involved in the project. The project manager and interior designer were on hand to answer questions. The result was positive coverage of the project. (Of course, it helped that the residence hadn't been refurbished in 25 years and the old orange and green decor had long passed its prime in terms of style.)

Heading off the potential crisis

When a situation emerges that could turn into a potential crisis, the first order of business is to try to mitigate its impact.

A good strategy is to discuss the situation with your immediate supervisor, top aides, and other advisors — in other words, your crisis management team — as the situation may warrant. Some issues require more confidentiality than others, but your campus chief public affairs officer and legal affairs advisor are important contacts if legal or public relations issues are likely to be involved. It is important to involve them early on, before the problems erupt into the public eye.

A wonderful editorial cartoon appeared in the *San Francisco Chronicle* after the *Exxon Valdez* oil spill in Alaska. It showed the tanker spewing oil into the ocean, with the following message coming from the bridge: "Mayday! Mayday! Get me public relations!" Of course, by then, it was far too late for public relations to do anything other than damage control.

We can learn a lot from the mistakes of others when assessing the potential for crisis and how to respond. Several years back, indirect cost issues would not have seemed to have the potential to create an institutional crisis, especially if practices and policies were completely within the law. But after Stanford University received prolonged negative attention about how it spent federal funds intended to support the indirect costs of research, this became a national "hot button" issue. Even though a court later vindicated Stanford in its use of federal "overhead" funds, the damage had been long since done. The image of Stanford University "wasting" federal money on flowers and yachts remains strong in many minds.

In this case, had someone recognized a problem, there could have been a review of how these funds were being used. With the application of some "common sense" policies, the crisis could have been averted and the damage avoided — even if the problem came to public attention.

When it became known that a few University of California faculty members were running government grants through a nonprofit foundation and getting paid substantial amounts, in addition to their faculty salaries, UC administrators responded swiftly by issuing new, less ambiguous guidelines about federal funding procedures. The chancellor wrote a letter to every faculty member outlining the steps he had taken to review and deal with the situation.

When the regents and the press were apprised of what had occurred, they also had in hand information on how the campus was dealing with the situation, including the chancellor's letter. A potential crisis was averted: it was just a one-day story in the local media.

It is important to note, however, that the faculty who were affected were very unhappy with the way the situation was handled, creating a very challenging situation for the dean and department heads, who found themselves caught in the middle. No matter how you may handle a problem, it's unlikely that all of your constituents will be happy. They may minimize the situation or disagree with your assessment of the gravity of the situation. But avoiding conflicts, unpleasant decisions, and controversial actions can lead academic administrators into a "crisis" situation.

For example, when a sexual harassment scandal hits the courts and/or the media, we often discover that administrators were aware of the problem, but either did not take it seriously or did not want to take action that might embarrass a colleague. But if such a case reaches the scandal stage — or crisis proportions — the fallout will be much more damaging both to the colleague and to the department or institution.

Preparing for a crisis

Many large organizations have proactive strategies for dealing with a crisis situation. An increasing number of college and universities have "crisis management" plans. It would be wise to search out such a plan from your administration if one exists and then tailor it to your needs.

The crisis management plan

The following are the vital ingredients of a crisis plan (Larson 1995):

1. A statement of your campus' general philosophy of crisis management

2. Instructions for your crisis response team to follow. This section should include the following:

   - A list of team members and their responsibilities
   - A list of people to notify immediately, with the phone and fax numbers
   - A phone tree showing who will call whom when the crisis hits
   - A statement about who is authorized to speak for the campus

3. Phone numbers for the fire department; county, state, and campus police; poison center; utility companies; disaster relief agencies; and other such groups

4. Guidelines for spreading the word on and off campus. This section should include these items:

   - Instructions for notifying faculty, staff, and students
   - The location of up-to-date mailing labels for various constituent groups (such as alumni, donors, and parents) you may need to reach during and after the crisis
   - Contact names and telephone numbers for local and regional media, including the student press
   - Instructions for posting information electronically, such as through your campus computer bulletin board or the Internet

5. Procedures to follow if the crisis involves the loss of electricity, telephone service, or access to the campus

6. Location of and instructions for setting up headquarters for the media. The site should insulate reporters from the incident but provide facilities for press briefings, computer and phone services, parking for TV vans and satellite uplink units, and so on. Be sure to include plans for an alternate site in case the campus is inaccessible.

7. Instructions for organizing media briefings and news conferences

8. Your campus' policy on releasing names of injured or dead people, with instructions for coordinating release with legal counsel

9. Background on your campus, such as the number of employees, the size of the physical plant, and other facts reporters may ask about

10. A current campus map

This recipe for a crisis management plan clearly anticipates dealing with a crisis of major proportions — murder, earthquake, flood, etc. In such an eventuality, most academic administrators will be "cogs in the wheel" as top campus leaders deal with the situation. But there are elements of the above plan that any unit should develop, whatever its size:

- Know your campus' philosophy of crisis management and get a copy of the crisis plan, if there is one. Know your campus spokesperson.

- Establish your own crisis response team, consisting of your top aides, advisors, and key colleagues. (Of course, you may add people depending on the particular situation.) Carry their phone numbers with you at all times. Leave word with them about where you can be reached if you are out of the office.

- Make a list of people to notify should a crisis hit. You will want important colleagues, friends, government officials, alumni — and your bosses — to hear about what's going on from you before they read it in the newspaper.

- Have background information on hand about your unit.

- Obtain campus policies regarding open records and confidentiality of information.

- Keep a list of the names and phone numbers of your own key media contacts, especially reporters and editors whom you may know and with whom you have good professional relationships.

- Keep handy a list of tips on dealing with the news media. (See preceding chapter.)

Going back to our earlier definition of a crisis, it is clear that media and public attention are often key elements — if not determinants — of a crisis situation. Joyce Carol Oates (1991) gave this perspective of media influence over our perceptions:

> There are shared experiences, like elections, or emergencies of the order of the Persian Gulf Crisis; there are profoundly devastating national tragedies, like the assassinations of John F. Kennedy, Robert Kennedy and Martin Luther King, Jr. Like contemporary neighborhoods, we may be most passionately linked to one another by dramatic crises, which by their very nature are unpredictable, thus especially frightening. Indeed, it may well be that crisis, with its myriad faces and names, will become our communal rallying-point of the 1990s. The rituals attending them will be media-generated, media-ordained. Tocqueville's insight of the mid-1800s — that the media make associations — is true now in a way that he could never have anticipated.

Since Oates wrote that insightful statement, we have had the Oklahoma City bombing, the O.J. Simpson trial, the assassination of Israeli Prime Minister Yitzhak Rabin, the crash of Commerce Secretary Ron Brown's plane in Bosnia, the pipe-bomb in Centennial Park during the Olympics in Atlanta — media events that have tied our nation, and our world, together into a small neighborhood.

Through the media, your "neighborhood" will share in your crisis. Media coverage will play a large role in predisposing that audience to sympathy and understanding, or hostility and criticism.

Because the flavor of media coverage that surrounds your crisis issue is so critical, it is important to understand that your crisis will be viewed by the media in some *context*. If your institution or some department has a good reputation for working with the

Anticipating media interest and influence

media and is open and forthcoming with information, that will be to your benefit in a crisis situation. If not, you will have to overcome some issues of trust and credibility. And if your crisis resembles some situation on your campus or elsewhere that has already attracted negative media coverage, your circumstances could become more difficult, so you should think through your strategy for media relations even more carefully.

Remembering internal audiences

Sometimes those closest to the situation become the last to know in a crisis. Caught up in the moment, one sometimes forgets the most obvious constituents — internal. When crisis hits, employees, colleagues, students, and close friends of the unit need to know what is going on. Once the news hits, they will be asked about it and, quite understandably, they will be considered credible sources of information. If they don't have accurate information, they could compound your problems.

Many campus administrators make it a point to fax information to a key list of people when some important news — good or bad — is about to go public.

If there is an accident or incident affecting a student, it is important to be current on rules of confidentiality and to be sure that the student's family and friends, as appropriate, are notified of what has occurred before there is any public notice of the incident. These seem like obvious statements, but in a crisis it is easy to be neglect some of the most basic, common-sense issues.

This is where a plan and a team are invaluable; when you can review points in writing, you won't forget important items, and each member of your team will bring important information and perspective to your approach. Don't be shy about consulting with your colleagues at other institutions as well. If they have gone through a similar situation, they may have valuable insights and advice to offer.

Rehearsing for a crisis

Some campus administrators actually rehearse in anticipation of a crisis. This is especially true for medical centers, large labss, and other facilities at which natural disasters or major accidents are more likely.

Consider the following incident and reaction (Sabo 1995):

> In November, 1993, as brush fires crept ever closer to Pepperdine University [CA], a group of senior administrators gathered to discuss their next step. One looked around and said, "You know, I could swear we just did this."
>
> In fact, Pepperdine's crisis management team had coped with a fire — albeit a pretend one — during a drill just a few months earlier. When the real thing started engulfing homes and destroying property, the team's well-rehearsed response was practically second nature.
>
> "There isn't enough time in the day to go through every scenario, but you can practice for the most likely crises," says PR director Jeff Bliss. "In our case, those are brush fires and earthquakes. In addition to an annual drill that involves evacuating part of the campus, the university periodically invites speakers from the fire and rescue squad to give briefings."

When the crisis hits

When a crisis hits, you have little time. You must get your message through to the media quickly and be as open and candid about the situation as possible. Particularly if the crisis involves human tragedy, media interest will be very strong and coverage is likely to be very sympathetic to the victims.

But the media can also be a real asset in a crisis. If there has been a rash of computer thefts on campus, for example, the media can put employees on the alert and help spread the word on how best to prevent computer theft. If a disaster has occurred, the media can get out the word on what steps are being taken to aid the victims and what the public can do to help.

Because the media play such a key role in a crisis, it is important to use the strategies outlined in the preceding chapter on dealing with the news media. Crisis communications, despite the stress of the moment, should be the same as normal communications — delivering accurate information as promptly and truthfully as possible. Remember: a reporter is your conduit to the public, so speak as though to the public.

It is also important to remember, however, that there are issues of confidentiality involved. Be careful to check out what you can say and what you can't say. Reporters will respect these boundaries if you make them clear and give the reporters some idea of when they can expect to be told more. This does not mean "No comment": be as open and honest as possible, but don't be afraid to say "I can't tell you that" or "I don't know."

Your campus public relations director has undoubtedly worked hard to develop a relationship of trust with the media. For that reason, when a crisis hits it is imperative to involve her or him in your media strategy and news relations.

The first step is to convene your team to review your situation and, referring to your plan, decide what needs to be done and who should do what. The team should prepare and release a comprehensive written statement outlining all the known facts surrounding the incident and the actions planned to address it (Anderson 1992). Clearly designate a spokesperson for the unit who will handle all calls and deal with the media — you, the campus news or public relations director, or someone else in your unit or institution. Your team will need to consider issues of timing, confidentiality, internal communication, action by the unit, and media relations.

To avoid problems of miscommunication internally, use whatever means are appropriate — an emergency departmental meeting, an email, a telephone tree, etc. — to alert those closest to you and closest to the situation about what is happening. This would certainly include campus administrators, regents, lawmakers, and public officials (perhaps), as well as key alumni and donors. Depending on the nature of the crisis, there may be need to reassure your internal audiences, in which case the personal touch is critical.

The University of Illinois hospital in Chicago had two cases of Legionnaire's disease in 1993 (Sabo 1995). John Camper, who was in charge of public affairs, recalls:

> We were so busy dealing with the media that we did an inadequate job of reassuring our employees that they were safe. Leaving aside the fact that they deserved a better explanation, this also caused media problems. The TV coverage featured one of our doctors saying that people were safe, followed by an employee saying he was scared and nobody was telling him anything.

Roger Anderson (1992), president of Adirondack Community College (NY), presented a well-received seminar on media relations in time of crisis to State University of New York community college presidents. We have abstracted his points regarding media relations:

> The clear message should be that the crisis is being addressed in an open, forthright manner, that the campus or academic unit is on top of the situation — to help calm fears, instill confidence, and stabilize conditions. Leaders must try to project a commanding presence that inspires credibility.

> It's desirable that inquiries be referred to the designated spokesperson, but any attempt to muzzle other personnel who want to speak will backfire. Staff can be reminded, however, that they're not under any obligation to answer questions posed by the media or anyone else.

Key points in dealing with the media:

- When you don't know an answer (or, for legal reasons, can't comment), say so. Try to avoid "No comment": it suggests that you are hiding something.

- Don't get drawn into speculations.

- Never lie or twist the truth. Credibility and sincerity are a campus leader's strongest assets. Withholding, avoiding, or massaging facts does far more harm than good.

- Avoid overreacting. The incident will pass and media will tend to remember how the campus and/or unit and its leaders reacted during the crisis rather than the crisis itself. (To most people today, "Watergate" signifies the cover-up, not the original burglary.)

- Don't force the media to use the Freedom of Information Act to obtain data or documents they want. A stalling tactic will merely arouse curiosity. Provide information as soon as possible. But it's perfectly appropriate to ask to meet with a reporter or reporters (even in advance of your release or press conference) to explain the administration's point of view.

- Be aware that specific legal protections, particularly applicable to students, may absolutely prohibit the release of certain information to the media.

- Don't become defensive with the media. As an old saying goes, "Anyone who angers you, conquers you."

- Consider writing a letter to the editor or a guest column in the local newspaper to present the institution's side of events or to respond to a situation.

After the crisis has passed, assemble the crisis management team to evaluate how the crisis was handled and to identify ways to improve your procedures. Survey key media representatives as well for opinions and suggestions. This review is especially important if it's your first major crisis. What lessons you learn, file away for the next time. (The authors would add: be sure to thank all of those who helped you in your "hour of need.")

Is a crisis all bad?

We tend to think of a crisis as a very negative thing, but it can in fact have some positive effects. In a crisis, people very often put aside personal differences to pull together toward a common goal. Such situations foster a sense of teamwork and community that can be very positive, even in the midst of a very negative situation.

Crises require the kind of strategic communications that are necessary to be successful in other situations — whether it is marketing your department to prospective students or launching a new fund raising effort.

Communications and the "quiet crisis"

"Crisis," as we have been using the term so far in this chapter, implies a time of great danger or trouble — an emergency. But in *Webster's New World Dictionary*, there is another definition of crisis: "a turning point in the course of anything; a decisive or crucial time."

This definition better fits most "crisis" situations likely to face campus administrators, such as budget cuts, losing a major grant, employee strikes, problems of adding much-needed facilities, divisive political issues on campus, a disputed hiring or firing, or the defection of a star faculty member. These situations also call for a careful strategy when it comes to communication with key audiences.

Cutting budgets

A common situation in higher education these days is dramatic budget cuts. But early, open, and continuous communication with constituencies can help lessen the shock and mitigate the damage.

Whether you are dealing with budget cuts or another stressful circumstance, here are several communications tips:

- Communicate openly about the situation and its impact on the institution or unit.

- Solicit input, if appropriate, from affected constituencies.

- Seek advice, if appropriate, from others within your institution or at other institutions who have dealt successfully with similar circumstances.

- Look for solutions that will minimize the impact on unit personnel.

- Develop a timeline for implementing the solution in phases. Make all constituents aware of the timeline.

- Report regularly to constituents and, if appropriate, to the public on the status of the situation.

Making these responses part of an *organized plan of communications* is one strategy. For example, when Perkins was faced with a 5% budget cut in her department at Midland University, she pulled together key colleagues and departmental staff in a brainstorming session to look at the situation and how to handle it.

The group members first decided on several principles to guide them through the budget cuts. They decided that service to undergraduates should not be reduced; i.e., all course offerings would be retained. They also decided it was important not to cut graduate student support and to preserve faculty sabbaticals. Since salaries were controlled by the central administration, they were out of the department's control. Everything else, they decided, should be open for consideration.

As chair, Perkins then sent out a memo to all department staff and faculty, which explained the situation and how much the department would have to cut from its budget. She made clear that this was a permanent base cut and set a date for a departmental meeting to explain the situation more fully and discuss options for dealing with the cut.

She asked faculty and staff to submit, prior to the meeting, their recommendations for coping with the cut. She also informed her alumni "board of advisors" of the situation and solicited their advice as well.

Prior to the meeting, she distributed the suggestions she had received, both for cutting the budget and for supplementing the department's budget with other revenue. At the meeting, all options were discussed openly, questions were answered, and a further decision was made to avoid staff layoffs if possible. A small working group was then formed — with staff, faculty, and students representatives — to recommend cuts.

Based on those recommendations, in consultation with her advisory committee and the dean, Perkins then made the final decision. She communicated the situation both internally, through a departmental memo, and externally, through the college newsletter (which was cut from four to three issues per year as part of the budget cuts). In addition, she provided updates through the year on the budget cuts and their impact.

This created an atmosphere of openness and trust that paid off in several ways — student recruitment remained strong because of the department's pledge not to affect course offerings and student support, alumni and parents provided more support for the department through gifts and sponsorship of a lecture series previously supported with state funds, and travel and mailing budgets were tightened somewhat without appreciable impact on the department.

Cutting staff

Academic administrators face a more difficult situation when employee layoffs are forced by budget constraints or union woes.

The University of Minnesota-Waseca faced the ultimate in downsizing in 1990 — closing down completely under a Board of Regents edict. There, too, administrators practiced an open-book policy, coupled with a multi-faceted personnel services program to lessen the trauma for students and staff. Acting Chancellor Nan Wilhelmson breathed into the campus staff a spirit that "this place — as long as it lasts — is for the students."

That spirit took the sting out of student protests, but relations with the faculty hit a rocky period when Wilhelmson had to decide who was and wasn't essential for the final year of operations. Wilhelmson eased the pain by establishing criteria collectively and broadly publicizing them.

Beyond a good communications strategy, you also ease the process for yourself and others if you keep several other points in mind:

- Make a plan to cover terminations.

- Follow carefully all applicable federal and state laws, campus policies, employee handbook guidelines, state policies, union contracts, and other relevant documents.

- Document any performance-based terminations with a paper trail of appraisals and counseling efforts.

- Check all procedures with your campus legal staff and personnel officers.

- Arrange severance packages, when appropriate, and out-placement services.

- Be sensitive to the needs of both the institution and the personnel.

- When dealing directly with targeted employees,
  be both firm and kind.

- Be honest with the news media — and use them
  to convey information to your personnel.

Finally, since downsizing is frequently accompanied by shifts in organizational priorities and goals, we should not underestimate the amount of "cultural change" that is required. And using communications is very important to prepare the campus for change.

Susan M. Schaffer (Massy and Meyerson 1993), consultant and former vice president for administrative services at Stanford University, emphasizes the importance of creating "formal and frequent opportunities for staff to understand and discuss the mission, focus, and issues that face their unit, the administration, and the university."

Timothy R. Warner (Massy and Meyerson 1993), Stanford's associate vice president and director of university budgets, describes the program of continuous communications that was built into the university's budget-restructuring travail. His description invokes an image of continuous communication and sensitivity to all impacted parties.

The rumor mill

This planning and communication strategy can pay off in a variety of ways, but one of the most important is slowing the rumor mill — a force that can be exceedingly destructive to any organization. Many times a situation can worsen into a crisis when rumors develop and spread.

Negative rumors tend to grow, worsening the institution's position and damaging not only employee morale, but potentially undermining private support, political support, and student and faculty recruiting. The best antidote to the rumor mill is a swift, effective campaign to "set the record straight."

The key guide to responding in any crisis — whether "quiet" or front-page news — is to follow the basic tenets of good communication covered in detail in previous chapters of this book. Consider the situation, consider the audiences, develop a message, use every appropriate means to convey that message consistently to all audiences, have a media strategy in mind should that become necessary, and then make a plan and follow it through systematically. This strategic approach will pay off, usually by mitigating the damage or fallout from a challenging or problematic situation.

Communications in a campaign

Organizing a campaign is also an exercise in continuous, strategic communication, albeit under much happier circumstances than the crisis situations above. Campaigns generally consist of image-boosting activities centered around an event — such as a major anniversary or other milestone — and fund-raising drives (capital campaigns). Each type of campaign provides opportunities for your unit and institution to make the public more aware of your mission and accomplishments and to improve your relationships with important constituencies.

Documenting your impact

It's hard to imagine conducting a capital campaign or celebrating a major anniversary without taking the initial step of preparing documentation on the powerful impact that your institution or unit has had on the community, region, state, and beyond. This document will be included in the information materials that you use repeatedly during your campaign as you prove your value to colleagues and constituents.

The features that you highlight will depend on the nature and purpose of your unit and your campaign. For example, your emphasis may be on your contributions to overall state education — K-12 up through adult education. Or you may emphasize your success in stimulating new businesses or drawing new industries to the region. An institution's impact statement will likely cover a broad spectrum that includes the winning of national awards, generation of patents and licenses for new technologies, creation of international programs and linkages, and contributions to improved agricultural production and environmental quality, to name a few possibilities. You may want to itemize how you have shared your expertise with governmental bodies and helped solve civic problems, and document how your cultural activities and facilities have improved the region's quality of life.

You may want to talk about the variety of your curriculum offerings and about your students, their quality, and their success in finding jobs after graduation. How many stay in state? How many have become CEOs of major companies? These are items of interest to a range of constituents.

You should not only describe these accomplishments, but, wherever possible, convert them into the dollars and cents that your unit or institution generates for the economy. If you are not sure how to proceed, talk with one of your fiscal administrators or, if you have a school of business, talk with your business faculty. They can show you such things as how to determine the economic multiplier effects of outside grants and monies and how to calculate the rise in local residential real estate values resulting from the public's access to your institution's theater, cultural facilities, and libraries.

Set goals and objectives

Begin with a core group representing your administration and your faculty and, if you are embarking on a fund-raising campaign, your development office. Use this group to come up with ideas about exactly what you want to accomplish. For a capital campaign, this means deciding which programs you want to build up and how much money you need to do so. Since units within an institution may have competing purposes and interests, it is important to resolve these differences and come together as a group before you kick off your campaign.

In putting together an agenda of activities that will be the backbone for a six-month anniversary celebration or a fund-raising drive, your goal is to get constituencies to think about — and better understand — who you are and what you do. As you plan, you will see the possibilities for building stronger bonds with constituents of all kinds.

Your plan might include, for example, a strategy to reposition your unit and forge an identity as a leader in your state or region or in your discipline, and, to clarify your relationship with state government, a religious denomination, or the surrounding community.

Settle on an organizational structure

With celebratory campaigns, a member of the institution's or the unit's administration is usually the coordinator. He or she works with designated representatives from departments and campus services — and perhaps with a student intern and a temporary aide or two — to make things happen. The institution's public relations and graphic design personnel are commonly enlisted to assist with much of the detailed planning and promotional materials. If these offices cannot accommodate the extra work, they (or you) may hire additional staff for the duration of the campaign.

In fund-raising campaigns, an institution's development office generally takes the lead, with the individual units providing support as requested. Often a marketing consultant or agency is hired to help the development office or to handle the entire project.

Though a development operation can gain substantial benefit from coordinating its activities closely with campus media operations, many do not. This is a decision we have never understood, since campus news services and other campus communicators can often time their production and release of news stories, publications, and so on in ways that reinforce fund-raising activities.

Whatever the arrangement, have a clear chain of command and maintain regular communication with participants to keep everyone informed.

Identify key audiences and their concerns

As we stressed earlier, you can't deliver an effective message (or request) if you don't know who the people are that you need to reach. The public, the media, faculty and staff, students, the local community, and state legislators are some of your most important audiences. Be sure you know who is out there, how much they know about your institution, and what they think of it.

If your public profile seems flat, try to boost awareness with a planned series of events, media stories, and the like. If you make people more aware of who you are and what you do, your celebration or campaign will likely have greater success.

In a fund-raising campaign, major donors are the key people: 90% of the dollars come from 10% or fewer of potential contributors. Reaching donors in the high-end category requires a different strategy from those used to reach people who contribute less than $1,000. Raising funds from major donors depends almost entirely on person-to-person contacts often cultivated over many years. Contributions from small donors are solicited by direct mail and telephone or telemarketing programs.

Yet, it's important not to overlook constituents on the lower rungs, including your faculty, staff, and recent graduates. In fact, you may offend them if you don't invite them to contribute, particularly if they are being bombarded by news of the campaign in various campus publications. They may be able to donate only a modest amount, but it is still a significant statement that they believe in the institution. Welcome these donations graciously, even if it means you get less bang for the buck from your fund-raising budget. It has been shown, moreover, that major contributors were most likely at one time minor contributors. If you can establish a pattern of giving, it will benefit you in the long run. People who donate a little bit this year will probably donate again next year, too, and perhaps boost that level of contribution.

Develop campaign themes

Just as a parade needs a theme around which to build its floats, a campaign needs a theme around which to center its events, publications, lectures, and other activities. Whether it's "Opening the Door for Tomorrow's Generation of Engineers" or "Celebrating a Century of Progress in Agriculture" or "On Our Way to Becoming the West's Leader in Technological Innovation," choose a theme that reflects your campaign's goals and your unit's or institution's mission. Weave the theme into all your campaign messages and materials.

Then design a logo to accompany it. The logo and theme are your identity package and should appear on all your materials throughout the duration of the campaign.

Establish a timetable and select geographic markets

Campaigns of every kind need a timetable that sets out when and where each event will occur. Timetables allow a logical progression of activities and also tell you when supporting materials, transportation, or other services must be lined up. Timetables need to be set early — commonly two years or more in advance. Of course, the fine details do not need such a long lead time, but if you want a national figure for your gala speaker or if you want to reserve the only large auditorium in town, you definitely need to look far ahead.

Capital campaigns generally occur in three phases.

What is called the *pre-announcement phase* is actually a planning phase, during which campus needs are determined, dollar goals are set, and then feelers are sent out to determine whether the goals are realistic, whether the donors are out there, and which well-connected friends of the institution can help in making the approach to the donor.

This is followed by a *quiet phase*, during which potential major donors are approached. Personal contacts and face-to-face interactions, of course, are crucial in actually soliciting donations. In fact, the campaign has not yet been publicly announced. During this phase, the organizers have the opportunity to revise their target sum, depending on the commitments they receive from that important 10% of donors that we mentioned earlier. During this phase, a substantial amount of money is raised.

With a better sense of what's a reasonable target (no one wants to shoot too high and then come in embarrassingly low) and at least 30% of the campaign goal in the bank, the campaign goes into its *public phase* — usually with the announcement of a major gift that was promised during the quiet phase — and with optimistic statements about reaching the goal. Because of the sums of money involved and the need to carefully lay the groundwork for each request, capital campaigns often have a timetable spanning several years or more.

Selecting geographic markets for your campaign means focusing your media messages on those areas where the constituents that you want to reach live. Are they primarily close to campus? Are they concentrated in two or three counties? Are they in the suburbs, the cities, or both? Are they simply any and all of your alumni? Again, the more you know about your audiences, the easier it will be to aim your message at them.

Choose your communications vehicles

How do you get alumni to participate in your unit's anniversary celebrations? How do you get the surrounding community to recognize the importance of your unit's contributions? How do you get donors to contribute to your campaign? The answers largely depend on your creativity in the messages and events that you generate, your ability to get cooperation and support from the mass media, and your personal contacts throughout the campus and community.

Campaigns use many of the media vehicles and techniques that we have already described in this book, including special campaign newsletters, brochures, and tabloids. You can send viewbooks, alumni magazines, and other existing periodicals to constituents, particularly if the publications include material on your unit or your campaign activities. Special events of all kinds — open houses, visits to field stations, special presentations for elementary and high school students — are good ways to tell your story. Photo exhibits, videos, and selected oral histories have great appeal as well, and can be used by electronic media in brief or extended pieces. In all these ways, you can humanize your institution or unit and gain audience interest, even from people who have not had a direct connection to you.

Use your personal connections and influence to get positive editorials or a comment on the evening news. Personal contacts plus good timing can often go a long way.

Seattle University capitalized on the interest created by the institution's centennial celebration in 1991, with the public announcement of its capital campaign following the final centennial event. President William J. Sullivan visited editorial boards at local newspapers and news directors at TV stations, and PR director J. Paul Blake made a three-day trip to contact media representatives in eastern Washington. Among the results: an article in the *Seattle Times* titled "100-Year-Old Seattle U. Is on a Roll."

For the capital campaign, the *case statement* is a key document. It is basically an embellishment of your sustaining message. It lays out your philosophy and your dreams of where you want to go and what you want to achieve. It presents your accomplishments and indicates how the campaign will enable you to move forward.

Writing a good case statement is an art. The statement must be tight but approachable, motivational but factual and sincere.

Your department's mission statement is a major component in your case statement.

Gary A. Best and Alice V. Watkins (1991), respectively chair of the division of Special Education and associate dean of the School of Education, California State University-Los Angeles, have used to good effect this case statement outline:

- *State the need.* Why does the department exist? What is its mission? Why is it important?

- *Document the need.* Number of students, declining state support, cost increases, etc.

- *Share your strategies.* How are you positioning your department or program such that it will be special and its needs more compelling than those of others? What is its quality? How have its graduates fared? What is its standing within the institution?

- *Identify the beneficiaries.* Who will benefit from the gift? Students? Faculty? Alumni? The whole campus?

- *Guide the donors.* How can they easily make the gift? What about a bequest? What are the tax and legal ramifications?

- *Encourage the philanthropic impulse.* It feels good to be generous. What have other donors made possible for your department? How will this donor's money benefit not only your unit, but the institution and society?

A case statement that includes these elements can be a very useful communications tool, not only for your fund-raising efforts, but also for your own internal communications program. It would be worthwhile trying to write such a statement and then seeing how it resonates with colleagues and students. From a group discussion of these elements may come a sharper focus for the unit and its role.

Before you and your development officer prepare a case statement, we suggest that you collect recent statements from other institutions and study them. If you plan to hire consultants to help with the campaign, be sure to examine other case statements that they have prepared to see how effectively they "make their case."

Budget your campaign

It's hard to conduct a campaign without funds. No matter how many volunteers are willing to devote time and talent, some things — such as facilities rentals and anniversary publications — require cold hard cash. Some units, in anticipation of a campaign, set a little money aside each year for several years in advance. Some institutions have reserves for such circumstances. Even so, the first job of a development officer or unit head who wants to undertake a campaign, often, is to find a donor to underwrite the costs of getting started. With some seed money in hand, it is easier to leverage additional funds from campus administrators or other private donors.

Remember: it's always wise to budget some flexible money. Campaigns are planned far in advance; plans and costs can change significantly between the time of conception and execution.

Monitor your progress

Constantly evaluate your progress and the success of your strategies. Meet regularly with your professional or ad hoc communications staff — and also with impartial observers — to assess how things are going. If, for example, you intended to distribute a ten-part series of profiles on outstanding engineers trained in your college, and none of the media to whom you sent the first five profiles have printed a word, you would do well to cancel plans to write the other five or think of some other outlet for your stories. If, on the other hand, the historic photo feature you sent out is wildly popular with the print media, consider putting the photos on a 30-second video with voice-over for distribution to television, as well. Look for opportunities you hadn't anticipated and don't waste resources if ideas don't work out.

Have fun

Campaigns are stressful and often an unwanted additional burden to your already considerable responsibilities. But if you enlist plenty of help and do a good job of delegating, you may find that you actually enjoy the chance a campaign affords to meet new people and see old friends, to work cooperatively with colleagues, and to interact with your local media, civil servants, and merchants in a common purpose that few other activities offer. Reacquainting yourself with your unit's or institution's history and achievements and with its many graduates can give you a shot in the arm that will carry you cheerfully through darker days for a long time to come. Also, take advantage of the opportunity to enlist volunteers in your efforts to lessen the workload on you and your staff and form tighter bonds with key supporters.

Learning from others

Every academic leader at some time in his or her career will face a situation — be it crisis or campaign — when these basic communication strategies will come in handy. One final tip to remember is not to try and reinvent the wheel. Undoubtedly for any situation that comes up, you have friends and colleagues who have "been there, done that." Don't be afraid to learn from their experiences and to adapt what has worked for them. There are very few new ideas around and many of the old ones — in one guise or another — have worked for higher education for decades. Talk to your colleagues or seek out those who have conducted successful campaigns or survived crises with limited damage to their institutions and learn what might work for you.

For further consideration ...

A case study in crisis communication

Patricia J. Gumpert (1993), Stanford professor of higher education, recounts a true story of a communications counter attack that worked beautifully:

At an unidentified "Eastern University," an art education program was targeted for elimination in a campus-wide 'restructuring' drive. It was saved through the charismatic leadership and savvy of the program's director, who managed to realign it with the entrepreneurial orientation of programs not on the block.

First, she renamed the program:

> Our name is a misnomer. We should really be called 'arts management.' Of over 100 students in our program, only six are in training to be teachers. The program is *really* arts administration, as in museums.

Then the director mounted a public relations campaign:

> We collected five notebooks of faxes from all over the world in 72 hours. From research institutes, corporations, industry, and alums. The letters showed the extent to which this program consistently meets local, national, and international needs. We mobilized all the resources we could with lightning speed. We also justified the program by showing its heavy interdisciplinary reliance on the liberal arts. What seemed most compelling was that we ranked second nationally in the country and there is no program duplication in the state. The administration was shocked when they realized they might be alienating their corporate sponsors. Our work is valued by them, as many of the faxes spelled out, in training people for computer graphics and 'management of high arts.'

Meanwhile the school of education was unable to coalesce: "We did it without the dean's help. He was out of the loop."

The result? "Arts management" was the only school of education program saved. Today it resides within this Eastern university's school of architecture, well across campus from the ex-school of education.

Celebrating a big anniversary

Sooner or later your academic unit will have a significant birthday: 25th, 50th, 75th, 150th, even 200th. Don't miss such an opportunity to retell your unit's story to your external audiences, and to stimulate an internal reassessment of unit ideas and ideals.

Some academic leaders have been so fortunate — if that's the right term — to have participated in two or even three anniversary celebrations. What their recollections reveal can help you face the challenge of figuring out how best to be "x" years old.

At the outset, don't "kiss off" as a mere "public relations ploy" the chance to focus public and faculty attention on your unit's record, needs problems, and possibilities. Everybody responds to a birthday "news peg." And give yourself plenty of lead time. Three years is a good bet, if only to write a definitive history and to squirrel away the necessary funds that even a modest celebration will require.

It's best to get an able anniversary chair or director — a lieutenant with imagination and finesse. Give him or her adequate administrative support and establish a broadly based committee to help him or her ensure participation among faculty, staff, students, alumni, and external constituencies.

Contemplate a celebration no more than a semester in length: human interests and emotions can't be sustained indefinitely. Above all, make your memorialization indigenous; that is, an academic celebration should be as much at home on a campus as a sophomore or a dean. Its motives, techniques, and events should be as thoroughly educational as the academic unit or institution it honors. Instead of merrymaking for a few days, develop a sustained commemorative program of extraordinary efforts in every phase of your unit's work.

While your celebration will look backward, of course, make its main thrust clearly one toward the future — the occasion for fundamental strides in functions and policies. As one president sounded a centennial keynote, "We plan to celebrate, not by glorification of the past, but by a relentless search for ways we may best serve in our second century the people of the state, the nation, and the world."

Try to cultivate a "grass roots" level of energy. A central committee can guide and prod, but it can't order a celebration. At best it will offer financial support and administrative aid to projects conceived and carried out from the bottom up, projects that mesh with traditional public functions, institutional practices, and the academic calendar — commencement, for example.

Do whatever you can to make your anniversary mean something to all the constituencies of your unit and realize its full potential in arousing public interest and support — as with the kickoff of a fund drive. Focus on people — hallowed professors, successful alumni, students with unbounded enthusiasm, supportive legislators or donors or trustees, and so on — and honor them appropriately.

Whatever the formality of the occasion, don't ignore "bumper-sticker" trimmings — such as an emblem and a slogan, to be emblazoned on an escutcheon for a speaker's rostrum, to be enlarged as a banquet or concert backdrop, and to illuminate anniversary publications. As a corollary, think up print media feature articles and TV sound bites. An anniversary that doesn't make news is no celebration at all. But the theme of your communication program should be focused on those institutional efforts that encourage units to rethink azimuths and recharge their aspirations.

This is the least, and the most, you should aim for in capitalizing on any anniversary: that it be a true mirror of the record, that it face the future as well as the past, and that it serve to identify your unit with all its publics to salutary effect.

chapter thirteen

Driving the Information Superhighway
Leadership communications in the electronic age

We may not be living in the middle 1400s, but we are witnessing an equally revolutionary time. In the past 15 years, the evolution in communications has been just as dramatic and had as much impact on the lives of many of us in academia as did Johann Gutenberg's invention of the movable type press and the printing of the first book on that press in 1457.

The development of the personal computer not only is radically changing the ways in which we communicate, but the speed and volume of that communication. Computers and other technology already have made almost unimaginable amounts of data available to us at the touch of a keyboard. They enable us to create lavishly illustrated documents — even books — in our homes or offices. Using computers, we can send long documents around the globe instantaneously at almost no cost. And we can have real-time conversations with people all over the world sitting at our keyboards, connected through modems.

Whether or not you personally cruise the information superhighway, it's important to know how new technology is affecting communications, how computers are changing the academic environment, and how you can use these new methods and media to further your goals.

It is possible using new video conferencing technology, for example, for faculty members at the Massachusetts Institute of Technology and UC Berkeley to team-teach a course to students in both locations. Courses from anthropology to zoology are now taught via an electronic bulletin-board system, by which students can read lectures and course materials, "talk" with professors, use simulations, and take tests with only a computer, a modem, and a telephone. More sophisticated computers will soon put video conferencing within reach of the average faculty member and student. Researchers at colleges and universities around the globe already instantaneously share research results and discuss their work electronically.

The "virtual college" or "virtual university" is a developing reality. By the turn of the century, students anywhere in the world may be able to tailor their college experience, taking courses at any school of their choosing and graduating with credits from institutions around the world.

Imagine taking music appreciation at the University of Indiana, engineering at MIT, English at Yale, chemistry at UC Berkeley, sociology at the University of Wisconsin-Madison, Shakespeare at Oxford, film history at UCLA, art history at the Université de Paris, and political science at Harvard — without ever leaving your home!! It may seem fantastic, but the technology exists to create such a virtual, international educational network right now.

Each week brings news of innovative ways that colleges and universities are using the new technology to improve teaching and to further research. There is enough happening to warrant entire books on this technological revolution and what it means to academia. Since our observations are confined to one chapter, we are limiting our discussion to the means by which new technologies can facilitate your communication with important constituents. We want to give you some sense of the power of this new age of the Internet and some examples of how deans, department chairs, and other college administrators are using these means to pursue their communication objectives.

Overcoming cyberphobia

You may be among the many in academia who have resisted putting one of those #$%@!!#* machines on your desk. Resist no more. The computer is today's equivalent of a telephone — another invention that many loathe. But trying to do business without a computer and a modem is rapidly becoming impossible.

This is especially true in academia, where computers were born, because today's students are so "cyberliterate." They communicate via computer. They do their papers and homework via computer. They even make friends and check up on the dorm's lunch menu via computer. It is important that college teachers and administrators be where their students are — in cyberspace.

But how to overcome a phobia about computers? Despite all the hype, there are really no manuals, books, or videotapes that can provide instant enlightenment and make you comfortable with computers. The best advice is to spend an afternoon with someone with whom you feel at ease who can show you the ropes.

Start with simple word processing tasks, if you are new to the game. As with anything else, don't walk away for a month and expect to come back to the computer, remembering how to use it. Use it or lose it.

Once you master the basics, start to use a computer regularly and you will gradually feel more at home with it. Once you've overcome your resistance to working with it, the rest will follow quite readily.

IDG Books Worldwide, Inc. has made a fortune on its series of computer books written especially for neophytes — *Macs for*

Dummies, Windows for Dummies, Internet for Dummies, and so on. These books take a very practical approach, with a wonderful sense of humor. They are a good buy, whether you are a "newbie" or a veteran.

Dan Gookin and Andy Rathbone, authors of *PCs for Dummies* (1992), start their book with this introduction:

> Welcome to *PCs for Dummies,* the book that answers the question "How does a computer turn a smart person like you into a dummy?" Computers are useful, yes. And a fair number of people — heaven help them — fall in love with computers. But the rest of us are left sitting dumb and numb in front of the box. It's not that using a computer is beyond the range of our IQs; it's that no one has ever bothered to sit down and explain things in human terms. Until now.

If that sounds like a good start, pick up a "dummies" guide. It will help ease the transition — and make very entertaining reading.

There are now two levels of computer literacy that relate to our ability to use computer technology in our communications programs.

The first is simply learning to use a computer and coming to appreciate what it can offer — the time it saves in drafting letters and reports; the ability to quickly and cheaply produce documents of all sizes; and the power to store, retrieve, track, and process information.

Up until five years ago, that was power enough! But today, we need to appreciate the power of computers not only to process information but also to deliver it. The past five years have seen the emergence of computer networking. (More to come on this, later in the chapter.) Using computers to send or receive information via the Internet is the second level of computer literacy and it is quickly overtaking the more conventional methods of communicating, such as phone, mail, and fax.

As Linda Weimer composes this sentence in the study of her home in California, it is possible not only to manipulate the sentence in *various* ways using her relatively primitive computer, but also — at the touch of a button — to send the text by electronic mail to the book editors in Wisconsin, two thousand miles away, instantaneously! They can read and edit the text and then return it, taking mere seconds instead of days, as with snail mail.

In some ways, computers have succeeded where diplomacy has failed: they are knitting the globe together into one huge community or neighborhood in which there are no borders, barriers, or obstacles, except language. Members can communicate with each other, uncensored, and all have immediate access to the same growing pool of information. The notion of a global community is finally being realized — on the Internet.

Computers as tools

In the mid-1970s, computers began to come into common usage in offices across the country. Though they had been used for research by academics for some time, it wasn't until about 20 years ago that computers started to replace the electric typewriter as the office tool of choice.

Weimer remembers this transition vividly, as one of her jobs as communications director for the UW-Madison Sea Grant Institute was to oversee the preparation of the annual, two-volume, 800-page funding proposal to the federal government. Within a few years, what had been a draining task, requiring many weekends for the communications office staff and several temporary employees to do the editing, typing, and corrections, became enormously simplified as the text, stored on computer, was simply edited on screen and printed out electronically.

Of course, now that same text can be supplemented with sophisticated graphics via computer, formatted in various ways, and then transmitted to Washington, DC via the Internet. Research proposals theoretically can be written, submitted, reviewed, re-turned, changed, resubmitted, and funded without ever going to "hard copy."

Unfortunately, the dream of computers making us a "paperless society" has not been realized. In fact, we have just the opposite situation, because computers make it so easy to draft and produce documents.

In fact, a California businessman was recently interviewed on television and he credited the advent of the computer with his remarkable success — he has built a multimillion-dollar docu-ment-shredding company. His crews travel to company work sites, such as investment firms and insurance agencies, to shred confidential documents — all generated by computer.

This document-production capacity has had the most profound effect on campus-based communications programs. Computers and sophisticated software have made desktop publishing a reality. Departments and divisions can produce their own bro-chures, pamphlets, posters, newsletters, and other periodicals "in-house" with ease — there is no need for an outsider to edit, typeset, design, and print the publications. Or is there?

Here is a look at some of the most prevalent ways that computers are helping academic offices communicate, followed by some tips on how to make use of them — and how not to!

Correspondence

The computer has been a tremendous boon in terms of handling correspondence. Computers have made it possible to easily tailor letters for target audiences, keep track of mailing addresses, and do sophisticated merge-and-print functions so that letters can be targeted very specifically to selected groups.

In mailing letters to prospective students, for example, Amanda Perkins is able to write three versions of the same letter — one to students from local high schools, one to in-state students who are not in the local area, and a third to out-of-state students. She tailors each version to the recipient: the first emphasizes the quality of the department and encourages nearby students not to feel they have to go far away to college; the second also emphasizes departmental quality, but stresses what a bargain in-state tuition represents; and the third favorably compares the quality of Midland's program with those of peer institutions around the country.

Perkins and her assistant are able to sort mailing addresses by ZIP code and thus, tailor the salutation and message to each individual student being encouraged to join her department. They then store the letters on a diskette, to be used again at the same time next year. In this way, computers have greatly reduced the drudgery of communicating with important constituencies.

Data bases

With computers it is also possible to maintain data bases of all kinds. We can check past correspondence at the stroke of a few keys or keep detailed records on important contributors to our institutions and units. We can also track budgets, plugging into campuswide computer networks that instantly track the expenditures of the department or division and give administrators up-to-the-minute accounts of their budgets and balances.

Newsletters

Computers also have made it relatively simple to produce regular newsletters and periodicals. By setting up a template, adorned with the newsletter name and departmental logo, the newsletter editor — often the department chair — can simply plug in the appropriate news in the appropriate frames and print off dozens of copies of the newsletter on the office printer.

Publications

As we graduate to more sophisticated publications, the value of desktop publishing comes more into question. Campus editors and graphic designers serve a function that goes beyond simply putting your ideas into print. They help with the conception of the message, the tailoring of the message to a given audience, providing readable (and even enjoyable) copy and giving the whole affair a polished, coherent graphic identity.

One sad result of desktop publishing is that there is more junk being put out by those of us in academia (and elsewhere) because it is so easy to do so. The adage "GIGO" ("Garbage In, Garbage Out") still prevails. If a publication wasn't worth doing "the old-fashioned way," then it probably isn't worth doing now in new ways.

The rise of "vanity" publishing is closely tied with the growth of computers. The irony is that people today — partly because of the glut of information coming at them — have less time to spend on brochures, newsletters, magazines, and other publications than in the past. This means that any publication must be more, not less, sophisticated. It is worth seeking some professional assistance for your publications program — at least to set it on the right course — before you and your staff get too enamored of the power of the new technology.

Cyberliteracy

Equipped with spell-checkers and grammar programs, word processing programs can also help academic administrators polish their documents and reduce the need for copyediting. Nevertheless, we have to be careful not to rely completely on the computer for good syntax and correct spelling, as we are reminded by this little ditty by Jerry Zar, Dean of the Graduate School, Northwestern Illinois University (1995):

An Owed to the Spelling Checker

I have a spelling checker
It came with my PC
It plane lee marks four my revue
Miss steaks aye can knot sea.

Eye ran this poem threw it,
Your sure reel glad two no.

Its vary polished in it's weigh.
My checker tolled me sew.

A checker is a bless sing,
It freeze yew lodes of thyme.
It helps me right awl stiles two reed,
And aides me when aye rime.

Each frays come posed up on my screen
Eye trussed too bee a joule
The checker pour o'er every word
To cheque sum spelling rule.

Be fore a veiling checkers
Hour spelling mite decline,
And if were lacks or have a laps,
We wood be maid to wine.

Butt now bee cause my spelling
Is checked with such grate flare,
Their are know faults with in my cite,
Of non eye am a wear.

Now spelling does knot phase me,
It does knot bring a tier.
My pay purrs awl due glad den
With wrapped words fare as hear.

To rite with care is quite a feet
Of witch won should be proud.
And wee mussed dew the best wee can,
Sew flaws are knot aloud.

Sow ewe can sea why aye dew prays
Such soft ware four pea seas.
And why I brake in two averse
By righting want too pleas.

Cruising the information superhighway

As much as computers help us shape and produce our messages,
they are proving an even more astonishing tool in helping us
deliver that message to audiences, far and wide. Computers and
their linkages have created a new medium for reaching out.

Even those of us who do not use computers are familiar with the terms "Internet" or "Information Superhighway." But just what is it? And how can you use it?

History of the Internet

The term "Internet" stands for interconnected computer network. It is a network of thousands — perhaps now, millions — of individual computer networks in countries around the world. It is, in essence, a network of networks that links tens of thousands of universities, colleges, businesses, government agencies, and research organizations, and millions of people.

What is now known as the Internet was first formed as a military computer network, ARPAnet — the Advanced Research Projects Agency network. Originally part of the Department of Defense, it was opened up to non-military users in 1970 when companies and universities doing defense-related research first were allowed access to it. During the 1980s, online traffic grew rapidly. In the 1990s, commercial uses of the Internet came into being.

In 1993, commercial providers were first permitted to sell Internet access to individuals; and traffic exploded on the information superhighway (a term that Vice President Al Gore is said to have coined).

The advantages of being linked to a network were readily apparent to users — to quickly and easily share data and information files, to send electronic mail, to run computer programs at remote sites or use software not available on their home computers, and to access data bases too large to fit on an individual computer.

Within the past few years, the U.S. government has officially turned the Internet over to the private sector, which means that no single authority now governs its use, although users voluntarily adhere to a telecommunications protocol. The fact that no single entity is in charge of the Internet gives rise to complex issues of privacy and censorship that are entering our courts, with the potential to clog our legal system. For the moment, it appears that materials on the Internet are subject to the same laws and standards that apply to published materials (as we discuss later in this chapter).

The Internet today

As of early 1996, 37 million people — 17% of the population of the U.S. and Canada over age 16 — had access to the Internet, according to a Nielsen Internet survey. That poll also showed that 24 million people had used the Internet sometime during the past three months and those who used it spent an average of five hours and 28 minutes a week on the 'Net. About a third (34%) of the Internet users are women. Also revealing in the survey: 25% of Internet users had family incomes in excess of $80,000 annually and 64% have college degrees.

The number of sites on the World Wide Web has grown from an estimated 1,000 in April 1994 to several hundreds of thousands. This explosive growth continues to exceed all projections and provides a glimmer of the awesome power of this new method of communication.

On several facts, however, most agree — there are millions of users now online, and the growth rate is expected to rise exponentially over the next few years.

The most ubiquitous use of the Internet is for electronic mail. Over 90% of people using the 'Net use it to communicate and/or to learn.

Communicating through the Internet

The fact that the Internet is a popular means of communication will come as no surprise to most academic administrators, to whom email has been both a boon and a bane.

The same technology that allows you to immediately spread the word to colleagues and students that your department has just gotten a nice gift from a grateful alum also overflows your "email box" with messages from others.

Email

As we mentioned in chapter 10, email provides an almost instant pipeline to thousands of specialists in virtually every field. We can send data, ideas, and queries to colleagues across the country and around the world, greatly facilitating collaboration. Emailing is far cheaper than long-distance calling, because you relay your message through a mainframe computer by making a call to a local service provider.

Email etiquette

In some ways, email — both around the world and around campus — has become too handy. It eliminates the need for person-to-person contact and can be used — when it shouldn't be — to handle interpersonal communications of a sensitive nature.

Many of the problems of email were covered when UC Berkeley reporter Kathy Scalise interviewed staff ombudsperson Ella Wheaton in the campus newspaper, *Berkeleyan* (1995):

> Everyone knows not to belch at the table, but not everyone knows using email the wrong way can be just as crude.
>
> And when it comes to people getting worked up over email, Ella Wheaton of the Staff Ombuds Office has seen it all. Wheaton says she knows when there's been an email problem the moment a staff member crosses her doorstep.
>
> "People walk in with files this thick," she holds her hands five inches apart. "They don't even have to tell me what the problem is, I already know." It's an email shootout.
>
> "We're like the pulse here," said Wheaton. "These days, email is becoming a very serious issue for us because it's a powerful mode of communication that can create relationship problems, conflict and, in some circumstances, liability." For issues that have emotion behind them, "email or voice mail or any electronic mode is not the best," said Wheaton. "It can lead to what I call electronic warfare: response, reaction,

response, reaction. I have seen some major mistakes at the touch of a button."

She especially encourages people to talk person-to-person when supervising and not use email to keep their distance. Or "you may just be trying to communicate with your staff because you're in a rush, but the employee starts to see it as being documented," she said.

"Staff see email as documentation. Staff feel compelled to respond because you're creating a record, whether you intend it or not. I have also seen staff compile extensive documentation on their managers, both with and without their knowledge."

Thus email takes on an unintended formality. Or sometimes the formality is intended, but it just makes for bad relations. One staff member having problems with her boss described it as "no communication, just a lot of nasty notes going back and forth." For her, the situation improved when her employer stopped firing off a slew of emails marked "urgent" five minutes before it was time for her to head home for the day. Whatever the situation, people can feel stressed under constant bombardment by email.

"Nobody would write me a letter, edit it, sign it and send it through campus mail asking me the kind of questions I get all day long on email," said one staff member. "In many ways, email makes it too easy to communicate."

It also makes it easy to pass along someone else's words inappropriately. A pet peeve is forwarding email without asking. Especially provoking is when email is edited, then forwarded. Sometimes phrases are taken out of context, but the original signature is left in place. People are outraged when they feel their words have been twisted.

Other times it isn't how you say it, but what you say. Junk email, otherwise known as j-mail, is the "$75 Nordic Track for sale" notice that has been haunting some screens or the "sublet available, call me." Putting out unsolicited email can be considered "noising up" everybody's mail boxes.

At UC Irvine, for instance, a heated debate broke out a while back when one department emailed much of the campus about its charity auction. The offending department was "flamed." In electronic jargon, to flame is the email term for sending angry messages when provoked by the bad manners of others. However, flaming itself is considered boorish.

For that matter, said Wheaton, "it could be that the etiquette of email is not so widely known. I think it's a little on the technical side to know that all capital letters is considered shouting in email. Our campus is just coming up on widespread use of email in the last two years." Those who would like a guide to keep them mannerly in all their email ways might want to check out an electronic publication on the Internet called "The Net: User Guidelines and Netiquette." It is available via the World Wide Web at the Web address: http://rs6000.adm.fau.edu/faahr/arlene.html.

A major issue in email communication is privacy. In public colleges and universities, they are considered public documents and the property of the institution. If, for example, a local reporter asks to see email communication between a dean and a department head on an issue, she is entitled to copies. And just because you erase email from your computer doesn't mean that it is gone. Almost all computer networks have "backup" systems that routinely save and store correspondence and documents.

Anybody using an email system should assume that the world may see any and all messages. Once a message gets into a network, it can be copied and forwarded for wide distribution, which can lead to problems.

Journalist Linda Ellerbe says she was once fired from a wire service reporting job because she inadvertently sent a letter she was writing to a close friend out over the wire service to a group of puzzled newspaper editors when she pressed the wrong key!

It also is wise not to put too much faith in a password. System administrators, not to mention proficient students, can get past such rudimentary system security measures.

It is important that colleagues treat email as something to be used for business purposes only. And, as noted above, email shouldn't be used to handle personnel actions such as criticism, perform-ance evaluations, warnings or involuntary separations — no matter how tempting it is to avoid a difficult face-to-face contact.

USENET, a collection of electronic bulletin boards that can be reached through the Internet and other computer networks, is popular with many academics. The bulletin boards are grouped according to discipline. For example, "bionet" contains bulletin boards primarily used by biologists, while the "soc" bulletin boards are used by sociologists. As you might guess, there is even a periodical covering bulletin board news, *Boardwatch Maga-zine*.

Electronic bulletin boards

The bulletin boards in so-called "newsgroups" may be moder-ated or they may not. Material submitted to a moderated group is first screened by an editor, who decides whether it's worth posting. Users of an unmoderated newsgroup get information more quickly, but may have to plow through a lot of extraneous material. Regular patrons of a newsgroup can decide by vote for one option or the other.

Networking is what intra-academia communication is all about these days. Merit Network, Inc., a consortium of Michigan uni-versities, offers help to those who want accesss to free, on-line Internet guides. Send an electronic mail message to NIC_INFO@NIS.MERIT.EDU.

*Keeping in touch
with the media*

Like academics, some journalists have been on the cutting edge of computer communication, while others have lagged far behind. In general, newspapers as an industry have been slower than colleges and universities to embrace the 'Net, but things are changing.

American Opinion Research, Inc. and the Foundation for American Communications recently completed a survey of 1200 randomly selected newspaper publishers, editors and advertising directors across the country (McCarthy 1995).

Only half the editors said they are currently using the Internet to do research and reporting, but 74% said they plan to use it within the next year. Likewise, 48% of respondents say they've investigated or implemented online services for their readers during the past year; 45% said they will institute these services in the next 12 months.

Campus news offices, on the other hand, have been quick to adopt computers and modems to communicate with the media. As early as the mid-1980s, the University of Wisconsin-Madison was sending press releases directly into the computers of the local newspapers. Not only did this increase the rate at which the papers picked up stories about the university, but also it reduced the number of errors in the coverage, since reporters and editors no longer had to edit and rekey the stories to get them into the local editions.

Computers now provide an opportunity to target the information to specific reporters — or media — and to get the message across right away.

Ed Tate, news bureau director at the University of Illinois at Chicago, is a big fan of computers. He routinely puts out feelers on the Internet and subscribes to several services that supply leads and experts to reporters. One story that his office posted on the SciNews-MedNews (science and medical information) network resulted in a cover story in the the July 1995 *Discover* magazine (Geuder 1995).

One of the first people to recognize the power of the Internet in communicating with journalists was Dan Forbush, who founded ProfNet while heading the news office at the State University of New York at Stony Brook, as we previously mentioned in chapter eleven.

Forbush has now spun off ProfNet as an independent "electronic cooperative" through which reporters post queries and campus PR folks respond with leads and appropriate faculty experts. Colleges and universities pay a modest fee to subscribe to the service, but journalists are given access for free.

The December 29, 1995 "issue" of ProfNet looked like this:

PROFNET SEARCH 1222

December 29, 1995
[Sent Friday at 1:00 p.m. EST]

———————————

SYSOP'S CORNER
HERE'S WISHING EVERYONE a happy and safe New Year's with all the best for 1996. Given the holiday, our next scheduled send will go out at the regular time Tuesday morning.

———————

SUMMARY
BUSINESS:
1. Marketing Magazines – Magazine Retailer

HEALTH/MEDICINE:
2. Weight Loss and Exercise – Weight Watcher's Magazine

LAW/CRIME/JUSTICE:
3. Attacks on Newspaper Carriers – Dayton Daily News

SCIENCE/TECHNOLOGY:
4. Safety of Front-Wheel Drive – Freelancer

———————

QUERIES

BUSINESS
**1. MARKETING MAGAZINES – MAGAZINE RETAILER.
Norm Schreiver is editing a new magazine called Magazine Retailer and seeks leads on experts who can discuss a variety of facets pertaining to the single-copy marketing of magazines in supermarkets and on newsstands. His specific interests: magazine reader demographics and profiles, innovations in inventory, store design, and magazine marketing. Seeks leads by February. E-mail: 75452.1340@compuserve.com Fax: 718-857-5899 Phone: 718-636-5992 (12/29)

HEALTH/MEDICINE
**2. WEIGHT LOSS AND EXERCISE – WEIGHT WATCHER'S MAGAZINE. Laurie Salomon seeks leads on experts who can discuss the "mind games" that those attempting to lose weight often play with respect to exercise and food. For example, she seeks experts who can set the record straight on the number of calories that we can expect various types of exercise to burn and offer suggestions on making these evaluations more realistic. Needs leads by the end of Tuesday. If forwarding leads between now and Monday evening, please use Laurie's fax at 212-687-4398. On Tuesday, please call her directly at 212-370-0644 x15. (12/29)

LAW/CRIME/JUSTICE
**3. ATTACKS ON NEWSPAPER CARRIERS – DAYTON DAILY NEWS. A person who delivers newspapers was murdered while on her route here in Dayton this morning. I'm interested in any studies that may have been done on the hazardousness of this occupation and/or any research on whether such attacks are becoming more frequent.

Janice Haidet Morse E-mail: Janice_Haidet_Morse@dni.com Phone: 513-225-2220 (12/29)

While it would not be economical for most individual departments or divisions to subscribe to such a service, it would be well to know if your campus news office has electronic links to the media. These are especially invaluable when there is a breaking news story to which your faculty might lend some expertise.

It is also important to note that electronic links are critical for radio and TV editors and reporters, too. Surveys have shown that

50% of consumers get all their news from television and 50% of people under the age of 30 don't read a daily newspaper. Although electronic media reporters have been slower to adopt Internet browsing as a method of getting sources or ideas for stories, that, too, is changing.

One of the most important, and most liberating, aspects of the Internet has been that colleges and universities can take their messages directly to the public. Most institutions — and many divisions and departments — have their own World Wide Web home pages, a sort of electronic front door through which people can visit them and gain access to all sorts of information.

Getting around the media

There are frequently pictures of the campus, course descriptions, faculty biographies, information about student organizations, and campus maps — even access to the library. The campus home page for the University of California, Berkeley, as an example, provides access to hundreds of campus information sites and receives 100,000 visits ("hits") each month. Cal's online catalog counts about a thousand hits a day.

Aside from making information available on the Internet to those who seek it out or those who just happen upon it, campus administrators are getting more savvy about using the Internet to reach out to selected groups — among them, alumni, donors, and other friends of the institution. It is especially cost-efficient and timely to reach alumni in foreign countries in this fashion. When keeping up with alumni, email addresses are becoming as important as mailing addresses.

The Office of University Relations at the University of California, Berkeley now routinely sends an electronic newsletter to key alumni and donors. It is called *Berkeley Online* and goes to about 1500 subscribers (up from about 100 a year ago).

The beauty is that it goes directly into each subscriber's mailbox — there's no need to search it out. Here is how it appears (1995):

BERKELEY ONLINE
22 December, 1995
v2.6

IN THIS ISSUE:

o Mooch is Back!
o Can You Say Top 25?
o Support Growing in Asia
o Looking for a Tax Deduction?

****

MOOCH IS BACK!

It was hailed as a great day for California football. For Steve Mariucci, it was a homecoming to the campus he loves and to the team he helped lead to a 10-2 record and national No. 7 ranking in 1991. Last Thursday [Dec. 14], the Green Bay Packers' quarterback coach and former Cal offensive coordinator was named head football coach of the Golden Bears.

"We're going to go out and recruit the best coaches and the best players, and I firmly believe we're going to make Cal a contender year-in and year-out in the Pac-10," said Mariucci, widely regarded as one of the most innovative offensive minds in the game. In the National Football League and at Berkeley, he is credited with cultivating remarkable quarterback talent, including current Green Bay QB Brett Favre and former Cal QB Mike Pawlawski, who earned Pac-10 Co-Offensive Player of the Year honors in 1991.

On a tangential note, Mariucci's nickname — "Mooch" — adds to the list of Cal's already colorful coaching staff that includes women's basketball coach Gooch Foster. Can you say "Coach Gooch, Coach Mooch" five times fast?

CAN YOU SAY TOP 25?

The Cal basketball team faces another highly ranked foe this Saturday in Chicago, when the Golden Bears take on the Fighting Illini of Illinois. Todd Bozeman's squad made its debut at No. 24 this week in the Associated Press Poll of top 25 teams.

The Bears, at 4-1, are displaying strong individual efforts, despite a loss to No. 9 Cincinnati on Wednesday. Bear fans hope the first loss of the young season will be instructive — before any Pac-10 action begins. The first Pac-10 game will be on Jan. 4 against the Arizona Wildcats at the Oakland Coliseum Arena. Tip-off time is 7:30 p.m. The Bears are also playing during the holidays in the Otis Spunkmeyer Classic, also at the Coliseum. Roll on you Bears!

SUPPORT GROWING IN ASIA

In recent weeks, UC Berkeley has been the recipient of $4 million in gifts and pledges from various corporate and governmental donors in Asia. Of this total, $3 million stemmed from the Berkeley-sponsored Asian Leadership Conference, recently convened in Indonesia. In addition to $1.5 million reported in last month's Berkeley Online [from NEC Corp., to support an NEC Distinguished Professorship], the University has also received:

- $1.5 million from Robert H. C. Tsao, chairman of United Microelectronics Corp. Of this, $1 million will support the UMC Distinguished Professorship in the fields of electronics, materials science, and physics. The $500,000 balance is a gift to the College of Chemistry for the construction of Tan Kah Kee Hall, Berkeley's new home for chemical engineering.

- $1 million from the Korean Ministry of Culture and Sports to establish the Ken Min Endowed Directorship for Taekwondo and the Martial Arts, honoring the man who began the campus's taekwondo program in 1969. Currently, 1,000 students a year participate in the Martial Arts Program on campus, taking classes and competing on teams. Cal, which has held the national collegiate taekwondo team title over the past six years, is credited with raising the stature of the sport worldwide. In the next two years, the university will work to attract an additional $1 million for the endowment.

LOOKING FOR A TAX DEDUCTION?

You may not have $1 million to give, but every gift counts. And it's not too late to give to Cal and get a tax deduction for 1995. You can mail your contributions payable to the UC Berkeley Foundation to the University of California, Berkeley, 2440 Bancroft Way #4200, Berkeley, CA 94720-4200. Donor lines are also open at University Relations until 5 p.m., Pacific time, Thursday, Dec. 28 - 510/642-4122.

****

Berkeley Online is produced monthly by UC Berkeley's University Relations. Cal alumni and friends may subscribe to the list from their computer terminals by sending the following command in the body of a message to "maiser@dev.urel.berkeley.edu": SUB-SCRIBE berkeleyonline. To unsubscribe to the list, send the following command in the body of a message to "maiser@dev.urel.berkeley.edu": UNSUBSCRIBE berkeleyonline

Send your comments, suggestions, and ideas to JLR@dev.urel.Berkeley.edu. Let us know immediately about any transmission problems. Please tell other Berkeley alumni and friends about Berkeley Online.

A little heavy on the sports and fund-raising, but perhaps that's to be expected in a year-end message to potential donors.

Taking advantage of online services

Many Internet access providers are now offering their services to alumni associations as a membership benefit and as a way of keeping alumni in touch with their colleges. These arrangements are usually mutually beneficial to the service and the institution, because the former gains access to a new customer, while the latter gains an inexpensive way to keep key audiences in touch with the program.

Online services also can be a boon to college and university administrators whose campus-based computer links are not yet fully developed or who are on the road a lot. For a nominal fee (about $10/month), an online service will provide access to the Internet, an email address, and a range of customized services.

Weimer belongs to America Online, which enables her, when traveling, to send email or read and answer email that has been forwarded from her office, simply by calling a local America Online access number. She can send a fax from her portable computer. In addition, there is a news browser feature which seeks out stories that mention the University of California, Berkeley and downloads them to her America Online mailbox.

Online service providers have gotten very competitive and often will provide free trial services. Avail yourself of the opportunity, but you will need a high-speed modem (14,400 bps or more) to really explore these services to maximum advantage.

Internet issues

While computers and the Internet have opened up a host of opportunities to colleges and universities and their component units, there are pitfalls as well. We will touch on some, of which academic administrators should be mindful.

While the wonders of new technology have opened up new avenues of fast and cheap communication, they have also made the job of communicating with constituencies even more challenging. You have friends and colleagues who *only* communicate online; and you have those who *never* communicate online. Eventually, you might train people to search for the information where you put it (on email, for example), but for now you may have to use more than one way to communicate your message. Putting out a newsletter online, for example, can be an effective project, but there are alumni of your department who will never see it; if that is your sole means of communication, it will be inadequate.

Who's missing?

In essence, cyberspace has not replaced other forms of communication; it has simply added another medium to be considered for your message. Using the parameters outlined earlier in this book, you can best determine how to effectively communicate online and with which key audiences.

The Internet also poses problems related to privacy. If students can crack the computer networks at some of Silicon Valley's most prestigious and high-tech businesses, they can surely crack yours. As was noted earlier in this chapter, one must be careful about placing sensitive information on the 'Net.

Privacy and the 'Net

Web policies

The Internet was once a place for unbridled creativity, but now colleges and universities are beginning to take a close look at what is on their computer networks and to develop policies governing content and access. It would be well to check with your university administrators to see if they have rules governing how the institution is to be represented in cyberspace and how your materials can be linked to the campus' home page.

Another area of growing concern is copyright. Although it is still a vague area, it is likely that the copyright laws which govern printed materials will govern the Internet as well. Be careful, for example, in using photographs in your "cybercations." Even if you have purchased the right to use them in print, you may not own the right to use them on the Internet. Even established entities like the Smithsonian Institution are unable to precisely tell you their policies governing the use of their images on the Internet — the whole area is so new that laws and policies are only just now being addressed. Undoubtedly, the Internet will provide a comfortable living to many students now enrolled in our law schools.

High tech/high touch

Fred Volkmann, vice chancellor for university relations at Washington University (MO), talks about the coming age of "High Tech/High Touch" (1995). He reminds us that no matter what, person-to-person remains the most effective and influential form of communication. Not all the computers or email networks or publications in the world can replace that one-on-one contact.

The most powerful use of computers and the Internet for constituent relations will be the capacity to more efficiently provide that *personal* communication — to quickly get out an email when the occasion warrants it or forward a message on to a co-worker, an influential alumna, a local policymaker, or a colleague in England. Perhaps the irony of the new age of electronic communication is that it will bring us back to a time when communities were "neighborhoods," when we had a common frame of reference, when we had more access to each other, more time for a chat and to exchange views. That would be the hope of this new age — that it can make our communications efforts a little more human.

chapter fourteen

How to Know When You Get There
Measuring the results of effective communications

From one perspective, effective communications is a good deal like faith — "the substance of things hoped for, the evidence of things not seen." That is, the effect or result of a single communications vehicle, or of a complete communications program, is not always or even frequently easy to determine.

Yet, once your communications program is under way, evaluation should become an ongoing process that enables you to make the adjustments, big or small, that keep you moving toward your goal. By using a battery of measuring devices, you can at the very least distinguish very successful communication from communication that is grossly ineffective. The trick comes in isolating the variables such that you know what it is you're measuring.

To some extent, evaluation derives from good planning and audience research, as discussed earlier in this book. If you don't have a plan or objective, no amount of measurement will let you assess your progress. But once you know where you are trying to go, there are tools to help you determine when you get there.

For many academic administrators, there are crude but important measures of the success of communicating with important constituents. Ask yourself these questions:

- Are we recruiting the students, faculty, and staff we want?

- Are we getting the support of our college administrators?

- Are we successful at getting extramural support for our department or division?

- Are more of our alumni staying in touch with us?

- Are we raising more money in private gifts?

- Are people feeling good about our department or division?

- Is our reputation measuring up to our quality?

- Do people know about us?

- Do they think well of us?

These are the sorts of questions that many academic administrators wrestle with these days. The answers tend to be highly subjective, depending on the source. Nevertheless, there are techniques that can be used to more objectively answer such questions and to provide the guidance necessary to refine your communications methods and programs.

Scott Cutlip, Allen H. Center, and Glen Broom, authors of *Effective Public Relations* (1994), have suggested four key things that demand evaluation or measurement:

- Coverage — Did your message reach all the pertinent groups?

- Response — Did those groups respond negatively, positively, or neutrally to your message?

- Impact — Did your message have lasting, long-term effects on the audience?

- Influence — Did your message set into motion the social processes necessary to influence the opinions and behavior of its target audience?

Measuring communications results is difficult and inexact. Still, there are some empirical devices, which we will explore below, that yield results difficult to refute.

Pudding proof

In keeping with the aphorism that "the proof of the cook is in the pudding," if a communications program accomplishes its mission, it's hard to say that the program was somehow not effective. Of course, such a measurement is largely subjective, because you can't really distinguish which *who, what, when, where,* and *how* elements of the program were crucial and which were wasted. On the other hand, no other method is so definitive in the large.

Writing in *Newsweek's* special edition on "The World War II Generation and How it Changed America" (1993), James Michener recalls that "not once in the years 1941-1945, did I hear a single American inveigh against the war." While the distinguished author may have missed somebody, what he says has become an accepted public belief. It can be taken as a given, then, that the massive communications program undertaken by the Office of War Information was successful in helping to develop what Michener calls "an extraordinary total national effort" marked by "moral dedication and incredible bravery."

On a much less grand scale, we can all point to fund-raising drives or similar campaigns in which success was clearly visible in dollars raised, legislation passed, or other desired outcomes. But when the mission is less specific (such as for a program to generate a positive public attitude toward a particular division or department), determining the effectiveness of the program will also be less specific.

Because so much communication falls into this imprecise area, you should not hesitate to take full credit for those of your programs that are clearly successful, since in many other undertakings you will find it hard — if not impossible — to show a direct connection between successful outcomes and your communications effort.

Bean-counting

Are your news releases making it into news media? Scrutinize the media or contract with a clipping service to do it for you. Then add up the number of stories in print, on radio, and on TV. Total up column inches and/or minutes of air time and you've got a very pragmatic measure of your ability to satisfy the needs of news media gatekeepers. If you photocopy the evidence and distribute it periodically to campus officials and key alumni, you will maximize that coverage; don't assume that your positive news is necessarily being noticed.

Also, don't make this the only measure of your success with the media. Recently, Gary Ratcliff and Roger Williams (1995) did a study at Penn State University of "benchmarking" in public affairs programs at fifteen universities, primarily in the Midwest. Public information was one of the three areas that they studied, and this was one of their conclusions:

> While the media placements data are reasonably accurate, we should, however, avoid using the data as a benchmark of the performance of public information offices. The tabulations do not distinguish whether a mention in a newspaper was the result of the initiative of a public information office or a reporter at the other end. ... The data points to the obvious: while a public information office can expand on the number of mentions a university gets in an elite newspaper, its job is made that much easier if the university's faculty is regarded as excellent across all programs. The data suggest that a university's endowment, which is a very

good indirect indicator of faculty quality, or faculty membership to the national academy of arts, sciences, medicine, and engineering are both excellent predictors of a university's placement in an elite newspaper. Geographic proximity to major media markets also seems to have a positive influence on the frequency of media placements.

There are two other important factors to consider. First, one story — if it strikes the right note with the media — can generate hundreds of inches of coverage. Second, clipping agencies will count negative news inches in the same way as they count the positive coverage. It is important not to confuse *activity* with *productivity*. Is your desired message getting through via the media? Is it swaying the hearts and minds of readers, listeners, or viewers? True, gatekeepers are supposed to have a nose for news and for what appeals to their readers. But to measure the real impact of your messages, you need to use more penetrating forms of assessment.

Tracking

A full-page ad in a recent issue of *The Chronicle for Higher Education* promoted a new IBM Academic LANKit, configured for a Local Area Network (LAN) so "You can free yourself from doing a host of tedious tasks or from waiting for the computing center to send help." For more information, the ad tells us to "call 1-800-IBM-667, Ext. 713."

We don't know for sure, but it's very likely that the extension number is a code that will tell IBM that we found this ad in *The Chronicle*, as opposed to a similar ad running in another higher education periodical.

IBM is likely "tracking" its ad, a simple yet effective means of measuring the ability of a message in a particular medium to stimulate the desired audience response.

Gary Penders, now director of summer sessions at UC Berkeley, explains (1992) how he used tracking to measure the effectiveness of his advertisements in recruiting registrants for the summer programs when he was summer sessions director at UCLA:

> Tracking begins with a mechanism attached to each marketing project [catalog, magazine ad, etc.] which tells you which project produced an inquiry. In display ads, for example, if there is a coupon the student mails to you, it should carry a simple number or letter code which identifies not only the marketing project, but the particular newspaper and perhaps even the date. On radio or TV, in public service announcements or other general approaches, a special phone number or a staff member's name can be used to track the inquiry. (When distributing a series of catalogs, or mailing one catalog on different dates), the design of a catalog should allow you to include a code of some kind which tells you which mailing produced the response. We have found it useful to place the catalog registration form on the inside of the back cover. When it is torn out and returned, the mailing label and code are on the other side, ready to key.

Penders goes on to suggest that admissions directors can integrate their marketing and registration data to find out not only which students responded to which marketing project, but also which of those students actually went on to register.

As he says, "Tracking has one critical function — to educate you."

Split runs

While tracking will distinguish which media of communication are more effective, it won't tell you which message appeal is the more effective. To do that in a controlled fashion, you can use the "split run" technique.

Let's return to our example of the IBM ad above. IBM could have prepared three ads for its LANKit, each with a different allure and then asked the *Chronicle* — for a fee — to run ad #1 in one part of its press run, ad #2 in a second part, and ad #3 in the remainder.

The split run measuring device is particularly adaptable to any direct-mail project, as the following situation illustrates.

In 1962, Wilson B. Thiede, professor and associate dean of the UW-Madison School of Education, was appointed editor of the *Journal of Educational Research (JER)*. The *JER* provided a valuable service to the field but circulation was declining. So Thiede called on Clay Schoenfeld to help improve and market the journal.

Thiede and Schoenfeld began by revitalizing the editorial board, adding issues and pages per issue, and introducing new features, particularly a "What's New in Educational Research" executive summary — all to make the journal both more substantive and more readable.

Through an analysis of current subscribers, they found that the *JER* appealed most to superintendents and principals of public K-12 schools and to professors of education. This discovery prompted Schoenfeld to obtain two mailing lists rich in potential subscribers — the membership of Phi Delta Kappa, the professional association of leading school administrators, and the Educational Research Association, the society of active scholars in education research.

With the advice of Thiede, Schoenfeld drafted a brochure outlining what the *JER* is, for whom it's published, what it can do, and what coming issues would contain. Since he didn't know for sure what "unique selling proposition" or "case statement" would attract attention and produce new subscribers, Schoenfeld drafted four cover letters. Each employed a "pitch" used regularly at that time in direct-mail campaigns by four national periodicals aimed at executives; each played to a different emotion or drive.

The four lead-ins were as follows:

1. How to get ahead in education — Subscribe to the international *Journal of Education Research* — NOW.

2. What you might not know CAN hurt you, so read regularly the international *Journal of Education Research*.

3. Save $2.45 by subscribing NOW to the bigger, better *Journal of Education Research*.

4. What's the mark of the "pro" in education? A personal copy of the international *Journal of Education Research* on your desk.

To evaluate the effectiveness of the brochure and the four covering letters, Thiede and Schoenfeld formed a "focus group" (which we describe later in this chapter), consisting of a metropolitan elementary school principal, a suburban high school principal, a small-town K-12 superintendent, three professors of education from three universities, and a school of education librarian.

At an extended luncheon meeting, the seven consultants discussed the materials. With some modifications they found the brochure effective, but disagreed about which cover-letter headline would work best. Two liked #1, two liked #2, and three liked #3. The only thing they agreed on was that #4 was not only unappealing, but also, in some ways, offensive.

Lacking a focus group consensus, Thiede and Schoenfeld decided to do a split run test mailing to their two lists, randomly using each of the cover letters, with coded return coupons so they could measure the "pull" of each version. Strictly as a control, they included the letter the panel had rejected.

When the coupons were counted, one appeal had outperformed the other three combined, racking up an impressive 12.7% return.

It was #4!

When he launched the *Journal of Environmental Education* as founding editor, Schoenfeld used the same appeal to equal effect. In still another case, it didn't work at all.

Schoenfeld used this exercise as a teaching device for many years in his journalism classes to emphasize the importance of "writing for the reader." Invariably, students were unable to pick the winning headline.

There are several lessons to be drawn from this example:

- Pre-testing a communication, particularly using a split run, is a highly effective way to measure audience attitudes, opinions, and actions in response to a particular communication concept.

- A focus group is not always effective. In this case, its members were unable to recognize that *Fortune* magazine's "prestige" or "status symbol" selling proposition would work equally well with education administrators and scholars.

- The results of any measuring device are fixed in time and place. What works in one situation won't necessarily work in another.

- A headline or lead-in can make a compelling difference. In this case, all the brochures and letters said the same thing. Only the boldface lead-ins were different.

- In direct mail advertising, the product's inherent utility and the mailing list's selectivity are usually necessary precursors of any successful communication campaign.

Critiques

You would seldom consider submitting a scholarly paper or research report for publication without first running it past a panel of peer reviewers. Why not do the same with communications materials?

Often there are positive "political" advantages in seeking critiques. For example, when Schoenfeld was an administrator dealing with school/college deans, he habitually submitted a draft communication for review to one of the deans, who happened to be an English professor. Not only did the dean make invaluable (albeit sometimes blistering) comments, but he acquired a certain "ownership" of the communication and would hence support its message. Seeking a critique from superiors is another way of reminding them that you are executing their wishes and keeping lines of communication open.

Members of your target audience also make for important reviewers. If you are writing an annual message to the alumni, pass it by some alumni friends for their opinions. If you're trying to get a message across to students, ask a few of them to look over a draft and give you some feedback before you polish it and send it out. Just make sure that your reviewers are fairly representative of your target audience. Otherwise their comments could be misleading. If, for example, your student reviewer works in your immediate office and knows everything about the subjects you cover in your letter to her colleagues, she won't be a very good barometer of the effectiveness of that document.

Questionnaires

When Schoenfeld was wearing two hats at UW-Madison, as an administrator and a professor, he liked to use the advanced journalism students in his class in specialized reporting as "guinea pigs." For example, when Schoenfeld drafted a brochure for "special" or non-degree students, he submitted it for review to students in his mass communications class at the time.

Rather than ask them simply to critique the semantics, he gave them ten minutes to read and assimilate the material and then subjected them to a pop quiz, testing their grasp of the facts that the brochure was intended to convey.

Although the results of such an exercise can be very sobering, it is an excellent device, provided the test cohort is reasonably representative of the target audience. In the above case, the test cohort proved to be representative in *most* areas, but not all. After the brochure was sent out, an analysis of phone calls coming into the unit office indicated that the regular degree-candidate students — the guinea pigs — were familiar with certain terms that proved to be very confusing to the uninitiated "special" students. So the brochure was rewritten.

Assuming you have a data base of "before" opinions, a questionnaire is also a utilitarian device for measuring the "after" effect of a communication campaign designed to change or at least modify those opinions. If you send such a questionnaire by mail to a random sample of people, however, be aware that the active responders may not be representative of the total audience. The same questionnaire administered via a telephone poll can be more accurate because you are reaching a random sample of people and the respondents are not self-selecting.

Focus groups

If you have used a focus group to analyze public opinions prior to a communications campaign, you can assemble the same group after the campaign to assess any changes.

For example, you may recall that the "MacNeil-Lehrer News Hour" periodically assembled the same focus group electronically throughout the 1992 presidential campaign, to capture any shifts in public attitudes toward the candidates.

A focus group can be used as a critique panel or as a questionnaire cohort as well. However, if a focus group begins to think of itself as a panel of experts instead of as a group of representative citizens, its views can become contaminated. For example, Schoenfeld once covertly used a mixed gang of faculty golfing friends as an effective sounding board for assessments on his campus communications behaviors, until one day he inadvertently revealed what he was doing. From then on, the threesome was useless.

When Steve Grafton, now director of the University of Michigan Alumni Association, was having trouble attracting young alumni back to events at Mississippi State when he was alumni director there, he formed focus groups to find out why (1992). He discovered that "young alumni like informal, low-cost events" and so he tailored his programming and communications accordingly.

Chemeketa Community College in Oregon regularly conducts focus groups on programs, publications, and procedures to assess student, staff, and community satisfaction (Koch 1993). Composed of ten to fifteen people representing a particular population, a typical session is an informal but facilitated seventy-minute meeting in which participants respond to open-ended questions.

A couple of things result from focus groups, says Chemeketa director of marketing, Alan Koch, who has conducted dozens of such group sessions in the last several years to pre-test and post-test campus communications: "You get direct feedback and the act of going through the process makes you a better listener, more mindful of what your constituencies think and want." For example, as a result of a post-publication focus group, Chemeketa's course catalog and class timetable have been made more acceptable to intended users.

When do you convene a focus group? Whenever you're contemplating a change or assessing a key decision-making point, Koch says.

Reader surveys

To analyze the effectiveness of their publications, communications professionals regularly survey their audiences. You can do that, too.

For example, a group at Emory University surveyed an internal audience to assess the timeliness and usefulness of the university's biweekly campus tabloid, *Campus Report*. (Gleason and Treadaway 1990) They also wanted to know what the campus community thought in general of Emory.

Although largely positive, the survey results showed room for improvement. The internal audiences recommended a review of the tabloid's distribution system and a reinstatement of campus job listings. Based on their experiences, the surveyors offer some suggestions for other academic leaders interested in surveying their internal audiences:

- *Find survey research expertise.* Try the business school, the journalism or sociology departments, the institutional research or alumni offices.

- *Develop a clear understanding of your objectives before you start.*

- *Determine the project cost.* Depending on survey methods, an internal audience survey can cost almost nothing or thousands of dollars.

- *Calculate the time involved.* Depending on the survey's size and scope, you may have to spend several months to a year developing and conducting it and analyzing results.

- *Watch out for researcher bias.* One advantage to using outside helpers is that they have no stake in the result.

Sometimes simple surveys can be combined with membership or readership renewals.

Touchstone, a University of Wisconsin-Madison research magazine, had a public mailing list of about 2500 readers beyond its internal campus distribution. To purge the list of those who no longer wished to receive the free publication, and also to determine the magazine's usefulness to off-campus recipients, the editors published an issue with a wrap-around cover containing two tear-out postage-paid postcards.

The postcards were printed side-by-side and each was labeled with the recipient's name, title, and address. One postcard affirmed the recipient's desire to stay on the mailing list and asked for an address update. The other postcard was optional and asked several brief questions to determine how thoroughly the magazine contents were read and how the recipient would rate the publication overall. Several lines were left for comments, which drew many explicit suggestions for areas in which the respondents wanted to see more news.

Questionnaire response was good and might have been even higher if respondents could have remained anonymous. But the editors wanted to know what types of people — corporate, academic, students, and so on — in their very mixed audience held particular points of view. It was not a sophisticated survey, but very effective. And it was a relatively simple way to make contact with an otherwise amorphous group of readers.

The most important thing to remember about reader surveys is that they are helpful only if you react to the results.

Informal evaluations

There are other good techniques for assessing audience attitudes.

Professional feedback

Academic conferences, scholarly media, reports from the field — each can at least occasionally provide clues on how your communications are doing. If, for example, you've broadcast messages about an innovative teaching technology in your unit, and you subsequently see that development cited in a journal or a convention paper, you get some sense that your communication fell on fertile ground. If you get email requests for more information on the topic or get a mention in *The Chronicle of Higher Education,* you can feel even more secure that your message is having effect.

Communication feedback

Phone calls or letters to your unit will also tell you something about how well you're doing. If people continue to be puzzled about things you thought were perfectly clear, it's time to reassess the message and/or the media. Have your clerical staff keep a log of the content of questions, phone calls, e-mails, and letters to the unit office from students, faculty, and the public that relate to communications problems or issues.

Linda Weimer just helped launch a magazine for the University of California, Berkeley, replete with many avenues by which readers can provide feedback on the project, including email address, street address, and phone number. When the receptionist turned in a phone message from an alumnus who liked the magazine so much he wanted to donate money to it, the magazine team knew it had a winner.

Advisory committee input

Although it may be dangerous to deflect the attention of your academic unit's general-purpose advisory committee from more profound matters, you may find it desirable occasionally to ask members to assess your unit's communication effectiveness. If you do, keep them focused on evaluating the strategic nature of the message, not on tactical editing.

To make your advisory committee more effective in this and all other areas, constantly work to keep it a representative group. As vacancies arise on the committee, fill them with younger people, minorities, special students, and other groups that best reflect your constantly changing constituencies.

Random sampling

Don't dismiss opportunities for chance evaluations of your communications. If you are developing a memo to faculty, take the draft to the faculty club and solicit comments over coffee. When you grab lunch at the student cafeteria, ask your table mates what they thought of a certain public service announcement on TV.

Schoenfeld used as his polling place the country tavern at the corner of Highway 14 and County Trunk J in Wisconsin. He would slide onto a stool, recognize his farmer friends, and get around to asking them what they thought of the story in the local weekly newspaper about the outreach activities of his academic unit.

With all such informal means of evaluating communication efforts, it's well to remember the essentially fragile nature of their credibility. Take their credibility with a grain — or sometimes a shaker — of salt.

Measuring results can be time-consuming, frustrating, and deflating, but also at times exhilarating, surprising, rewarding, and reinforcing. It's the name of the game in assessing how well you're reaching out to your publics and hitting your marks.

chapter fifteen

The Sum of the Parts
The interplay of multiple communications strategies

When he was president of Princeton, Woodrow Wilson once remarked that nobody specializes in the interrelationship of things. When he became president of the United States, he saw even more clearly, no doubt, the importance of that undertaking.

This, in essence, is the job of effective administrators, whether of nations or of colleges. They must be able to see how the whole can be greater than the sum of the parts and to understand how each piece fits into the bigger picture. As Amanda Perkins might put it: Effective leaders are ecologists, not taxonomists.

Colleges and universities are complex organizations and the units that fit within them are complex as well. They are composed of individuals who have a myriad of interests and viewpoints — some congruent, others conflicting — and who have a multitude of motivations, needs, insecurities, and talents. To approach any academic issue from a unilateral point of view is to court failure. Only by continually appreciating and balancing multiple perspectives can one achieve some measure of consistent success.

How many academic leaders, when hit with a problem, consider that the issue has been blown all out of proportion or reflexively deem the solution to be simply "better PR!"

All too often the term "public relations" is used to describe a set of superficial values and techniques — a concoction of sleight-of-hand stunts and glib slogans with which press liaisons and public affairs folks are expected to cure all varieties of academic aches. In reality, as we have shown in this manual, public relations actually is a reflection of the institution's conduct and only secondarily a matter of publicity.

The leader's role

Notwithstanding the vital role played in public relationships by every member of the institution, the catalyst of campus conduct is the leader — usually the president or chancellor, but also the chair of the board of trustees, the provost, the vice president, the head of the academic senate, the college dean, or the department head.

Each leader must understand and synthesize the many dimensions and viewpoints that embody his or her organization, and then make some overall sense of it to the outside world. In his or her actions as well as words, the leader must represent this diversity with a constancy of message and behavior that anchors the institution and its image.

Too often, leaders interpret this to mean that everyone must sing the same institutional tune, but that is not an effective — if even achievable — approach.

You might think of an academic institution as a symphony orchestra with you, the leader, as its conductor. It would be incredibly boring to insist that each instrument play the same part and the talented musicians you hired wouldn't stick around long under those conditions. At the same time, you can't have everyone going off to select his or her favorite work to perform.

As the leader, you need to select a piece of music (or message) that the orchestra can get behind, then inspire each musician to do his or her best, most creative work. The talent of the conductor or academic administrator is in bringing forth the best from each musician or academician to create a melody that pleases and resonates with the audience.

This is a difficult and complicated task, as any leader knows. To stretch the orchestral analogy a little further, certain instruments will take priority over others at given points in the concert. But, overall, they will be integrated into a unifying, harmonious theme.

You, as administrators, will find yourselves functioning as musicians in the president's orchestra. It is important to understand and integrate that role as you set your goals and plan your communications. You will get further if your messages and themes resonate with those coming from the institution and its president. In fact, the communication outlets that convey the president's priorities (internal newsletters or newspapers, alumni magazines, student newsletters, etc.) are more likely to pick up your message too if you echo the themes of the institution. If, for example, the president is promoting new technology, you can capitalize on that by highlighting ways that technology is improving undergraduate life and learning in your unit.

Within academic institutions, we are very aware of the many fairly autonomous units that form the whole, but to the outside world it is all one. The territorial boundaries that we are so conscious of within our institutions melt away as soon as you walk away from campus.

Wherever you find outstanding campus leaders, you will find people deeply conscious of the varied voices that each express a unique version of campus function and policy, and you will find people skilled at bringing these voices together. You also will find that these leaders are deeply sensitive to public expectations and have an uncanny ability to grasp them, to adapt their goals, and to meet those expectations, not only in words but in deeds.

Meeting public expectations

What is the public's expectation of higher education? The answer to that question is more fundamental than you might think to the question of how a college or university is perceived — good or bad.

Derek Bok, former president of Harvard University, in his 1989-1990 annual report to the board of overseers, wrote:

> People believe that a university so conceived is likely to yield important benefits to society through education and research. The freedom and independence these institutions enjoy and the tolerance and support they receive have the greatest chance of surviving if all of their actions and policies seem consistent with achieving the highest attainable level of teaching and scholarly inquiry. This is so for the obvious reason that education and research are the primary functions of a university and its principal contributions to society.

He added:

> When universities act in ways inconsistent with the pursuit of education and research, they do not merely compromise their mission; they threaten reservoirs of confidence and trust on which their welfare ultimately depends.

Every instance in which the academic mission of a college or university is compromised, Bok asserts, threatens the integrity of that institution, the commitment of faculty and students, and the confidence of the public.

Bok makes an important point. When colleges and universities espouse a philosophy or act in ways that reinforce their commitment to students, to quality, to research, and — at least in public institutions — to public service, they are well-received by their various publics or audiences.

But higher education institutions run into trouble when their actions seem to run counter to those values that conform to public expectations — such as when, for example, their faculty are perceived to be more interested in making money than in teaching students. Public expectations are tied to public trust and public trust is critical to higher education.

The kinds of public relations problems that have plagued educational institutions in recent years are tied very directly to public expectations and violating the public trust. Bad publicity stems from trends such as: the skyrocketing cost of college (making it less accessible to students); the misuse of government overhead funds and high administrative salaries (putting money first and students second); tenure issues (reinforcing the false notion that there are a lot of professors on our campuses who are not effectively teaching or doing research); and putting untrained teaching assistants in the classroom, especially those for whom English is a second language (giving the students an inferior alternative to faculty instruction).

Good publicity stems from those stories of students thriving or accomplishing something exceptional (including athletic achievements) because of their college experience; stories of important research discoveries that promise to help us improve the quality of life; and stories of faculty and staff performing services deemed to have value to the public at large — be it writing a book, working in a free clinic, or simply giving a free public lecture or concert.

Public expectations of higher education are not necessarily realistic, just as the cases we cited above are very much oversimplified. But, unfortunately, perception too often is the reality.

When a leading state university ran into a budget buzz-saw recently, it promptly decided that "what this university needs is better public relations" and it appointed a public relations committee. The PR committee consulted a group of representative citizens. "What shall we do to be saved?" the committee asked, confidently expecting to be told such things as: "You need a fancy new videotape about the university" or "You need to do TV spots about the university" or "The president needs to make more public appearances," or "You need better lobbying in the state capitol."

But the consultants were not misled as to the institution's real public relations problems. They said:

> The university's difficulties are basic in their origins. There is widespread concern with the caliber of undergraduate instruction, freshman counseling, and residence hall conditions. There is concern about too many graduate students teaching classes — and that some have such heavy foreign accents, they can't be understood by the students. There is a lack of sympathy with current emphases in the university's building priorities. There's a feeling that budgetary procedures are slipshod, if not scandalous. Crime on campus is a pervasive worry. There is a nagging suspicion that some 'politically correct' faculty are having an undue influence on campus culture. And there is wonderment why, despite apparent NCAA rule infractions, the university's football team still can't seem to beat its historic rival in the state next door.

In other words, the citizens diagnosed the university's public relations problems as having little to do with the frosting — but everything to do with the cake itself.

Public relations is about living up to the public's expectations. Correctly conceived, it is no bag of publicity tricks; it is inextricably linked to sound administration in all its aspects.

A thousand points of light

Public relations can't be the responsibility of a single individual; every contact between institutional personnel and a constituent is a thread in the tapestry that forms the institution's image.

Recently focus groups were held with members of the general public throughout the state of Michigan to gather their impressions of the University of Michigan and to better understand how people get their information about the university.

The surveyors found that the general public holds the university in very high esteem, but that their specific knowledge of U of M was shallow, indeed. When pressed to explain why they had the impression that Michigan was excellent, many couldn't say. Some who were alumni could single out a U of M department or college that was excellent, but couldn't give any more specific details. Many, by the way, did mention the high quality of Michigan's athletic programs.

But of interest to the point of the interplay of multiple communications strategies was the fact that, for the most part, those participating in the focus groups said they got their information about the university, and formed their impressions, through first-hand experience. Traditional forms of mass communication — newspapers, television, radio, even alumni magazines — seemed to play a lesser role in shaping their impressions.

If this is so, it reinforces two ideas — that we must bring some harmony to the many messages emanating from the campus and that actions speak louder than words. If undergraduate education is a high institutional priority, but students can't get in to see an advisor or are frozen out of the classes they must take to graduate in their major fields, then their parents, relatives, friends, and neighbors will believe that the expressed institutional priority is a sham and they, in turn, will spread that word to their relatives, friends, and neighbors.

The more likely scenario is that people across your campus are making friends for your institution every day in ways that might never be visible or acknowledged: a friendly "hello" on the telephone, a Rotary Club speech, a little extra help for a struggling student, advice on a new business concept, tutoring a third-grader from a nearby school. What former President George

Bush termed "a thousand points of light" are alive and well on our campuses — and they are our most potent weapon in the battle for positive public opinion.

A personal perspective on public relations

As you are "reaching out," using the 14 points in this guide, don't overlook the importance of "reaching in" as well.

This guide has emphasized that communication should be a vital part of the activities of the campus and that campus leaders must reach out to their constituencies to inform them and build support.

At the same time, you should want for yourself what you want for your institution or unit. That is, you should communicate to your superiors, inform them of your activities, and build their support for your programs. You don't need to sell. Just tell. Don't expect that those to whom you report will know enough about what you're doing or that somehow this information will radiate from your actions. Just as you strive to make the work of your unit or institution known to your key audiences, make your contributions and those of your staff known to your boss.

Document what you do and, in your reports, pay the same attention to substance and style as in your communications with constituents. If you feel uncomfortable with the idea of self-promotion or personal public relations, reflect on the message in this chapter and throughout this book: *publicity* is like *reputation* — what you say you are or are thought to be — while *public relations* is like *character* — what you really are and do.

You and your boss will be more comfortable if you focus on communicating your deeds and their impacts; you will be less comfortable if you simply hype your reputation.

Higher education is notoriously unforgiving of the huckster. We all have known faculty and staff who, despite their remarkable achievements, were not well-respected by their colleagues because they were considered shamelessly self-promoting.

Adopt an approach with which you feel comfortable and that fits your campus culture and environment. Stick to the basics: prepare a straightforward narrative about what you did for a specific project, the circumstances, the reasons behind your strategies and tactics, the steps you took to implement your plans, those with whom you worked, and the results of your efforts. Attach copies of the materials you produced with documentation of results.

This should become a routine — an efficient and effective way to let others know what you're doing. Just think of it as the final phase of any communication project, as a chance to give yourself a little pat on the back ... and a little extra motivation to keep up the good work!

The elements of effective communication

Whether you are a college president, a new department chair, a seasoned administrative assistant, or head of a million-dollar research program, you are communicating your vision, your goals, your activities, and your accomplishments to multiple constituencies in dozens of ways.

We hope that *Reaching Out* will help make that task a little easier. We also hope that this guide outlines principles and methods that you will want to pass along to your colleagues and staff members.

It is more than self-interest that motivates this suggestion. More than at any time in its history, higher education in this country relies on the goodwill of its alumni, neighbors, students, parents, employees, and the public to get its essential work done. Despite theories to the contrary, that goodwill does not spontaneously generate merely by having a nice viewbook or a winning football team. It requires all campus administrators, as well as many other employees, to make a conscious effort to reach out within and beyond the campus to inform, welcome, engage, and inspire people, who may then be supportive of the institution.

This guide is built around 14 elements that can help anyone achieve an effective communications process:

1. Recognizing your mission, goals, and context, and building on substance. The purpose of any communications program is to support the mission and the attendant goals of the unit or institution. It also operates within the broader framework of the campus' mission and goals and should be in harmony with them. Analyze the institution, your unit, and the program or project you are promoting. Successful communications programs are built around what is there, not what one wishes were there.

2. Identifying key audiences. Unless you have a very large program, you can't afford to communicate with everybody all the time. Focus on those audiences most crucial to your success and assess how best to reach them.

3. Researching your audiences' attitudes. Assess the knowledge and attitudes of your target audiences so you better understand how to reach them and how to have an impact on them. Ideally, you will want to do more than educate them — you will want to motivate them to take some action on your behalf.

4. Becoming familiar with available media. Discover which media are best suited to carry your message to the folks you are trying to reach. Knowledge of communication vehicles — and their cost-effectiveness — is key to the success of your efforts.

5. Defining your needs and formulating a communications plan. Knowing your mission, assets, message, communication tools, audiences, and audience attitudes, you should be able to describe in writing how the pieces of your communications program fit together coherently. Be specific and realistic. Without a plan, you risk engaging in a lot of random, hit-or-miss activity that will not move you toward your goal.

6. Marshaling communications assistance. You don't need to go it alone. You have many colleagues who are willing to help you with your program if you will reach out and bring them into the process.

7. Finding and budgeting funds. Tight budgets on campuses across the nation make this no small challenge. But the most successful communications programs aren't by definition the most expensive. You may have to start small and launch your program in phases, but each success should help you win more funds.

8. Distilling and shaping your message. Reduce your information down to a compelling nub that can be adapted for various constituencies. Some call it the "elevator" message. Advertisers long ago found that short is sweet and simple is successful.

9. Matching your medium to the audience and your message to the medium. Choose the media that are most likely to reach most of your target audience in a timely way. Then make sure your message is tailored to the selected medium in tone, style, content, and format.

10. Treating the news media as a special audience. Take the time to understand what the news media finds newsworthy, and then uncover the newsworthy angles to your program. Working effectively with reporters and editors can greatly increase your chances of success in putting your message across to the public.

11. Understanding communications in campaigns and crises. Every campus leader will confront times of crisis and opportunity. Whether seizing the chance to celebrate an anniversary or facing the public in a time of crisis, a strategic approach will benefit your communications program.

12. Getting out and driving the information superhighway. We are in the midst of a communications revolution. Computers, the Internet, multimedia technologies — all are changing the way we communicate and giving us more direct access to the important audiences we want to reach. This rapidly changing environment promises to prove a very cost-effective way for colleges to communicate.

13. Measuring results and assessing effectiveness. This step calls for the same caliber of analysis that went into formulating your plan. It calls for a readiness to change tactics based on feedback and evaluation. The test of successful campus leaders is not that they don't make mistakes, but that they don't make the same mistakes twice.

14. Understanding the interplay of multiple communications strategies. An appreciation of the interrelationship of things and the variety

of signals being broadcast by your campus can improve your own communications efforts.

Communication is leadership and leadership is communications. This is the mantra with which we began this guide and the way in which it seems most fitting to end it.

Where you find outstanding leaders, you invariably find outstanding communicators. Outstanding leadership and outstanding communications programs, with all the new possibilities that today's knowledge and technology have to offer, promise to bring with the new millennium a golden age for this nation's colleges and universities.

For further consideration ...

Top 10 public policy issues for higher education

The Association of Governing Boards of Universities and Colleges (1996) has looked into its crystal ball and identified ten public policy issues facing colleges and universities:

1. Cost containment and productivity. To control costs, some states may place caps on tuition and examine faculty work loads and productivity. The idea of "learning productivity" will catch on in some regions.

2. Affirmative action. The location of this battleground seems to be shifting from campuses to courtrooms. Administrators will cope as well as they can with ambiguities related to hiring, firing, promotion, and admission policies. Administrators will also be watching the U. of California as it prepares to eliminate racial, ethnic, and gender preferences in favor of alternative strategies for hiring and admissions.

3. Student financial aid. The debate continues. Are federal and state programs adequately funded? What kind of financial aid programs should continue? Should they be revised? If so, how?

4. Governance and privatization. What is the proper role of governing boards? Should some public institutions privatize — or at least privatize specific services?

5. Federal tax debate. Various tax proposals will continue to be in the news, and the tax exemption for private institutions is still an issue in some states.

6. Economic development. Several states will discuss higher education's role in stimulating economic development. In many states, business and higher education leaders are working together to lobby for funding for economic development programs.

7. Federal research issues. There are really two separate issues here: the level of federal funding for university and college research, and the nature of policies for recovering indirect costs.

8. Distance learning and technology. More and more institutions and states are exploring how distance learning can help cut costs while increasing productivity.

9. Campus climate. The incidence of crime and the deterioration of both race and gender relations — plus the shrillness of debates about them — could affect public policy implications through the courts and legislation.

10. Regulation and accountability. Both federal and state governments are seeking the right balance between accountability and regulatory reform.

Epilogue

As this book was going to press, Clay Schoenfeld, its senior author and guiding spirit, passed away in his sleep at his cabin in the woods near Black Earth, Wisconsin.

Clay was an "alumnus" of an earlier — some might say, a simpler — era in higher education.

His roots in the federal land grant tradition were deep, as his fictional character Amanda Perkins illustrates. The telephone was purely a utilitarian invention for Clay. When he was done talking to you, he hung up — even as you were poised to add one last thought. He never used a computer, banging away at this last manuscript on his old typewriter, and he loved playing the role of curmudgeon, though always with a twinkle in his eye.

Did Clay live in a simpler time for higher education? I don't think so. Colleges and universities are mostly about people and people aren't simple — they never have been.

The communications skills that Clay used as a successful faculty member and dean are as relevant today as they were thirty years ago. Know where you're going, know why, have a plan, stick to it, and above all, have integrity, constancy, and common sense.

This book is not only *by* Clay, it's *about* Clay. His own experiences form the subtext of each chapter (except the one on computers!). His six decades as a consummate communicator are distilled into the drams of advice we offer here.

Clay was colorful. As a teacher. As a colleague. As a writer. As a friend. We miss him, but fortunately he is here in these pages for you to know, too.

Linda Weimer

May 13, 1996

References

Anderson, Roger. 1992. When it hits the fan. *The Community Technical and Junior College Times* (December 1): 2.

Association of Governing Boards and Colleges. 1996. *AGB public policy paper no. 96-1*. Washington, DC: Association of Governing Boards and Colleges.

Banning, James H. 1995. *Journal of College and University Student Housing* (summer).

Barbalich, Andrea. 1991. Bouncing back. *CASE Currents* (September): 50-56.

Barton, Laurence. 1993. *Crisis in organizations: Managing and communicating in the heat of chaos.* Cincinnati, OH: South-Western Publishing Co.

Barzun, Jacques, and Henry F. Graff. 1992. *The modern researcher.* 5th ed. Orlando, FL: Harcourt Brace Jovanovich.

Bennett, John B. 1991. Academic program evaluation. *The Department Advisor* (Spring): 5-8.

Best, Gary A., and Alice V. Watkins. 1991. Fund-raising: Biting the bullet. *Academic Leader* (August) 7(8): 1-2.

Birnbaum, Robert. 1992. *How academic leadership works.* San Francisco: Jossey-Bass.

Brill, Leslie. 1993. Quid pro quo vadis: Gathering resources for your department. *The Department Chair* (winter): 14-15.

Buchanan, Peter M. 1991. Campus chiefs focus on PR. *College Marketing Alert* (October 15): 204-205.

Burrell, Barbara C., and Theresa A. Neil. 1992. *Survey construction and use.* Administering the Summer Session, Proceedings of the 43rd

Annual Conference. Chicago, IL: North Central Conference on Summer Schools.

Carter, Lindy Keane. 1993. Righting the wrongs. *CASE Currents* (February): 46-47.

Conklin, Richard W. 1989. The role of public relations. In *The President and Fund Raising* by James L. Fisher and Gary H. Quehl. New York: ACE/Macmillan.

Cutlip, Scott M.; Allen H. Center; and Glen Broom. 1994. *Effective public relations*. 7th ed. Englewood Cliffs, NJ: Prentice-Hall.

Cutlip, Scott M. 1993. Personal correspondence with Clay Schoenfeld.

Dalbey, Marcia A. 1993. Seeking resources, obtaining forgiveness. *The Department Chair* (winter): 1, 20.

Dentzer, Susan. 1992. A wealth of difference. *U.S. News & World Report* (June 1): 45-47.

Doyle, Robert. n.d. Personal communication with Clay Schoenfeld.

Duderstadt, James. 1995. Personal communication with Linda Weimer.

Eble, Kenneth E. 1990. Communicating effectively. In *Enhancing Departmental Leadership* edited by John B. Bennett and David J. Fuguli. New York: ACE/Macmillan.

Evans, Michael R. 1993. Planning for results. *CASE Currents* (January): 40-47.

Geuder, Maridith Walker. 1995. Media mentality. *CASE Currents* (November/December): 46.

Gleason, Jan, and Dan Treadaway. 1990. Reading internal audiences. *CASE Currents* (October): 19-21.

Gookin, Dan, and Andy Rathbone. 1992. *PCs for dummies*. San Mateo, CA: IDG Books Worldwide, Inc.

Grafton, Steve. 1992. Commitment-shy young alumni. *CASE Currents* (June): 11-14.

Gwaltney, Corbin. 1992. The nation. *The Chronicle of Higher Education Almanac* (August) 26: 3.

Gumpert, Paticia J. 1993Retrenchment. *Journal of Higher Education* (May/June).

Hardin, John T. 1993. Quoted in "On line," *The Chronicle of Higher Education* (March 10): A19.

Harkavy, Ira. 1993. Quoted in "Urban universities: 'In' or 'of' their cities?" *Administrator* (January 2): 1-3.

Harris, April L. 1992. The money question. *CASE Currents* (July/August): 36.

Harvey, James. 1995. Quoted in "Public Perceptions of Higher Education Vary, Study Shows," *Higher Education and National Affairs* (February 27).

Higgerson, Mary Lou. 1992. Communication strategies for marketing the department. In *Academic Chairpersons: Celebrating Success, No. 39 in National Issues in Higher Education* edited by William Cashin. Manhattan, KS: Kansas State University Center for Faculty Evaluation and Development.

Hollister, Peter H. 1992. Neighborly advice. *CASE Currents* (November/December): 47-50.

Kearns, Kevin L. 1991. The economic orthodoxies offered U.S. Students won't prepare them for work in world markets. *The Chronicle of Higher Education* (March 27): B1-3.

Koch, Allan. 1993. Quoted by Kim Christiansen, "Functional Focus Groups." In *Shaping the Community College Image* edited by Steven W. Jones. Greeley, CO: National Commission on Marketing and Public Relations.

Kramer, Gary L. 1992. Using student focus groups to evaluate academic support services. *NACADA Journal* (fall): 38-41.

Larson, Wendy Ann. 1995. Are you ready? When crisis strikes on your campus, will you be prepared? *CASE Currents* (September): 10.

———. 1991. 50 ways to stretch your dollar. *CASE Currents* (September): 36-42.

Machlup, Fritz. 1991. Recipe for a good graduate department. In *Interpreting Public Issues*, by Robert J. Griffin, et al. Ames, IA: Iowa State University Press.

Massy, William F., and Joel W. Meyerson, eds. 1993. Strategy and finance in higher education: Surviving the '90s. Princeton, NJ: Peterson's Guides.

McCarthy, Peter. 1995. Cyberstats. *CASE Currents* (November/December): 9.

Mena, Jesus. 1995. Public Information Office, University of California, Berkeley.

Messner, Fred R. 1992. *Business to business communication handbook.* New York: Association of National Advertisers.

Michener, James A. 1993. After the war: The victories at home. *Newsweek* (January): 26-27.

Millard, Richard M. 1991. *Today's myths and tomorrow's realities: overcoming obstacles to academic leadership in the 21st century.* San Francisco: Jossey-Bass.

O'Shea, Catherine L. 1991. Necessary losses. *CASE Currents* (September): 58-62.

Oates, Joyce Carol. 1991. Quoted in *Crisis in organizations: Managing and communicating in the heat of chaos,* by Laurence Barton. Cincinnati, OH: South-Western Publishing Co.

Office of University Relations, University of California, Berkeley. 1995. *Berkeley Online* (December 22) 2: 6.

Parker, Pat. 1994. Long-distance recruiting. *CASE Currents* (September): 40-45.

Penders, Gary. 1992. *The evolution of marketing skills.* Proceedings of the 43rd Annual Conference of the North Central Conference of Summer Schools. Chicago: NAASS.

Pendleton-Parker, Billiee, and Sammy Parker. 1993. *Perceptions of motivation, evaluation, and rewards for faculty: Faculty interviews and administrative analysis.* Paper presented at the 10th Annual National Conference of Academic Chairpersons, February 1. Orlando, FL.

Pobojawski, Sally. 1992. Letters. *Science Writer* (winter): 24.

Ratcliff, Gary, and Roger Williams. 1995. *Process benchmarking.* Department of Public Information, Pennsylvania State University. February.

Rodgers, Joann Ellison, and William C. Adams. 1994. *Media guide for academics.* Los Angeles: Foundation for American Communications.

Rosovsky, Henry. 1991. *Annual report of the dean of the faculty of arts and sciences, 1990-91.* Harvard University.

Ruderman, Judith. 1992. How to find a find and catch a catch: writing the winning grant proposal. In *Writing and Publishing for Academic Authors,* edited by Joseph M. Moxley. Lanham, MD: University Press of America.

Ryan, Ellen. 1991. Waste not, want not. *CASE Currents,* (September): 26-31.

Ryan, Ellen. 1993. Program the market, market the program. *CASE Currents* (February): 32-38.

Sabo, Sandra R. 1995. When the unthinkable happens. *CASE Currents* (September): 14.

————. 1995. Lessons learned: PR pros offer their best crisis-management advice. *CASE Currents* (September): 17.

Santovec, Mary Lou. 1992. The annual report: An often overlooked management tool. *Administrator* (April 20): 1.

Scalise, Kathy. 1995. What you need to know about email. *Berkeleyan*, University of California, Berkeley (February 22).

Schoenfeld, Clay, and Karen Diegmueller. 1982. Effective feature writing. New York: Holt, Rinehart and Winston.

Schoenfeld, Clay, and Robert J. Griffin. 1992. Pitfalls and possibilities in communication: A review of research literature. *International Journal of Education and Information* 2(1): 3-17.

Schoenfeld, A. Clay; Robert F. Meier; and Robert J. Griffin. 1989. The role of the press in constructing a social problem. *Social Problems* (October): 38-61.

Seldin, Peter. 1991. Personal and professional. *The Chronicle of Higher Education* (May 8): 15-17.

Seppe, Nathan. 1992. Flawed hubble far from useless. *Wisconsin State Journal* (November 24): A1-2.

Smith, Mason W. 1993. Communicating beyond the tower. *CASE Currents* (June): 39-44.

Strunk, William, Jr., and E.B. White. 1959. *The elements of style*. New York: Macmillan..

Stuhr, Robert L. 1989. The case statement. In *The President and Fund-Raising*, edited by James L. Fisher and Gary H. Quehl. New York: ACE/Macmillan.

Taylor, Karla. 1993. Writing and editing for results. *CASE Current*, (January): 40-47.

Teitel, Lee. 1994. *The advisory committee advantage: Creating an effective strategy for programmatic improvement*. ASHE-ERIC Higher Education Reports, the George Washington University. Washington, DC.

Thieblot, Bernice Ashby. 1994. Name that campaign II. *CASE Currents* (November/December): 64.

University of Chicago Magazine. 1986. (October): 5-17.

Todd, Barbara Tipsord. 1992. SAAs: The adviser's view. *CASE Currents* (May): 12-18.

Topor, Robert S. 1993. *Marketing communications.* Mountain View, CA: Educational Catalyst Publications.

———. 1993. *Media and marketing: A powerful new alliance for higher education.* Mountain View, CA: Educational Catalyst Publications.

———. 1992. Thriftypubs: A new concept for higher education publications. *Publications Newsletter* (September): 2-3.

Tucker, Allan. 1984. *Chairing the academic department: Leadership among peers.* New York: ACE/Macmillan.

Tucker, Allan, and Robert A. Bryan. 1991. *The academic dean.* New York: ACE/Macmillan.

Tyson, William. 1993. Personal correspondence with Clay Schoenfeld, March 24.

Volkmann, M. Fredric. 1995. Personal communication with Linda Weimer.

———. 1995. High-tech or high-touch? *CASE Currents* (May): 56.

Walsh, Edward. 1992. The economy, stupid! *The Washington Post National Weekly Edition* (November 9-15): 7.

Webb-Lupo, Anita. 1992. Budgeting basics. *Administering the Summer Sessions.* Chicago, IL: North Central Conference on Summer Schools.

Weimer, Linda L. 1995. Spring Initiation Banquet, Order of the Golden Bear, University of Calfornia, Berkeley, personal notes.

Widmeyer Group. 1992. The essentials of a strong media operation. *Career Education*(December): 15.

Yoe, Mary Ruth. 1992. Getting it down to a science. *CASE Currents* (November/December): 8-12.

Zar, Jerry. 1995. Personal communication with Linda Weimer.

Index